FACE YOUR FEAR

ALSO BY RABBI SHMULEY BOTEACH

Dreams:
Learning to Interpret Your Visions of Night

The Wolf Shall Lie with the Lamb:
The Messiah in Hassidic Thought

Wrestling with the Divine:
A Jewish Response to Suffering

Moses of Oxford, Volumes 1 & 2:
A Jewish Vision of a University and Its Life

The Jewish Guide to Adultery:
How to Turn Your Marriage into an Illicit Affair

Wisdom, Understanding, Knowledge:
Basic Concepts of Kabbalistic Thought

Kosher Sex:
A Recipe for Passion and Intimacy

Judaism for Everyone:
Renewing Your Life Through the Vibrant Lessons of the Jewish Faith

Kosher Emotions

Kosher Adultery:
Seduce and Sin with Your Spouse

Why Can't I Fall in Love?
A 12-Step Program

The Private Adam:
Becoming a Hero in a Selfish Age

The Psychic and the Rabbi:
A Remarkable Correspondence (with Uri Geller)

RABBI SHMULEY BOTEACH

FACE YOUR FEAR

Living with Courage
in an Age of Caution

ST. MARTIN'S PRESS
NEW YORK

www.stmartins.com

LIBRARY OF CONGRESS CATALOGING-IN-PUBLICATION DATA

Boteach, Shmuley.
    Face your fear : living with courage in an age of caution / Shmuley Boteach.
        p. cm.
    ISBN 0-312-32672-6
    EAN 978-0312-32672-2
    1. Courage. 2. Courage—Religious aspects—Judaism. I. Title.

BJ1533.C8B57 2004
177'.6—dc22

                                                    2004048695

First Edition: November 2004

10 9 8 7 6 5 4 3 2 1

To the memory of both my grandmothers,
Chaya Bluma (Ida) Paul and Eshrat Boteach,
both of whom passed away during the writing of this book
and who led lives of inspired moral courage

And to Debbie,
who—when I am afraid—is never far away

CONTENTS

PART ONE:

The Case Against Fear

1

1 Fear: The Dragon in Eden   3
2 Fear: The Ultimate Terrorist   12
3 What Stuff Are We Made Of?   18
4 The Media's Campaign of Fear   29
5 Fear's Futility   36
6 Busting the Myths About Fear   59
7 Move Toward the Light   72
8 Tell Yourself Not to Be Afraid   80
9 Fear Is the Hammer That Beats Our Lives into Dust   88

PART TWO:

To Conquer Fear

91

10 Strengthen Your Inner Immunity   93
11 Principle #1: Dedicate Your Life to Something Higher   97
12 Principle #2: Believe in Your Destiny   104
13 Principle #3: Become a Leader   112
14 Principle #4: Face Your Fear   116
15 Principle #5: Keep Hope Alive   122
16 Principle #6: Redefine Vigilance   126
17 Principle #7: Replace Caution with Courage   130
18 Principle #8: Embrace the Superrational   138
19 Principle #9: Create Your Own Reality   144
20 Principle #10: Fight Back Against the Darkness   150

21 Principle #11: Do Something   154
22 Principle #12: Kill Your Television   161
23 Principle #13: Choose Righteousness   169
24 Principle #14: Have Contempt for Evil   174
25 Principle #15: Recognize Holiness   179
26 Principle #16: Connect Your Life with Others   191
27 Principle #17: Do Good   195
28 Principle #18: Connect with Family   200
29 Principle #19: Develop a Primary Relationship   206
30 Principle #20: Raise Fearless Children   220
31 Principle #21: Build Your Community   234
32 Principle #22: Knot Your Spiritual Umbilical Cord   242

Conclusion: Living Life in the High Places   253
Acknowledgments   257

PART ONE

THE CASE AGAINST FEAR

1

Fear: The Dragon in Eden

The word of the LORD came unto Abraham in a vision, saying, Fear not, Abram: I am thy shield, and thy exceeding great reward.

—GENESIS 15:1

Fear defeats more people than any other one thing in the world.

—RALPH WALDO EMERSON

I'm writing this book because I am afraid.

I have struggled my whole life against fear, as many of you have. I have known fear of failure, fear of humiliation, fear of injury, and sometimes fear of death, either for myself or a loved one. Most of all, I have wrestled against the fear of not mattering, of being cast out because I did not fit in, of being overlooked because I was not significant, and of being shamed because I was not worthy. I have at times been paralyzed by this feeling. I have let it hold me back. And what I now want most is liberation from that fear. I believe that I have found many of the keys that free us from the terrorism of fear. And I am going to share them with you.

To be afraid is to suffer. Fear constitutes the most intense form of human oppression. When you are afraid, you cannot be happy. Fear is the single most destructive emotion in the heart's armory, the single biggest roadblock that you will encounter in your search for fulfillment and happiness. If you live with fear, you can be sure that you will die with most of your dreams un-fulfilled. Unless you conquer fear, it will conquer you. Fear not only prevents you from fulfilling your greatest destiny, but it threatens to rob you of your very identity by destroying everything about you that is unique. To be afraid is to be transformed from a human being of destiny to a creature with no future.

Fear is a permanent tormentor. Unless the world vanquishes it, fear will lead to the rise of more people like Osama bin Laden, who will exploit fear in order to gain power. Unless we overcome superstition, we will never find a true G-d. Fear is an epidemic sweeping America and the world. We are more afraid now, with less cause, than we have ever been before, which largely explains why we are so unhappy, so easily shaken, so easily stirred.

It is time to fight back, to declare that we are not at the mercy of our fears. It is time to join battle in a constant and daily struggle to conquer our apprehensions: to understand why they plague us and to find a way to purge them from our lives so that we can finally be free.

In the modern world, there are tremendous forces bearing down upon us: financial pressures, work pressures, political pressures, familial responsibilities, the fear of random and inexplicable violence, and the fear of illness, just to name a few. We are constantly confronted with the horrors of history and of life: senseless hatred, poverty, famine, lovelessness, loneliness, and death. In a world empty of G-dliness, bereft of soulfulness, we feel hollow on the inside and so succumb to outside pressures.

Learning to Equalize External Pressures with Internal Strength

Of course, if these terrible external pressures were all there was to life, you wouldn't be able to continue. You would collapse under their weight. But if you can fill yourself from within—with a connection with G-d, with the people who love you, with a sense of purpose, with the certainty of destiny, and with the conviction that you profoundly matter—then you grant yourself immunity to those outside forces and win back your life. You are liberated from fear and can begin to really live. Imbuing your life with substance will empower you to withstand the weight of those pressures.

Like a deep-sea diver, who must equalize himself internally with the outside pressure if he is not to be crushed by the water's force, all of us need to equalize ourselves with the external challenges that threaten to unnerve us. We cannot do so if we don't understand what we're up against.

Know this. There is one root cause of all your fears: the fear that you don't matter. The fear that we're one big zero is what animates most of our actions. It's what makes Donald Trump buy gold toilet seats. It's what makes otherwise content men run for the presidency. It's what makes teenage girls agree to have sex with sleazy boyfriends. And it's what made me want to write this book. The scarlet thread running through all these actions is a desire to be noticed, to be recognized. To refute once and for all that inner worry that we don't matter that eats away at us.

That fear looms larger than ever right now because we are largely detached from all that is eternal. We have become unmoored from the stabilizing forces in our lives that grant us a sense of permanence.

We have become fixated on the ephemeral and transfixed with the transient. Bigger home alarm systems, a stronger military, and a better diet are how we have responded to an age of terror and heart disease.

We have forgotten that real security comes from a feeling of inner connectedness, a sense that we live not only for ourselves but for a higher purpose. Without an anchor to moor us, we are easily traumatized by the evil around us. Immersed in an age of uncertainty, thrown into a sea of material confusion, we have developed precious little immunity to fear. The emptier the carton of milk, the easier it is to shake it. The weaker the roots of the tree, the easier it is to uproot it. And the more disconnected you are from meaningfulness, the more easily you are persuaded that your existence can be easily terminated.

Many people believe fear is an emotion too primal to govern, a reflexive emotion as outside our control as jumping when you are surprised by a loud noise, as intuitive as the fight-or-flight response. This is the most dangerous myth about fear. Living in fear is a choice, much as living in a hot or cold climate is a choice, and if you try, you can create a reality without it: in fact, you must, if you are to survive with your hope intact. To move beyond fear, you must recognize that the Band-Aids and dressings you are applying to your fears aren't helping but are actually making your wounds even worse.

The foundation of all serious achievement lies in overcoming fear.

Human greatness begins where submission to fear ends. You cannot become wealthy like Bill Gates without first casting aside the fear that you will fail, without risking capital and prestige. You cannot become a Winston Churchill if you are intimidated by the evil power that you must fight. You can't get a college degree if you're afraid of taking tests, and you can't win an Olympic gold medal if you're afraid of losing a race.

**It is courage, not caution,
that leads to great success.**

Much more important than the ephemeral victories of money and honor are the inner triumphs. You cannot marry your soul mate unless you first overcome your fear of commitment. You cannot become the parent you wish to be unless you first transcend the fear of bringing a brand-new life into a cold and uncaring world. And you can never maximize your potential if you live in the permanent fear that you just won't measure up.

I have written several books before this one, but this is the first time that people have thanked me when I told them my subject. People are desperate to get out from under these paralyzing fears. As the stories poured out of people, I realized they were all saying the same thing: "So little of what I do in my waking life is what I actually want to do. Most of what I do is motivated by apprehension. I have no authentic identity. I'm a robot controlled by my fears."

The nurse at my doctor's office looked sad one day and told me that her boyfriend did not wish to marry her. She said she had read my book *Why Can't I Fall in Love?* to find out what she should do. "What book are you working on now?" she asked. I told her I was writing a book about overcoming fear. "Oh, I prefer your books on relationships. One on fear won't apply to me. I'm pretty courageous." "Really?" I said. "But you just told me that you can't get your boyfriend of four years to commit. If you weren't afraid, you would have resolved the situation long ago. You would have given him an ultimatum or at least confronted him strongly about how miserable you are. But you have refrained from doing so because you're afraid of losing him, being alone, not finding someone you love as much, or all of the above. You're stuck in the mud only because you're afraid of moving either forward or backward." She stared at me in silence and then went back to her work.

A friend of mine who is an assistant rabbi at a synagogue told me that he doesn't get along with the senior rabbi. "The man is mean and unfriendly. He treats me like garbage." "He's not mean or unfriendly," I chimed in. "He's only afraid. He's afraid you'll upstage him, steal the spotlight. So he tries to undermine you. He's probably a decent guy. But his fear makes him mean."

We are so afraid that we have been numbed by fear; we have made ourselves blind to the grip it has on us.

How many of us worked hard at school not because we loved learning, but because we were afraid of bad grades? How many of us became workaholics, sacrificing our personal relationships, not because we loved our work but because we were afraid of ending up as big nobodies? How many of us allow our marriages to languish because we're afraid to confront the emptiness of our relationships?

Overwhelmingly, human action is motivated by fear.

If you are honest with yourself, you realize that most of what you will do in life is motivated not by something positive but by the negativity of fear and insecurity. Rather than running to the light, you're running from the darkness. Are you staying in that dead-end job because you love it, or because you're afraid to take risks? At a dinner party at which people have political views sharply different from your own, do you refrain from disagreeing with them because you can't be bothered, or because you're afraid of appearing out of sync? Have you avoided that conversation with your teenage son or daughter about whether they've taken drugs because you don't care either way or because you're afraid of hearing the answer? I know a mother whose two children are careening out of control. One has a dirtbag boyfriend who once slapped her face hard in the presence of her mother. The other has terrible friends, several of whom are junkies. I've softly encouraged the mother to do something to rescue her teenage girls from their downward slide, but she always tells me that I exaggerate how bad the situation is. The mother is not blind; she can see as well as I can exactly what's going on. Rather, she is afraid; She's terrified that she has failed as a mom. It's easier to deny the situation than to face that fear.

Fear is usually self-fulfilling; it leads to the realization of what it's designed to ward off. A man who goes to a job interview fearing that he won't get the position will usually oversell himself and become tiresome, or undersell himself and appear unmotivated. A man who wants to date a woman who, he fears, doesn't reciprocate his affection will either never ask the woman out or overdo his overtures. Virtually every survey indicates that women find self-confidence to be the most attractive quality a man can have, after a sense of humor. Yet many men cannot even summon the courage to ask a woman her name, because they fear rejection. Often a man will tell me that he saw a woman at a party to whom he was attracted but could not summon the courage to introduce himself. "Why not?" I'll ask him. "She was out of my league" is the stock reply. "You mean she was out of your league for even a conversation? What kind of insecurity has gripped you that you think you aren't worthy to talk to another human being?"

To live with fear is to live with your potential permanently imperiled and imprisoned, and to overcome fear is to set yourself free. In his award-winning book on the Rwandan genocide of 1994, *We Wish to Inform You That Tomorrow We Will Be Killed with Our Families*, Philip Gourevitch tells the story of Thomas, a Tutsi marked for slaughter, who somehow survived the machete-wielding Hutu executioners:

> Thomas told me that he had been trained as a Boy Scout "to look at danger, and study it, but not to be afraid." And I was struck that each of his encounters with Hutu Power [who perpetrated the genocide of the Tutsis] had followed a pattern: when the minister ordered him back to work, when the soldiers came for him, and when they told him to sit on the street, Thomas always refused before complying. The killers were accustomed to encountering fear, and Thomas had always acted as if there must be some misunderstanding for anyone to feel the need to threaten him.

In life it may be true that people will try to kill you, but they stand a far greater chance of succeeding if fear has already transformed you into a victim.

The instructions for overcoming fear that you will find in this book do not consist of abstract concepts, appropriate only for meditation and inapplicable in the real world. This book is a spiritual book that seeks to identify the underlying causes of fear. But, it delivers extremely practical strategies and techniques that you can use in your everyday life to put fear behind you, even while you walk in dangerous times.

Fear Has No Redeeming Quality. Period.

To make use of these techniques, you must first abandon all thoughts that fear serves a useful purpose in your life. This book will make an important demand of you, without which you will not mine its usefulness: you must accept that fear is not only harmful but evil, not only unhelpful but deeply destructive. Fear has not a single healthy application in any area of life. Period. Many argue for the redemptive qualities of fear. No, fear is wholly corrosive; there are no positive consequences to fear that could not be realized through much more positive means. Sure, fear of an accident will get you to drive more carefully, but so will a love of life and health. Fear of a heart attack might get you to watch your cholesterol, but it will also make you into a hypochondriac who runs to the hospital every time your left arm is sore.

My goal in this book is to get you to confront your fears and base your life not on dread and insecurity but on courage and confidence.

Love and Fear: Two Rivers and Their Tributaries

Love and fear are like fire and water, wholly incompatible, mutually exclusive, entirely antithetical. These two primary emotions are two rivers running through your life, and from each there are tributaries. Paranoia, envy, bitterness, self-consciousness, insecurity, and egomania flow from fear, while graciousness and gratitude, joy and happiness, confidence and contentment stream from love. If you can divert the flow of your energy away from the negativity of fear and toward the positive stream of love, your fear will be swept away in its rapidly moving current.

To be sure, I am not arguing against shoring up our external defenses. In this age of terrorism, we should strengthen our military and aggressively pursue the cold-blooded killers who stalk us. In this age of economic instability, we must find ways to establish greater financial security. And in this age of unpredictable health scares, we must seek to exercise, eat sensibly, and lead more balanced lives. But none of these external remedies can ever compensate for the far greater inner vulnerability to fear. Once the fear of Osama bin Laden or of cancer creeps into your soul, even the 101st Airborne and the Mayo Clinic can't give you a good night's sleep. Whether you live or die becomes immaterial, because you have already become the living dead, petrified by each new dawn, terrified by the advent of night. You must fight an inner battle against fear and conduct a personal assault on insecurity, inner fear by another name. I'm certainly not telling you to throw caution to the wind, mortgage your house, and put all the money in the stock market, or to walk the streets of Riyadh wearing an "I love George Bush" T-shirt. But I am telling you to scrutinize your fears objectively, refute them, and lead your life based on wisdom and intelligent analysis rather than on irrational trepidation.

We're Worried We Can't Cope

In my own ongoing battle against fear, I have gained an important insight. Here's why: None of us is ever really afraid of something happening to us. Rather we fear our response to the occurrence. Our great concern is that we won't be able to cope. For example, no woman ever fears breast cancer.

Rather she fears her inability to deal with it. She fears her reaction when she is forced to confront it. She doesn't think that she'll be strong enough to fight it. Similarly, everyone knows that one day his parents will die. That thought alone is not what frightens a man; what he fears is that he won't be strong enough to handle the loss.

No outside force has the power to make me afraid. Fear is a wholly internal emotion based entirely on personal choice.

No man ever fears not being able to support his family. Indeed, all developed countries have social services designed to ensure that children never go hungry. Rather the father fears that he will not be able to live with the humiliation of having failed to provide for those he most loves. No country is ever afraid of an organization like Al Qaeda. Every country has enemies, and accepting threats is part of life. What the country really fears is the response to the sacrifices that will have to be made in order to confront the danger. And no child is ever really afraid of the dark. Rather they fear what their imagination will invent to fill the all-consuming blackness once the lights go out.

A friend called to tell me how frightened he was that a former employee of his was going to file a sexual harassment suit against him. He asked me how he could cope with the fear. I told him, "I don't believe you're afraid of the suit. You're afraid of how you will react to the public humiliation and the possible repercussions. And you're afraid of what this says about you, both in your own eyes and in the eyes of your wife. It's not the event that scares you, but your response. So the secret to overcoming the fear is to master the response. Before any suit is filed, don't be paralyzed. Act now. Get in touch with the woman in question quickly. If the allegations are true, make full and honest restitution. Win her over by showing her that you are a changed man and that you want to make it right. Then go to a spiritual counselor and with him do some real soul-searching: ask yourself why you don't respect women enough to see them as your equal. And if the matter does become public, prepare yourself for that eventuality as well. Tell yourself you're a good man who happens to have a significant flaw. Don't worry what people will think of you. If you make your character better and feel good about yourself, then you'll live this down, put it behind you, and eventually people will forget. But whatever you do, don't be paralyzed with fear."

The understanding of fear as something entirely within your control is immensely liberating. You can take a stand against fear by refusing it a foothold in your life. You must convince yourself that there is no challenge you cannot meet, and you must strengthen yourself internally by expanding and deepening your connections with those things that are essential to the inner life of the spirit: family, friends, community, and G-d.

This is the most important book I have ever written.

**Freedom is the essential blessing of life
without which all else is cursed.**

And freedom is achieved primarily by liberating ourselves from the prison of fear. The American colonists were not free until they liberated themselves from the fear of George III. And today's American people will not be free of Osama bin Laden until we see him for the desperate thug he is. To be sure, there is no quick fix in the battle against fear. Just as the battle against darkness and death will stretch from here to eternity, so will the battle against its tributary, fear. That truth should not be disheartening. Engaging in the battle against fear is life-affirming and thrilling. Nothing can make you feel more alive than the everyday triumphs over fear. The impossibility of ever triumphing completely against fear means you get to be part of a jailbreak every day. With every victory over anxiety and fright, you will feel born anew. You do not take one big breath and subsist on it for ten years. Life is expressed through constant activity, constant struggle, which keeps you warm and generates light. And the light of life pushes away the darkness of fear.

I am not so naïve as to believe that total immunity to fear can be obtained from a book, just as I do not believe that love of G-d comes from reading the Bible alone. This book should serve as the catalyst by which you can unearth your own dormant resources to combat fear. G-d did not will us to live in a constant state of panic and alarm, and human beings are stronger and more resilient than most of us realize. You have a glorious destiny that is yours to fulfill, but you will not reach the Promised Land unless you are courageous enough to climb up and peer over the mountain. Let the strategies in this book serve as the ladder. The view is entirely your own.

2

Fear: The Ultimate Terrorist

And Abraham said, Because I thought, Surely the fear of G-d is not in this
place; and they will slay me for my wife's sake.

—GENESIS 20:11

Dolendi modus, timendi non item.
To suffering there is a limit; to fearing, none.

—SIR FRANCIS BACON

When I start to write a book, the topic I have chosen becomes the filter
through which I see the events of the world around me. When I first
committed myself to writing a book about fear, although I understood the
enormity of the task, I thought I had a reasonable understanding of fear as a
limited motivating force and roadblock to human success. As it turned out, I
didn't have a clue.

In the course of writing this book, I have rediscovered every day just how
enormous an influence fear is in our lives. Only after living with the topic for
more than two years have I felt that I've even begun to approach the vastness
of this emotion and the control it exerts on the human consciousness.

More fear exists in our lives than we're prepared to admit. I was astonished by how driven by fear I found myself, my family, and my friends.
When I started listening carefully, every person I counseled, every dinner
guest who dropped a name, every friend confessing an indiscretion, every
former student who got in touch for professional advice was really saying the
same thing: "I am afraid." The woman who argued that her husband was not

loving was saying, "I am afraid that I no longer interest him." The dinner guest who was telling me that he worked with Rudy Giuliani was saying, "I am afraid that on my own I would not be very welcome in your home." And the student who complained that he hated his job was saying, "I am afraid that I am wasting my life." Lawyers today have unprecedented control of our personal lives and corporate strategies because people are so afraid of being sued. I have more than once had to delete benign anecdotes in books because publishers told me that the lawyers would not allow it. Indeed, the fear of lawsuits is as American as apple pie. I recently saw that bottles of soda now contain a warning that the tops can pop off and take out your eye. Fear of lawsuits in America has forced us into being afraid of plastic bottles.

And it's not just that my circle is filled with scaredy-cats. My friends reflect the mood of the culture at large. New Yorkers now have Botox parties, modeled on the popular Tupperware party concept. Women used to gather to buy plastic containers; now they gather to buy plastic faces. They choose a mask over a face capable of expressing joy, surprise, or sadness, in the fear that these emotions might leave their trace on their faces. Why would a woman literally inject poison into her forehead, robbing herself of the ability to show emotion, if not out of the terror of looking old? And why shouldn't she be afraid? She reads everywhere of captains of industry like Donald Trump and Jack Welch trading in devoted wives for younger women without rumples. They read in the Nielsen ratings that advertisers aren't interested in anyone over thirty-five (which means that I'm already a write-off). They see on magazine covers that the only women who get attention are those with firm bodies and silicone breasts. If I were a woman, I would be damned scared of growing old. Heck, even as a man I have become frightened of growing old. And isn't that tragic? Rather than looking forward to the mature years, when wisdom will save us from screwing up so much, we instead dread the advantages of age and fear flabby skin.

When I was a kid, I used to calculate how old I would be at the turn of the millennium. It seemed such a proud milestone to live through. But then, as I approached the awaited day in my thirty-third year, rather than enjoying it, I heard from the media that the world was going to come to an end with the effects of the Y2K computer bug. Dams were going to burst, jet airliners were going to plunge from the sky, and nuclear power plants were going to melt down. We were all going to die of radiation poisoning. I had several friends who stocked up on bottled water and canned beans. We got through that crisis, and then along came the mother of all fears: terrorism. September 11, 2001, exploded in our faces, and fear became a permanent fixture in our daily lives. When I suggested to friends that we all go to see the dropping of the ball in Times Square for New Year's Eve, they looked aghast and said, "Are you nuts? Times Square is a really high-profile target." A target! These normal suburbanites were talking like General Tommy Franks, planning their Saturday night as if they were mobilizing troops!

Now, I have no problem with sitting home on New Year's Eve and doing nothing. Heck, I prefer it. But that decision should be made because you love your home rather than because you fear terrorists. You and your spouse, not Osama bin Laden, should decide what you want to do on New Year's Eve. I was left wondering: How did this happen? How could a country as strong as the United States—with a tradition of more than two hundred years of independence and freedom—suddenly be brought so low? How has a band of hate-filled, nomadic cave dwellers so focused us away from our blessings and onto our deaths?

We're like the stock market. There's good news one day, and we're on top of the world. Bad news the next, and we're buying duct tape. There's no stability; we're insanely volatile. In the weeks after September 11, friends of my wife flew in from Australia to Canada. We asked them to fly down to New York for a day so we could see them. Their response: "New York is way too dangerous. We're staying in Canada." I had to explain to them that "Bronx Bombers" referred to the New York Yankees, a baseball team, rather than to live terrorists. You'd think that explosions were a regular feature of riding the New York subway. You'd forget even thinking of visiting a country like Israel. Leaders of the Reform movement of Judaism in the United States created a furor when they canceled all their summer programs to Israel in the summer of 2002 because of the fear of suicide bombs. Just imagine. Jews have prayed for two thousand years for a return to their homeland and a state of their own. And now American Jewish kids are being prevented from visiting the Holy Land by Jewish organizations because of fear. We're being held hostage by fear. We don't let our children walk to school anymore for fear that that nut who kidnapped Elizabeth Smart has a psycho cousin coming after our kid as well. Capable and honest men and women, who would make great leaders, refrain from entering politics for fear that the press will dig up the hit of ecstasy they once took at a college rave. On Internet dating sites, women are constantly warned to meet men from the Web sites in wide-open places, which just reinforces the impression that rather than being normal, most men are ax-murderers.

Last year I was scheduled to speak at a Jewish leadership conference in Montreal, Canada, and my wife and children were going to come up with me. My radio cohost at the time, my dear friend Peter Noel expressed shock—live on the air—that I would endanger my kids by taking them to Canada, a country larger than the United States, amid the SARS "epidemic."

Never mind that there had only been a handful of infections. Never mind that those infections had all been in Toronto, a city eight hours' drive from Montreal. One caller to our show had the temerity to suggest that I wear a face mask during my lectures. Imagine that. People come to hear a rabbi give an inspiring lecture about hope and perseverance, and he delivers it looking like Jason in the Halloween movies. Listeners to my show were telling me that I should deprive my kids of an inspiring, religious weekend with their father at a nice hotel, of seeing him speak at an important conference, because of some minuscule threat, the product of hype and our irrational obsession with fear.

Immunity to Fear Is Not a Product of a Strong Military

We Americans have left ourselves at the mercy of external events because we rely exclusively on external defenses—our face masks and our 21,000 pound MOAB (Massive Ordnance Air Blast) bombs. I'm certainly not arguing against strong external defenses. As long as there are Osama bin Ladens and Kim Jong Ils in the world, I'm proud that we have a MOAB in storage, just in case. But the more importance we attach to them, the more we are subject to these external whims. After all, there are plenty of extremely poor countries in the world that barely have bullets, let alone MOABs. Yet they do not seem nearly as frightened as we. Spain is one of the world's wealthier countries with a well-developed military. As soon as their trains were bombed by Al Qaeda in the horrific 3/11 massacre, they threw out their prime minister because they thought him too belligerent. All of their rifles, jets, and attack helicopters did nothing to immunize them against fear, because the real defenses against fear are not bulletproof vests and flak jackets but an indomitable spirit, which the Spanish sadly seemed to lack. By caving in to terrorist pressure and changing governments, they may indeed have taken themselves off Al Qaeda's radar screen. But they did so at the expense of locking themselves in a dungeon of fear.

Just as a hurricane gets stronger the longer it stays over warm water, Kim and Osama get stronger by hovering over our fear. They feed on our rotten emotions, like maggots that feed on rotten meat. And the same is true of all the other miscreants who are a threat to all that is dear to us.

Look at how we react to external threats. A kidnapping in another state? Lock the doors and keep your kids inside. Heightened terrorism alert? Cancel those travel plans. Bad economy and unstable markets? Transfer your equity holdings to bonds. While these strategies may well work in the short term, they're nothing more than a mask against SARS. The real tragedy is that we have allowed a flimsy piece of cloth to triumph over the human spirit. Amidst our power and our wealth, can we really call ourselves successful if our principal bequest to our children is a life lived in fear? Of what value is more than two hundred years of sacrifice in this country if, amid all our prosperity, fear snuffs out the pleasure we derive from our blessings?

Fear Creates a Class System

The German philosopher Georg Hegel said that at the beginning of history, two combatants fought a primordial battle for ascendancy. At some point in the battle, one of the men became afraid that he would sustain injury or lose his life. And, Hegel says, it was at that precise moment that the relationship between master and slave was born. The world's very hierarchical structure is based not on wealth and resources but on fear, bullying, and intimidation. The great French philosopher Jean-Jacques Rousseau famously wrote in *The Social Contract*, "Man is born free, and everywhere he is in chains." To be sure, the chains he was referring to are many, but each of their links is made of fear.

To choose fear is to choose slavery. This is what President Franklin Roosevelt meant when he said we had nothing to fear but fear itself. When we succumb to this poisonous emotion, we allow it to curtail our liberty, our single most precious possession. As long as we allow fear to dominate our decision-making process, and our dread to overshadow all that is good and wholesome in our lives, we are simply living corpses, the proverbial dead men walking. By allowing fear to dictate the way we live our lives, we lose them entirely.

We must immunize ourselves against the virus of fear, or it will infect us all.

Some argue that the world is becoming scarier and that our fear is justified. I disagree. Are AIDS and the SARS virus more frightening than the bubonic plague that according to some estimates killed three-quarters of the population of Europe and Africa over a twenty-year period in the fourteenth century? Is terrorism more of a threat to the future of our country than the threat of the former Soviet Union and a nuclear holocaust that had decades of schoolchildren going through drills of running into bunkers and ducking under their desks? Is the economic slowdown we're currently experiencing comparable to the Great Depression, which had one out of every four Americans out of work? Our world is far better off now than at almost any other time in history.

The only thing that has changed is us. We are more easily frightened, more easily rattled today than before. Who would have predicted that the most prosperous and wealthy generation, with the best health care and most comprehensive education, would also be the most frightened? We must diagnose the virus of fear and discover an effective antidote. If we fail, the outbreak will become a plague. We must examine the culture of fear that's grown up around us and understand how this toxic emotion stands in the way of our success.

3

What Stuff Are We Made Of?

And the LORD appeared unto him the same night, and said, I am the G-d of Abraham thy father: fear not, for I am with thee, and will bless thee, and multiply thy seed for my servant Abraham's sake.

—GENESIS 26:24

The man who fears suffering is already suffering from what he fears.

—MONTAIGNE

Terrorism, the economy, myriad incurable illnesses, car crashes, or any of the other bogeymen we invoke when we're justifying our night sweats aren't really the things that are scaring us. These are the symptoms of our fears rather than the causes. And I don't think that we'll be able to eliminate fear from our lives until we come to terms with the root cause of our fears, what's actually scaring us.

If it were true that our fears were objectively linked to external threats, we'd have little reason to be afraid. How many of us, statistically speaking, have to worry about being blown up at brunch? Are we concerned that a mouse or a cockroach can cause us physical harm? Of course not, but it doesn't stop us from screaming and climbing up onto the nearest chair when we see them. And what is the probability, when our husbands are a little late coming home, that they've been hit by a Mack truck? Isn't it more realistic to think that they've just forgotten to call? What is the statistical probability that a man in his forties has colon cancer? Yet in early 2004 the *New York*

Times reported that there is a waiting list of up to two years in some parts of the country for a colonoscopy. Of course it's better to be safe and have things checked out, but we're talking not about people who love health but about people who even in the prime of their lives are already fearing death. There is nothing rational about it.

If fear isn't subjective, then why are some of us so much more afraid than others? Why would our individual fear barometers fluctuate so wildly, regardless of objective truths? Doctors tell me all the time that their male patients are much more scared of things like needles than women. One doctor told me that a male patient had fainted on him when the doctor cut his ingrown toenail. Now of course the pain of a shot is a lot less than that of hitting your knee on the corner of the coffee table; why don't we live in fear of stubbing our toes? Fear is in the mind. It's not out there; it's in here.

People are very frightened today, but it's not terrorism, the economy, health considerations, and (insert your pet fear here) that's really scaring us. Rather there is one fundamental fear that underlies all others and makes us vulnerable to manipulation and attack.

**Yes, we're afraid of death and losing our jobs
and public disgrace and smallpox in the subways.
But those fears are just stand-ins for the mother of
all fears: the fear that we don't matter.**

The Nile River of fear from which all tributaries flow, the central trunk of trepidation from which all branches protrude, is the fear of nothingness and insignificance.

Come on. It's time to understand yourself and get honest. Are you haunted every day by the fear that you're a great big zero? Isn't that why you get so insulted when an acquaintance sees you in the supermarket and doesn't say hello? Do you really need her greeting to make your day worthwhile? Or is it that you're constantly searching for validation against the fear that you don't matter? Do you feel that when people take the time to say hello, it means that you must be worth something?

You're no different from the rest of us. We're all afraid that ultimately we don't matter, that our lives are meaningless, accidental, and capricious, that our existence is negligible, temporary, and unimportant. We fear our own ordinariness and our lack of uniqueness.

Isn't this truly the fundamental force that drives your fear?

You're afraid that your life is purposeless and directionless. You're afraid that nobody cares about you because you're not worth caring about. You seethe with bitterness when you think of past boyfriends or married girl-friends, because they moved on without you to people who, in their opinion, were better. Isn't that why you spend the majority of your life trying to prove that you matter? Isn't that why you flash your positive test scores at your parents, drop the names of important acquaintances in conversation, try to get into an Ivy League college, try to make money or become famous, and try to fall in love? All in an effort to prove that you are not ordinary but special, not pedestrian but distinctive.

Virtually every human undertaking is motivated by a desire to prove that we matter.

When I had just turned twenty-two, I became the rabbi at Oxford University—forgive me for sounding arrogant here, but it's in order to make a point. (Okay, so it's not. It's in order prove to you that I matter.) During the next eight years I distinguished myself as an innovator in the field of student activities and programming. Professionals came from around the world to learn from our events, and I was profiled in newspapers everywhere on the globe. When I turned thirty, I felt an utterly inexplicable moroseness overcoming me. My wife made a big party for friends and family, and I ruined it by being down in the dumps. I felt old. I feared that my successes as a rabbi to students would no longer be special because I was passing from my twenties into my mature thirties. That's it. I was washed up. My best years were behind me. I remembered reading that all of Einstein's great theories came to him in his twenties, and after that he never really came up with anything profound again. That was it. My most creative years were behind me. I was already beginning to feel ordinary.

A friend of mine told me, "You have to accept that up until now, you were seen as up-and-coming. But now you've arrived, and there is not a lot you can do to make an impression. You're going to do more of the same. Just accept it." Such words reinforced my irrational feeling that I was a big loser.

Well, miraculously, I survived my thirtieth birthday and even managed to do a couple of new things over the past few years. But now that I am pushing forty, the same fears are returning to me. It's "feel like a loser" time all over again.

I have struggled my entire life against feelings of unworthiness and worthlessness. I'm not saying that I'm depressed. Thankfully, I was blessed with an abundance of energy and rarely ever get especially down. But I do spend way too much time trying to prove myself rather than merely allowing my inner talents to manifest themselves organically on the outside.

Fear of Death Is Animated by a Fear of Insignificance

Still not convinced that the greatest human fear is the fear of human ephemerality and inconsequentiality? Let me prove it to you this way: Who isn't afraid of death? Unless you're a freaked-out, fundamentalist religious fanatic whose idea of fun is blowing himself up on a bus, you are probably scared of dying. Now, why is that? You may think that you're afraid of dying because of the universal fear of the unknown; we don't know where we go when we're dead. But that wouldn't explain why atheists are also afraid of death. As Bertrand Russell, one of the most famous atheists of the twentieth century, said, "I believe that when I die my bones will rot and nothing shall remain of my ego." Another famous atheist actually had written on his tombstone, "All dressed up with no place to go." If you're not going anywhere, there's no reason to be afraid.

Here's the real reason you're afraid to die:

> **People are afraid of death because it is the irrefutable corroboration of their ultimate fear, proof positive that all along they really didn't matter.**

One day you'll die, you'll be no more, and guess what? Horror of horrors, the earth will continue to revolve on its axis without you! Sure, a couple of people will remember you. Some may even grieve over your passing. But after that they'll get over it and get on with their lives. Life will move along without you. Death reminds us that no one is irreplaceable. That woman who said she'd never marry again if you didn't come home from the war, well, a few years later, she's popping out kids and living at home with her hubby and the white picket fence. The nation will elect the youngest man ever to its highest office. He'll inspire them with soaring oratory about how they should not ask what the country can do for them, but what they can do for their country. It will seem like he's indispensable, that he alone embodies the vibrancy and youth of his people. But then one day he'll be driving in an open-air limo and an evil man will blow out half his brains. And an hour later, a man twenty years older than he will take over, and after him yet another man will take over, and still the nation will continue to grow and continue to prosper without that charismatic young president.

Death is terrifying because it makes you face the fact that the world will carry on even after you've stepped off. The kids you nurtured and raised will have children of their own. Your friends may occasionally raise a glass to your memory, but they'll find someone else to make them laugh. Seen through the cracks of your coffin, the belief that your existence makes a difference and that you are invaluable is nothing but comforting fiction.

We're not even afraid of death, the end of our lives, as much as we're afraid that we've made no indelible mark on the world. Even when we had veins and sinews, we were nothing but dust and ashes. We ask ourselves, "If I were to disappear tomorrow to a disease or a car crash, would anyone care? Would my loved ones recover, would children still play, would professors still teach? Won't lovers still congregate on the riverbanks for picnics? And if so, isn't that evidence that there was no special uniqueness to my existence at all?"

We're more afraid of not mattering than we are of anything else. And that's why we spend a lifetime trying to prove that we do matter.

> **Human existence is a lifelong quest for things that make us feel important, from valuable things like love and G-d to shallow things like celebrity and money.**

The Two Paths to Significance

As you live your life, you are confronted with a daily fork in the road between two paths to significance. The first is ephemeral and is suggested by fear. It involves feeling important through acquisition—of houses, cars, stock shares, and women or rich boyfriends—and through competitiveness, feeling important by outdoing others. This is the typical Donald Trump approach to life. You're important because you're rich and you can yell at people on national TV, "You're fired." Your entire life is driven by the fear that you are inconsequential, so you mistakenly believe that by acquiring trophy girlfriends, you will achieve significance. You make the error of believing that by putting other people down, you will automatically be raised up, so you're an uncontrollable braggart. A person like this spends his life trying to impress you and me. We are his masters. He's terrified that we will look at him and see an insecure vulgarian, so every day he tries to add to his holdings so that he can allay the fear that he doesn't matter. Of course even if he had all the money in the world, he would still be insecure, would still be controlled by his fears. He can't help it. When you deal with fear by indulging it, when you address insecurity by catering to it, it grows and grows.

There is another path, a way to overcome fear. That way is never to succumb to fear, never to buy the lie that you were born insignificant and now need to acquire things and prove yourself to others to start mattering. In the Bible Abraham is portrayed as being utterly fearless. He is commanded at seventy-five to leave his father's home and move to an unknown country. He does so courageously. Later he fights five wicked kings with a ragtag army and defeats them. He is not even afraid to confront G-d and haggle with him to save the lives of the inhabitants of Sodom and Gomorrah. What makes Abraham so courageous? He was the first person in history to find G-d. In other words, he was the first human being to consider himself as having stemmed from the infinite. He was the first to conceive of himself as always being attached to the heavens. Abraham was born feeling that he mattered. There was no money he needed to acquire, no degree he needed to earn, no important people he needed to schmooze in order to feel important. Being a child of G-d was enough. He never suffered from the type of insecurity that our generation, severed as we are from G-d, experiences.

As a parent, isn't this your most important job: to make your children feel, from the day they are born, that they matter? Is there any more important role you play as a father or as a mother than making your children overcome the fear that they're not important? And isn't the secret of making them feel like they do matter the gift of unconditional love?

Feeling G-d's presence about him at all times, Abraham felt loved. Thereby he was protected from the curse of fear.

Women Who Are Desperate for Male Attention

A thirty-something woman came to me, wanting to know the secret to finding a more successful relationship. I asked what had gone wrong in her previous relationships. She told me, "Guys really hurt me. They sleep with me and then about a month later they say that they're not in love with me. I want a relationship that lasts." I told her, "There are two kinds of women. One projects confidence and therefore draws a gentleman. The other projects insecurity and therefore draws a womanizer. You don't believe that you're special or beautiful. You compare yourself constantly to your thinner, more glamorous friends. Men see that and immediately notice the chinks in your armor, and it brings out the scumbag in them. You invite them to take advantage of you, because you're desperate for male attention."

I asked her if she had been close to her father, and she responded that she loved her father but that he had been physically abusive when she was a child. I have seen this a thousand times. When women are not made to feel validated by the healthy attention of their first masculine figure, they become desperate for male attention and open themselves up to being exploited by unworthy men.

Why have millions of young American women abandoned the feminist dream of being taken seriously by men and instead decided to gain male attention with degrading spectacles of their bodies? I am convinced that the principal cause is an increasingly weak link between fathers and daughters, an estrangement that tragically exacerbates daughters' fears.

In our society we have it all backward. Too much is made of the father-son relationship at the expense of the father-daughter one. The image of a boy being taught by his dad to catch a baseball or throw a football is commonplace, while the only mainstream image of a father interacting with his teenage daughter pictures the dad telling her not to come home too late when she goes out with her boyfriend.

Pop tarts like Britney Spears and Paris Hilton, who use provocative poses to advance their careers, are often close to their mothers, who may even serve as their managers, while their dads are nowhere to be seen. Where you do read about a father's central involvement in his daughter's career, the result is usually respectable women like Steffi Graf and the Williams sisters, all of whom resisted the offers for provocative photo spreads even after they became famous as tennis stars. This is not because mothers don't love their daughters but because fathers, understanding the male mind, are much more successful at protecting their daughters from other men. And when a daughter receives strong masculine validation from a loving and caring father, she is not fearful of being unimportant and is consequently not desperate for sexual attention from manipulative men.

In March 2004 the *New York Times* ran a front-page story of a fifteen-year-old girl who refused to have sex with her sixteen-year-old boyfriend. He promptly cheated on her. When the girlfriend found out, she told her boyfriend that they should both cut class and go and have sex. She did so, she said, "in order to keep him." This young woman was terrified that she was unloved and unimportant. When I read this story, I wondered where this girl's father was. Had her father been a strong male presence in her life, she would not have been so desperate for the affection of a scoundrel.

Even when I go to a Yankees game, I take my five daughters along with my older son. True, they often don't know the names of the players or even the score! But they know their father loves them and hates being separated from them. There is a special connection that daughters have with their fathers that even a mother cannot replicate, and that grants young women a startling immunity from compromising themselves with womanizers. Being raised by a loving father allows women to date men out of strength rather than weakness, out of confidence that they have something special to offer a man rather than the fear that they will end up all alone.

Indeed, when a daughter is close to her father and respects him as a man and a dad, she begins to judge other men by that same high standard. When she dates men, she will not judge them by their smooth tongues but by the depth of their commitment, because her own father was not a talker but a doer. She will not jump into bed with a man who has not married her in order to please him. She has high self-esteem, and she expects the men in her life to make an effort to please her rather than the reverse. Her idea of a relationship is not to come down to the guy's level but to raise him up to hers.

As for the criticism that too close a relationship with your daughter will impede her ability to later form close connections with romantic partners, exactly the opposite is true.

A young woman with an involved and loving father has the confidence in herself to begin a loving relationship with a man precisely because she has learned to trust men.

She is not afraid that men will abandon her. She can allow herself to be vulnerable, a prerequisite for romantic love, because her father has shown her an example of a man who can be trusted and relied upon. If she feels betrayed by her own father, she will often run to another man more to escape pain than to find love, which is what usually makes her a prime candidate for that revealing photo spread or for casual sex and abandonment.

Living Life to Escape Death

Of course, the disease of living a life propelled by fear of insignificance is not confined to young and vulnerable women. It has been exhibited by some of the most accomplished and self-assured people in history, people who, for all their successes, were robbed of the pleasure of their achievements because all their efforts were designed to escape death rather than enhance life. Many people have spent their lives trying to build something that will outlast their lifetimes, whether that's a billion-dollar business, a new contraption, their face on a hundred-dollar bill, or the name on a dormitory at a university. We undertake these things not to cheat death, nor even to achieve immortality. Instead we do them to escape fear. We fight our fear of nothingness by erecting monuments to our significance.

When death comes along and says, "See, John D. Rockefeller didn't matter. For all his millions of dollars, he is no more, and the earth has continued its journey through space without him," Rockefeller's foundations still dispense money as a way of saying, "No, Grim Reaper, you're wrong. Look at the work he's doing from beyond the grave. This guy still matters."

The fear that our lives are empty, irrelevant, and purposeless is also behind one of the other great fears of life, the fear of pain.

Given that one of the primal human fears is the fear of pain, why do so many women look forward to having children? All over the world, women excitedly submit to this gut-wrenching (literally) ordeal. If it were just pain that we fear, birth rates would dwindle to nothing. Meaningless pain, a purposeless ache, scares us. Birth is pain with a purpose. It enhances rather than diminishes us. Labor is a marathon you run with the understanding that at the end of it, you'll be a mother. And for this sense of purpose and identity, women will endure almost any hardship. I have never given birth, but I assume that I would risk terrible hardship and even death, G-d forbid—if the purpose of it was to keep my children safe. I suspect the same is true for you as well.

Our entire lives, we walk around looking for evidence that we're valuable. We do everything we can to ensure that we make a mark on the world. We spend a lifetime asking, "Do I matter?" We're thermometers instead of thermostats—reacting instead of in control—because we're never entirely sure what the answer to that question is going to be. Your boss yelled at you this morning, so today the answer is no, you don't. Your husband complimented your new hairstyle, so you do. When we're stuck in the grips of this reaction, we never overcome our core fears. We're always reacting to external phenomena to determine whether or not we matter. We're always choosing the wrong fork in the road, the path that grants us significance through externalities, acquisition, and competitiveness, rather than internal meaning, spirituality, and kinship.

Being Afraid Is the Equivalent of Asking, "Do I Matter?"

I read about a sociological experiment done at a university in New York. The question the experiment was designed to answer was, If you ask someone for something without offering a reason, will they give it to you? To answer the question, a sociologist got a bunch of his graduate students—healthy, able-bodied young people—to go out into New York City's crowded subways and ask people for their seats. It turned out that, in almost all cases, if someone was asked to relinquish his seat, he would do it, but that wasn't the most interesting finding in the experiment. The professor found it almost impossible to keep graduate students on the project. People kept dropping out. They found it was too hard to ask a complete stranger for his seat, even though it was in the name of science, and even when, as in almost all cases, the seat was willingly given.

I feel that I can relate. I was getting on a plane to fly from New York to Los Angeles, and I was hot and thirsty from waiting to board. I felt self-conscious and embarrassed asking the flight attendant for a cup of water; I know that the time before takeoff is busy for them and they don't like to be bothered. And sitting in economy, I'm not that important a guy, right? So when I asked for water, I told her that I had to take a pill. She gave me the water, and as I drank it, she teased me, "Where's that aspirin?" Shamefaced, I confessed that I'd just wanted the water. She said matter-of-factly, "Don't worry about it. This happens all the time. Everyone lies and says they have to take a pill."

I got to my seat and spent much of the flight thinking about the exchange. How is it that I'm too frightened to ask for a cup of water? Why was I like those students who couldn't ask someone for his seat? Why do I need a crutch, an excuse? And apparently I'm not the only one; everyone does this. What is really going on?

I think the answer boils down to this: although asking for a subway seat or a cup of water seems small and insignificant, in our eyes they're really not. If we're not yet fully convinced of our own intrinsic value as human beings and as children of G-d, we treat every interaction as an opportunity to ask the question, "Do I matter?" And so that flight attendant's answer becomes much more important than it really is. If what you're really asking is "Do I matter?" and she says, "Sir, I'm very busy right now, please go to your seat, and I'll try to bring you some water after takeoff," then I'm going to hear, "No, you don't matter. You're not important enough to get water. Those guys in first class don't even have to ask, but you're a zero. You're just a loser sitting in coach."

The students in the sociological experiment on the subways couldn't ask people for their seats because hearing the wrong response—"Fuggedaboutit"—would have challenged the very value of their entire existence. What they would have heard was not, "No, I'm sitting already and I'm tired. Get some other seat." They would have heard, "Who the heck do you think you are? If you were the mayor or some famous celebrity asking me for my seat, then it would be my pleasure to give it up. But since you're a nobody, you can jump off the train for all I care."

When you're always questioning whether or not you're valuable, you live in fear of having that debate settled in the negative. You hate to risk confirmation of your unworthiness. Our insecurities make asking a stewardess for water as scary as asking a beautiful woman out for a date, or asking for a raise: we have to undertake the risk of rejection, of being judged unworthy. Is it any wonder that we live in a state of flux when our entire sense of self-worth hangs in the balance every time we need to quench our thirst?

The less we can rely on finding a sense of meaning and purpose on the inside, the more desperate we will be to find a sense of meaning and purpose on the outside.

It is then that we become victims, hostages held for ransom by external events. That's how celebrities become so miserable and damaged. Their sense of self-worth is entirely outside their control, determined by a fickle public who may or may not buy their CDs or watch their TV shows.

When lawmakers came after Bill Clinton for the Monica Lewinsky scandal, Larry Flynt offered a million dollars for information on any members of Congress who were cheating on their wives. As a result there was a tangible sense of fear and trepidation among our elected representatives. But why? Flynt wasn't a terrorist. He wasn't planning to kill anybody. The fear was the fear of disgrace. These powerful politicians were afraid that they would be transformed from men of power and influence into discredited laughing-stocks, stripped of their titles and fancy offices and ashamed to show their faces in public. They had spent their lives accruing these symbols of power and prestige to stand as evidence that they mattered. Since they had no internal fortification, they were entirely dependent on external trappings to tell them that they were valuable, and those could be taken away with a single phone call to the self-described "smut-peddler who cares," Larry Flynt. If they had had real internal fortifications, they would have known they were valuable whether they walked the halls of power or not. (Of course if they'd been living moral, dignified lives, they wouldn't have had anything to worry about either.)

4

The Media's Campaign
of Fear

And Joseph said unto them, Fear not: for am I in the place of G-d?
—GENESIS 50:19

Neither a man nor a crowd nor a nation can be trusted to act humanely or
to think sanely under the influence of a great fear.
—BERTRAND RUSSELL

If the central human fear is that we don't matter, that we're not unique or special or inherently valuable, surely this is an age-old concern. So why does this issue of fear loom so large right now in America and the West? Why would we—the most powerful nations in the world, and the richest, thank G-d, of all time—be so afraid at the apex of our success? We are healthier, more prosperous, and freer than virtually any other nation. We're certainly not afraid because times are so much scarier than they ever have been before; all you have to do is look at our infant mortality statistics to see that in fact, the opposite is true. Our fears are disproportionately inflated: there's no correlation between reality and our level of fear. Even terrorism is a highly irrational fear. We stand a far greater statistical chance of falling down the staircase at home and breaking our neck than of being shot out of the sky with a shoulder-launched, heat-seeking missile.

And yet we cower under the covers. A two-bit thug living in a cave with a dialysis machine keeps us awake at night. Nomadic weirdos like "Emmanuel," who kidnapped Elizabeth Smart, prevent us from allowing our kids to walk to school for fear that they too may be abused or kidnapped. We're afraid of losing our jobs, and with them our houses and cars and ability to support our families. We're afraid of random acts of violence and larger, more deliberate ones. And in the process, some part of us dies.

If you ask a room full of Americans why they feel fear, you'll get a handful of answers, variations on a theme. "We're afraid because our soldiers are under attack around the globe." "We're afraid because the rate of diabetes is skyrocketing." "We're afraid because unemployment is so high." These things may be true, but they don't explain the national mood. If the sixties were the decade of love, then the turn of the millennium has been largely characterized as the decade of fear.

The Campaign of Fear

Why are we so much more afraid now? One reason is that we're on the receiving end of a great big fear campaign. Fear sells. Watch the network evening news on any given day, and all the headlines are about how the price of gas is skyrocketing, how the banks may repossess your home, and how you risk arsenic poisoning every time you take a drink of water. It serves corporate interests to keep us anxious and frightened: fear is a great, great business. If women are afraid of losing their looks, they'll buy more cosmetics. If Westerners are afraid of being killed in a terrorist attack, they'll watch more news to see how the war against terror is progressing. If they have major health concerns, they'll watch Peter Jennings to find out about new cancer screening techniques. They'll pay to go to gyms to keep in shape. If they're afraid for their jobs, they'll run to refinance their mortgages and borrow more money. Our politicians, our media outlets, and the people who would sell us stuff want us to remain insecure and unbalanced. Our governments feel that they must constantly warn us that a terrorist attack could come at any moment, so we can't ever say that we weren't warned.

The *New York Times* reported in December 2003 that the infiltration of pornography into every area of life leads men to fear that they have to live up to the stud stereotypes they see in the culture. They are taking Viagra at earlier ages to help them overcome performance anxiety. Do you think the pharmaceutical companies are falling over themselves to make men feel better about themselves? Fear of AIDS sells condoms; pushing abstinence makes nobody rich.

It seems that nearly everything today is designed to keep us worried and to sell us stuff. At my daughter's Bas Mitzvah party I hurt my back dancing. When I was a kid and my single mom covered all our bills, we had no health insurance, so even if one of my limbs was accidentally sawed off, I patiently waited at home for it to grow back rather than bug my mother to take me to a doctor she couldn't afford. But now, like any good American, I ran to the doctor to make sure I hadn't broken my spine, G-d forbid. He took an X-ray and told me that I had merely sprained a muscle. "But I should mention that there is some arthritis showing in your spinal column," he said. Great. I went to the doctor to hear that everything was fine, and instead I heard that my frail body is coming apart at the seams, and I'm not even forty. It was only after I started crying like a baby and insisted on sitting on his lap that he told me that the rate of erosion in the disks of my spine was actually normal for someone my age.

A few days before Christmas I heard an advertisement on the radio for a device, worn all the time, that allows the elderly to contact emergency services if they've fallen or had a stroke. The medical company selling it called it "the perfect gift." So now they're marketing even our Christmas gifts to our fears rather than to our joys. Imagine giving your mother a wrapped box containing not a gold chain or warm mittens, but a little gizmo that tells her that she may drop dead, alone and abandoned, at any moment.

To be sure, many of our fears are motivated by legitimate concerns. We are being terrorized by many in the Arab world because they hate our power, our rights, and our freedoms. They look at their glorious past, their hapless present, their less-than-hopeful future, and they blame Western infidels for all their troubles. The economy is uncertain, and a lot of people have lost their jobs. And we are being terrified by the media: rape, mayhem, and the latest killer disease sells more commercials than evenhanded journalism.

And we do have something to lose—on both an individual and collective level. Sociologists point out that since it was so common for parents to lose their children to disease a hundred years ago, parents made a point of not attaching themselves too strongly to their offspring. When we hear members of previous generations saying, "Mom and Dad were stern and rarely ever showed affection," they are recalling adults who may have been subconsciously immunizing themselves against the possibility that their children would not make it into adulthood. We are thankfully a generation in a country that has largely conquered infant mortality and disease. Exceptions are mercifully rare, but when tragedy strikes, it is sudden and unexpected, thereby magnifying its devastation.

Teresa, an acquaintance of mine, confessed to me that she had never been really, truly afraid of death—had never worried about bad things happening in the world—until she met someone and fell in love. When she thought about something bad happening to her husband, she finally understood what it meant to feel real fear. "If something happened to him, I couldn't continue with life. So I worry about him all the time." And those feelings were only in-tensified when she later became pregnant with their first child. Love in the modern era is always twinned with the possibility of loss, making it incarcer-ating rather than liberating. But maybe that's to be expected in a world where we have conquered infant mortality only to see an explosion in divorce.

Americans, of course, enjoy tremendous wealth and opportunity and more extensive freedoms than the citizens of any other country in the world, so as a nation, we do have a lot to lose. But the far greater loss, the one that crept in under our radar screen while we were looking for suicide bombers in the audience at *Thoroughly Modern Millie*, is that we have lost our freedoms to another terrorist entirely—fear.

The Destructive Notion That Fear Is Useful

In order to shake off the tyranny of fear, we have to determine why we are so afraid. What has left us so vulnerable? Here's a big clue:

We have allowed a dangerous idea to infiltrate our consciousness, namely, that fear is somehow positive, that it protects us from bad occurrences.

I know a fifty-something woman in London who is convinced that her job in life is to worry about her family. She worries for her husband's health (he has treatable prostate cancer), her children's finances (all three are married with kids, and each is struggling financially), and the state of the world (she is Jew-ish and is very anxious about rising European anti-Semitism). She is an ex-pert worrier, and it's ruining her marriage, her life, and her children's lives. Her own kids don't enjoy being around her. She is a pile of gloom. Rather than smiling, she spends most of her time sighing. Don't try to argue with her about it, because she is somehow convinced that in the absence of being able to cure her husband or give a million dollars to her kids, she has an obli-gation to worry. In the back of her mind she believes that worrying about her family somehow casts a protective shield over them, as if she were Scotty on the starship *Enterprise* ("Ay, Captain. The shields are up, but I don't know if I can hold them."). The same mistake is made by countless others who believe in the healing and protective powers of fear. We will examine this idea in great detail—and bust many of the "positive" myths about fear that have in-sinuated themselves into our consciousness.

Fear Is No Shield

There is a deeper reason for our rawness and vulnerability, one that leaves us completely unable to fight back against fear. We are much more afraid now than we ever were before, because we've lost our inner immunity. All the internal fortifications that used to shore us up have been eroded and replaced by pale imitations of the real thing. We used to worship a real G-d; now we worship movie stars as gods. We used to marry for life; now we marry until we get bored or someone better comes along. We used to have children; now we have our expensive dog breeds and our careers. Many of the things that anchored us both on the outside and the inside have been lost to us and replaced by plastic substitutes. As a result we are unmoored and adrift.

I know a man who is frozen to the core by the fear that he doesn't matter, only he doesn't know it. It has never dawned on him that his mistreatment of his devoted wife is a reflection of that fear. Since he is, he fears, worthless, how much more so is the woman stupid enough to marry him? It has never dawned on him that his neglect of his children is another manifestation of this fear. His kids, unlike his peers, can't make him feel important by giving him a promotion, an award, or inviting him to the right cocktail parties. It has never struck him that his horrible relationship with his sisters is also fed by that fear. They are more professionally successful than he is, so he treats them as adversaries rather than kin. He is convinced that once he makes his fortune, his life will be good, as if fear can be vanquished by external accessories. In his enslavement to his fears, this man has lost touch with every single thing that might actually render him immune to fear. The people to whom he really matters, and who could help him overcome his fear of worthlessness, are the ones whom he treats the worst.

Osama bin Laden Sought to Expose American Corruption

Isn't this what Al Qaeda is out to prove? Let's go back to the planning stages of the attack on the World Trade Center. Osama bin Laden, indeed anyone who could meticulously plan an attack of such complexity, is not stupid. Diseased, deranged, heartless, and evil? Yes, absolutely. Stupid, certainly not. As he was planning this attack on the world's most powerful country, he surely must have known that this pinprick—not to, G-d forbid, minimize the loss of three thousand innocents, but insofar as the continuity of the United States is concerned, a pinprick—would rouse a slumbering giant. Surely he knew that by attacking a country with a $400 billion annual military budget, larger than all the rest of the nations' in the world combined, he was opening the gates of hell for himself and his followers. Why didn't he attack another soft target, another embassy on foreign shores? Why did he go after the tallest buildings in one of America's largest cities? Why invoke the rage of the world's most powerful military machine? What was he out to prove?

I believe that what Osama bin Laden planned was to show, for the benefit of the Muslim youth that follow him, that we are empty and without real substance. Bin Laden is a fundamentalist whose purpose is to perpetuate radical Islam. Many Islamic countries are poor and underdeveloped, which makes it hard to convince young people that their way is better than ours. Bin Laden could have encouraged Muslims to rescue themselves from poverty and illiteracy as a way of gaining parity with the West. But that was too big a chore. So he took a shortcut. Rather than compete with the West, he sought simply to discredit it. Rather than raise Islam, he sought to denigrate the West by proving the corrupt and unhappy nature of Islam's adversaries.

By frightening us with the attacks on September 11, bin Laden was saying that for all our wealth and power and freedom, we are fundamentally hollow and therefore easily broken. He was saying to the young Muslims who follow him, "You see these wealthy Americans? Stop being envious of their lifestyles, and don't be seduced by their movies, their music, their clothes. It's all a big lie. For all their tall buildings and fancy homes, they sit inside them and tremble. They can't even enjoy their blessings. One attack and they're resorting to plastic sheets to protect their brick mansions. That's because they're hollow inside. Shallow materialists, so easily shaken. They live in cages they call estates. They have no G-d, no inner sense of conviction, no principles, and so they can be brought low by a group of cave dwellers. We who have nothing, no material possessions, can so easily frighten them because we are full. We have G-d on our side." In frightening us, bin Laden was out to prove to the Muslims of the world that they are the winners and we are the losers. They may not have air conditioning, but their faith cools them and they sleep better than we do because they have no fear. Hence, risking the wrath of the United States was worth it for bin Laden since it gave him such a profound moral victory. He predicted that we would substantially curtail our freedoms in order to prevent another attack. And today, every time I spend ten minutes trying to get into a building in Manhattan— past the security guards and the electronic surveillance—I think to myself that he was partially victorious.

To be sure, there are many Americans who have proven their immunity to fear, most notably our brave sons and daughters in the military. Later we will examine the ingredients in their lives that constitute an impregnability to fear that the rest of us lack. But bin Laden sadly is correct about many of us, and we cannot ignore the grain of truth in this criticism, however evil he may be. Right now, Americans are like saplings, buffeted by the winds of fear. Our roots are shallow, and our trunks are weak. We must reconnect with our deepest foundation so that we're more solid on our feet, less vulnerable to the hurricane of fear that swirls around us. We are of course right and bin Laden is wrong. Freedom will always triumph over tyranny. Good will always prevail over evil. Light will always dispel the darkness. But freedom does not mean the freedom to indulge a purposeless, materialistic existence in which our sense of significance comes from clothes and sports. With freedom comes responsibility.

5

Fear's Futility

Be strong and of a good courage, fear not, nor be afraid of them: for the
LORD thy G-d, he it is that doth go with thee; he will not fail thee, nor forsake
thee.

—DEUTERONOMY 31:6

The worst sorrows in life are not in its losses and misfortune, but its fears.

—ARTHUR CHRISTOPHER BENSON

So Americans are more afraid than they've ever been. What difference does it really make?

People tell me, "Americans can now afford to be more cautious. There's no life-or-death cause we need to fight for. Why would I brave terrorism by flying to Madrid to close a deal? I can teleconference instead, or let the deal go entirely. My family, thank G-d, won't starve." This is a dangerous delusion, a narrowing path that can only lead to a pathetically cautious generation.

Shakespeare said, "Of all base passions, fear is most accursed" (*Henry VI*). Fright is to the human condition what water is to fire, what death is to life, what kryptonite is to Superman, and what Waterloo was to Napoleon.

Nothing obstructs your ability to achieve your ambitions more than your own fears; nothing prevents the realization of your dreams more effectively than dread.

The physiological reaction to fear is to lose your breath while your heart races; fear literally steals the very breath of life.

Like depression, fear stands in your way: it immobilizes you, paralyzes you, forces you back inside yourself. It defeats you and stops you dead in your tracks. Fear diminishes you, literally. It makes you cower.

When we experience fear, we curl up and revert to the embryonic position. Our human development proceeds in reverse: we devolve instead of evolve.

And it feels terrible! Fear is certainly the most degrading and humiliating of all the human emotions. It even looks pathetic. It makes us numb to life and in that sense most resembles depression. Fear makes us feel insecure and unsafe—so insubstantial that we're sure that any blow from the outside will cause our entire structure to crack and collapse. Fear steals our substance, robs us of our content, leaving nothing but a rickety frame in its place.

If you live in fear, you will witness the gradual diminishment of your humanity. You will become less adventurous, less truthful, less forthcoming, and ultimately less alive. A married couple came to me for counseling on the brink of a divorce. Married already for twenty-seven years, they were odd candidates for a breakup. The husband said that he could no longer stand his wife's lies. He claimed she lied about how much she got done during the day, where she had been, how much money she spent, and what her friends said about him. Although his wife was in general an honest woman, she did lie to her husband about many things, not because she was a liar, but because she was terrified of the ogre who nitpicked everything she did and always made her feel stupid. Her fear of her very own husband—the man who had professed to love her—had made her dishonest.

Like freed animals who refuse to leave the safety of our cages for the unknown of the wilderness, we retreat to the safety of captivity through our fears. It's a terrible irony. As our freedoms increase, our willingness to exercise them recedes. As a result, we're living half-lives in the shadows.

Liberating ourselves before we become resigned to these half-lives is essential. "The truth shall set you free," or so the saying goes, but nothing on earth, not even truth, can set you free unless you have overcome fear. You can devour every self-help book in the universe, but you will never be what you envision being until you have transcended fear. You can seek advice about relationships from every love guru, but you will not find your soul mate until you have conquered your trepidation about being vulnerable. Sure, you might get married. Holding yourself back from divulging the contents of your heart will condemn you to sharing a partnership rather than experiencing a soul relationship. You can take all the self-esteem seminars in the catalog, but you will not feel triumphant until you have conquered the fear that you fundamentally don't matter.

Ralph Waldo Emerson said, "He has not learned the lesson of life who does not every day surmount a fear." If you haven't worked on conquering your fears, you have only two possibilities left, both of which will rob you of your ability to live a full and happy life. You can either be permanently afraid, in which case you will never know happiness, or you can select from a limitless menu of escape mechanisms—movies, drugs, alcohol, gossip, cheap sex—to help you forget your fears, in which case you are forgoing life and withdrawing into fantasy.

**Refusing to fight your fears may force you
to escape them instead.**

Isn't it easier to overcome fear?

The first step is to destroy the idea that fear is a productive emotion. Recognize fear for what it is—a useless immobilizer. It robs you of experience. It makes you suspicious and therefore mean, turning you into the living embodiment of your worst characteristics. Since it undermines your resolve, it encourages you to conform, stealing your identity more effectively than any credit card thief. Since it usually becomes a self-fulfilling prophecy, fear invites disaster. And since fear forces you to regress into an isolated bunker mentality, it is fundamentally selfish.

In writing this book, I confronted many of my friends with the simple challenge of providing me a single example in which fear is useful. They would say things like, "The fear of death makes us drive more safely. The fear of losing money on the stock market makes us invest more wisely. The fear of being caught stops us from committing adultery." But none of that is so. It is the fear that if we miss the first ten minutes of the Broadway show, our lives will end, or that if we come late to the meeting with the boss, our whole professional career will be destroyed, that has us driving too fast in the first place. It is the fear that without money we are unimportant that has us embracing silly rags-to-riches investments. And it is a fear that everyone besides us is having fabulous sex that has us pursuing cheap substitutes to fulfillment in our marriages.

Furthermore, there is no positive thing that can be brought about by fear that cannot be achieved by a far more positive means. If you love life rather than fear death, you won't drive recklessly. If you love financial security and hate reckless gambling, you won't be careless with your investments. And if you love your spouse and hate causing her pain, you won't be off having an affair with a stranger.

One woman told me that her fear that some men are dangerous made her adamant that any man she dated through the Internet meet her in well-lighted places like Times Square. Wasn't that a good thing? I told her that the opposite is true. If you arrive on a date afraid, you won't be able to be natural. You'll laugh nervously and display a restricted personality. You are certainly less likely to make a favorable impression. Does that mean that I think that women should just date any guy in an unsafe place? Of course not. If a woman values herself, she won't go out with just any guy in the first place. It's fear of loneliness and a desperate desire to be loved that has women finding idiots on the Internet to begin with. Better to go to respectable and dignified places to find good men, like synagogue and church, educational lectures, or charitable events, that attract a higher standard of man in the first place. In a comfortable and dignified venue, women are more naturally themselves and therefore make a far stronger impression.

We must debunk the myths we have so long used to justify fear's supremacy in our lives. Fear is not protective in any way. It is not an effective motivator, especially over the long term. If fear actually worked to motivate people, then the Soviet Union and the communist block would still be around, and the United States, which rewarded people rather than frightening them, would have broken apart into fifty autonomous countries. If fear were an effective motivator, then all those parents who beat their children would have obedient kids for the rest of their lives. And if fear really worked, then Hitler, rather than the Allied powers, would have won the Second World War.

Fear Always Has a Shelf Life

The fact that none of these things is true has everything to do with the limited shelf life of fear. After a while, the effects of fear wear off. People become numb to it. You can beat them with a whip a few times to get your work done, but soon you will have snuffed out the spark of their humanity, and all you'll have left is an automaton, someone more dead than alive. That's why, historically, one of the main arguments against slavery, aside from the obvious evil and immorality of the practice, was that it was financially unworkable. A whip provides no incentive to productive labor and eventually leads to disastrous economic results. The South was poorer than the North largely because of slavery. Even the economies of the communist countries, motivated as they were by fear, lagged far behind economies of the West, which were motivated by personal reward and professional career growth. There is simply nothing inspiring about fear.

Fear robs you of life. When you live your life consumed by fear, you're alive in only the most superficial biological sense. If you are always thinking about death, can you really be said to be alive? Fear renders you cold and immobile. It makes you sterile and impotent. You become about as warm and exciting to be around as a headstone.

Fear Robs Us of Our Mobility

When we speak of being afraid, we speak of being "frozen," like a panicked deer transfixed by headlights. This metaphor is particularly apt, because what fear does is immobilize us, preventing us from action. As Edmund Burke said, "No passion so effectually robs the mind of all its powers of acting and reasoning as fear."

There are countless historic examples of tremendous losses suffered as a result of fear. German Jews might have done something about Hitler, but he had successfully made them, over the course of nearly a decade, so desperately afraid that they were paralyzed. What might have happened if they had fought back at the first signs—the first vandalized cemetery, the first frozen business, the first broken storefronts? Or even later, when it became clear that Hitler was hell-bent on extermination? Of course, I would never pass judgment on the holy martyrs of my people, slaughtered mercilessly by the Germans who bear the sole responsibility for the genocide. But from their deaths, we can learn the price of fear.

The Iraqis could have rid themselves of that butcher Saddam Hussein, but he had successfully rendered them powerless through the tyranny of fear.

> To make a population afraid is an even better way
> of controlling them than to lock them all into prison,
> because from an external prison there can be an
> escape. But from the internal prison of fear
> there is rarely an escape.

When your heart gets locked in fear, there is no escape. The prison is now inside you. Philip Gourevitch referred to this phenomenon in *We Wish to Inform You That Tomorrow We Will Be Killed with Our Families*. " 'Rwandan culture is a culture of fear.' " Nkongoloi, a lawyer who survived the slaughter and later became Vice President of the National Assembly, went on. " 'These victims of genocide had been psychologically prepared to expect death just for being Tutsi. They were being killed for so long that they were already dead.' "

If this can happen to nation-states, it can happen even more easily to individuals. Fear rarely points you in the right direction. It obscures the true state of affairs. I have heard tales of countless men and women who might have made millions if they had pursued promising investment and business opportunities, but afraid of loss, they capitulated. Others, afraid that they would remain behind while their friends raced ahead in the game of wealth, invested recklessly and lost their hard-earned savings. Both groups abandoned rational evaluation and succumbed to fear. And I have many times counseled single men and women, still alone in their forties and fifties, who have confessed to me that they walked away from the perfect marriage partner decades earlier out of fear. They were afraid of marrying and making a mistake, or they were afraid of making a commitment too early when someone better might come along, so they allowed their soul mates to drift by, and they now live in permanent regret over the fear that denied them the possibility of lifelong happiness.

By paralyzing us, fear becomes the principal reason we don't get what we want from life. We're afraid of being humiliated, so we don't take risks. We're afraid of commitment, so we condemn ourselves to a life of emptiness and solitude. We're afraid of being deserted, so we don't speak out against things we know to be wrong.

**By freezing us in place, fear prevents our reaching
out to the things we really want and being
the people we really want to be.**

When we live in fear, we live in a state of permanent frustration. Since we are too afraid to actualize our dreams, soon their very existence becomes a burden. They haunt us, yet we can't overcome inertia to make them happen. Our dreams become permanent reminders of our impotence. So we cease to dream.

**Those who live in fear carry themselves around
like a fragile plant, always about to be damaged,
a crystal decanter about to be cracked. They lose the
lightness of being, becoming heavy and slow moving.
They forfeit the flexibility that allows them
to endure hardship without scars.**

Entrepreneurs Succeed Because They Are Courageous

In 1976 a young Harvard junior decided that the company he had founded a year earlier needed his full-time guidance, so he dropped out before graduating. The company went on to revolutionize computing as we know it. I'm not advocating that we all be like Bill Gates and not finish our education, which may well be vital to our future success. But had Gates not overcome his fear that without a Harvard degree he would not amount to anything, who knows what would have happened? He saw an opportunity and courageously seized it. More recently Arnold Schwarzenegger won election to the governorship of the most populous state in the country. His friends had reportedly told him not to run, that too much dirt about his past would be dug up, and the disruption to his life would be too significant. In short, they told him to be afraid. But this was a man who had already confronted his fears by coming as an immigrant to this country in his early twenties. He was going to run for the governorship. I of course don't condone Schwarzenegger's alleged fondling and groping of women, but I do admire his determination to stand up in the face of naysayers who tried to convince him that he should be afraid of his past rather than correct it and make proper restitution to those he may have harmed.

By paralyzing us, fear cheats us out of life's richest gift: the ability to experience life to its fullest.

It's time for some perspective. Recently when I was contemplating a trip to an island that had been threatened by Arab terrorists, a woman I know expressed concern that my beard and yarmulke made me an obvious target. I pointed out to her, a lifelong and die-hard New Yorker, that many people in the world are still afraid to come to New York. The streets she navigates unthinkingly every day, the subways she relies upon to get to work, the buildings where her friends live, the plays and movies and restaurants she loves—in the minds of many people all over the world, these are the dictionary definition of peril. They have read for years of all the shootings in New York, and now to top it off, there is the ongoing threat of terrorism. Is New York more dangerous than the Great Barrier Reef? Probably. But literally millions of people go about their business every day, living their lives, riding the trains and walking the streets without incident other than being importuned by street vendors selling knockoff Gucci sunglasses.

When you are afraid to come to New York, when you allow your fears to paralyze you, you miss an entire world of rich experience. You allow that fear to supplant the possibility of those experiences. What a great shame, especially since you could get a great deal on a fake Louis Vuitton handbag. If I had canceled my own trip to that island out of fear, the loss would have been my own. Those who refuse to visit Israel, one of the most mesmerizing and culturally rich countries in the world, because they are afraid are depriving themselves of exposure to the greatest crossroads of human civilization and religious belief. One of the things I most enjoy about visiting Israel is the defiance, the resolve to lead a normal life amid the dangers, the refusal to submit to fear. To walk the streets of Israel along with Israelis is to inhale courage and have it pulsate through your bloodstream. Here is a people who choose not to be afraid and who reaffirm that choice after every suicide bomb attack.

When we're frozen by fear, it blinds us to real dangers.

I recently read that a shocking 10 to 15 percent of all teenagers in America are obese. They don't call type 2 diabetes "adult-onset diabetes" anymore. Kids are eating so poorly and getting so fat so young that they're coming down with this entirely preventable disease in childhood. These same children will grow into adults with heart disease, stroke, asthma, joint pains—a legacy of weight-related ill health. And yet we forbid our children to walk to school because it's too dangerous. In the 1950s seven out of ten children walked to school; in the late 1990s the number fell to three out of ten, and I would bet that the number continues to decline. In our misguided attempts to keep our kids safe, we deny them precisely the kind of daily, routine exercise that could prevent obesity, even as obesity-related illnesses threaten to overtake those caused by smoking as the leading cause of death in this country. We're so busy watching the side door that we don't notice the thief marching in through the front.

I want my own children to have something better. I want all our children to have something better. It is chiefly when I am around my kids that I am best able to overcome my fears, because of my determination not to transmit my apprehensions to them. The same principle holds for any officer in the army, who cannot afford the luxury of fear because he or she is leading other men and women and trying for their sake to exemplify courage.

Fear Robs Us of Our Identity

Our fear has been greatly exacerbated in the modern era because of our culture of lovelessness. If you're not made to feel in your earliest years that you are of infinite value, then you will usually spend the rest of your life trying to prove that you are. Bad and distracted parenting is one of the principal causes of the culture of fear in which we all walk. When kids have to fight for their parents' attention, when they see that it is not they who bring their parents happiness, but rather good news from the office, they internalize a mentality of valuelessness. The fear that results from that sense of valuelessness can often animate their actions for decades to come.

A sense of valuelessness is constantly reinforced by our culture, which tells us that unless we are draped in the accoutrements of success, we're worthless.

The designers tell us, "You're nothing, unless you're wearing my jeans. Your own name is utterly unrecognizable; nobody's heard of you. I am somebody, while you're a nobody. So you'd better have my name on your butt." The culture tells us, "You're nothing, unless the plaque on your desk says vice president. You're nothing, unless you jump into bed with this rich and powerful guy. You're nothing, unless people will pay to buy a magazine that features photos of you naked."

And so our individuality is under assault, every minute of every day. A woman looks in a mirror, and instead of seeing the lines on her face as souvenirs of all the adventures and triumphs and tears and laughter that have marked her life, she sees an old hag, one who compares unfavorably with the Hollywood actress in the advertisements for an expensive skin cream. What makes her unique are her experiences; shallow lives lead to shallow lines. Celebrating her difference, her uniqueness, is really the way out of her insecurity. But her fears—of being undesirable, of being abandoned—lead her to try to conform to an ideal, a cookie-cutter stereotype. Soon she's got needles in her face, as if poking her head with sharp metal objects is going to make her forget her fears.

**Fear is the emotion of conformity.
Nothing is more responsible for the erasure
of our uniqueness than fear.**

If Abraham Lincoln was correct that we all come into this world as G-d's original but most depart as man's copy, then nothing is more responsible for the erasure of this dignity than fear. Of all the fears that currently plague our lives—fears of terror and death, aging and illness, professional setbacks and public humiliation—perhaps none is more tragic that the simple fear of being ourselves. Take a moment to think about that and to grasp how serious that is: we are afraid just to be.

Samuel Butler called fear "the static that prevents me from hearing myself." I counseled a twenty-something woman who had already experienced multiple rejections from men. She told me that she had become so uncomfortable in her own skin and so depressed about her life that she was even self-conscious around her own family. As a result she avoided family celebrations and holiday get-togethers. "My whole life involves being whatever others want me to be. I feel like I have no confidence, like I have no backbone. I often feel my life to be a burden."

I certainly know what it's like to be afraid just to be. When I was a boy of eight, my parents divorced and we moved from Los Angeles to Miami, where I was enrolled in the fourth grade of a Jewish day school. The boys, who had formed a clique since nursery school, bullied me mercilessly as a newcomer. The experience made me afraid—not of them but of myself. I couldn't for the life of me understand what about me was so hideous that they would so forcefully reject me. I remember well the experience: the terror of being myself. I did everything to conform, everything I could think of to fit in. I laughed at their bad jokes, shot spitballs at the uncool fat kids, who were rejects like me. Though I had a mother to comfort me, I did not have a father in my immediate vicinity who could give me backbone and inspire me to be myself and find a better circle of friends. My father loved me, but he was three thousand miles away in Los Angeles. The situation got so bad that— I'm embarrassed to say this even as I write it—I started buying these boys gifts just so they would be my friends.

It wasn't until the sixth grade that I developed the courage to do my own thing. I knew I was a better person than they were. Maybe not as cool, but more compassionate. I didn't want to treat other kids like garbage; it didn't make me feel good about myself to treat others cruelly. I rejected those miserable, mean-spirited bullies, and the contempt I developed for them made me unafraid, because they were now beneath me. I made a point of getting to know the new kids who came into our class, and I treated them as though they had been there for years. In the process I came to know that the bullies in my school were even more afraid than I was and could only feel good about themselves by passing on their fear to others. When my ten-year-old son recently went through a bullying experience, I told him neither to fight nor simply to ignore his tormentors. "Rise above them," I told him. "Look at them and determine never to become like them. Be everything they're not. Reach out to the kids in your class whom no one else takes an interest in, and soon the admiration you earn will make you a leader in your class."

Being Afraid to Be You

How tragic it is to be afraid to be you! A leading New York attorney told me that she disagreed with my philosophy of fear. "When I was in eighth grade," she said, "I had a teacher who hated me and always put me down. She always said that I wouldn't amount to anything. And it was that fear of failure that spurred me to work so hard. I graduated top of my class at law school and became the first woman partner at my firm. Her comment was always in the back of my mind, and it motivated me: I always wanted to prove her wrong." I responded, "That's ridiculous. Instead of a nasty teacher to react against throughout the whole of your life, you could have had a loving parent to make you believe you had a gift to give to the world. Instead you were led to believe that you had something to prove to the world. When you're inspired by fear and a need to show that you matter, you may eventually get to your destination, but one thing's for sure, you'll enjoy neither the journey nor the view once you arrive. There are many things that can motivate our success, but when it's motivated by fear, it is always accompanied by suffering."

Because we're afraid, we hide. We're afraid that if we let our real selves—our real beliefs, likes and dislikes, our thoughts and hopes and dreams—show, we'll be rejected for them. And that is too much to bear. It's too much exposure. It's easier to go with what the culture tells us we should like and do and think. We'd rather rely on pundits to tell us what opinions to have, on style mavens to tell us how to decorate our homes, and on advertisements to tell us what to wear. We'd rather surround ourselves with what's cool than with those things that address our individual needs.

We're afraid that we're not inherently special or unique, so we willingly cooperate in eliminating the things that make us special and unique.

This is how fear actually exterminates the part in us that is most worth saving. Fear causes us to conform, when in fact the thing we should be most afraid of is losing ourselves. If you're not going to be yourself, why come into this challenging world in the first place? And what do we really lose when we pretend to be someone we're not? Let's say that you never show your true face to your spouse. You hide your insecurities and preferences and deepest self because you're afraid of rejection. What have you really gained? Your husband or wife is in love with a stranger, a construct. Is there anything lonelier than the knowledge that you're not loved for who you are? You're really more alone than you would be if you showed that person your truest self and got rejected for it. Then at least you'd have the courage of your own convictions. So you have someone to watch television with in the evenings. Congratulations.

I counseled a husband who has an addiction to pornography. He came to see me because of my well-known opposition to porn and its destructive consequences for marriage and relationships. He was hoping through our conversations to wean himself off the corrosive addiction. When he told me how bored he was with his marriage, and how desperate he was for an erotic thrill, I asked him, "Have you ever discussed your erotic needs with your wife?" "I'd never do that," he told me. "She'd think I was a sicko." I have met countless husbands in the same boat. They're terrified that if they expose their male libidinous needs to their wives, they'll be rejected. So instead they develop a subterranean and damaging erotic life, one that pulls them further and further from their marriages.

**Our greatest fear should be not that we will
lose our lives, but that we never lived because
we became somebody else.**

I am certainly no stranger to the desire to conform out of fear, and I have struggled with this problem over and over again in my own life and work. This fear is sometimes magnified when you're part of a close-knit religious community. When I first published my bestselling book *Kosher Sex*, I never expected it to appeal to my own religious community. I wrote it for the world at large, to teach others how their romantic lives could become more intimate and fulfilling. I was amazed by the number of staunchly religious individuals, both Jewish and Christian, who wrote to me secretly, sometimes with fictitious names, telling me of their moribund sexual existences within marriage and asking for counseling. I remember the mother in Israel who confessed to me that she had taken a lover because she felt so alone in her marriage. I spoke to the husband who frequented prostitutes because he didn't feel attracted to his wife. I counseled the young married man who wanted to kill himself because his wife did not know he was gay. In most cases the people wrote secretly, in fear that their spouses would discover that this was an issue of importance for them. The men and women who wrote to me were embarrassed: they thought spiritual people shouldn't be so eager to fulfill a "base" physical need. It seems incredible to me that we can be so fearful in our lives that we tremble even before the person with whom we share our children and last names.

A Christian woman who had conducted a secret affair, regretted it, and was desperate to reconnect with her husband asked me what she should do. I told her, "It's essential that you tell him what happened. You have to repent, right the wrong, and regain his trust." "Impossible," she blurted out. "I'm terrified of his reaction." "By being afraid of him," I answered, "you wrong him doubly. It's bad enough that you betrayed him as your husband. Now you wish to betray him as a human being by portraying him as an ogre with whom you cannot share a confidence." As we talked further, it became evident that the principal cause of her unfaithfulness was her deep dissatisfaction with her marriage—and her inability to talk about that dissatisfaction with her husband. Finding a lover seemed a lot less frightening than confronting the problems in her relationship.

Another woman wrote to me that she is convinced, two years into her marriage, that she has married the wrong man. "I know that in your books you're completely opposed to the idea that we might have married the wrong person, saying that if so, we must have had the wrong children. But I'm convinced that in my case it is so. I was raised in a traditional home and did what was expected of me, including dating and marrying the son of my father's old schoolmate, whom my parents adored. I did not have the heart to let my parents down or challenge their presumption of knowing what's best for me. But I do not love or respect this man." This woman's fear of standing up for herself to her parents made her passive in the face of the most important decision of her life. I told her that she dare not compound her earlier error by being afraid to have an honest conversation with her husband about her unhappiness. In all likelihood his pained yet loving ability to hear her out would endear him to her, and she might discover that she had married the right man after all.

When we keep our true selves hidden away from public view like an embarrassing relative, we're cheating ourselves out of an authentic existence. Conforming in this way retards our progress as individuals. Instead of coming into our own, we're trapped in a kind of perpetual adolescence, looking to the table at the center of the lunchroom to tell us what to think. Teenagers, of course, put a great deal of stock in their rebelliousness. For all their talk of breaking away from the pack, they actually observe a rigid uniformity. Sometimes it's actually difficult for my fifteen-year-old daughter to pick her own friends out of a crowd because they all look so much alike, with their identical clothes, hair—even their posture. "I walked into the classroom today and realized that everywhere I looked, I was looking at me," she told me.

Outsourcing Bravery

It doesn't go away as we grow up, either. We're afraid of being seen as cranks, eccentrics, weirdos. And yet isn't it precisely those people who buck the system and walk out of step who so vividly populate our imaginations?

Isn't this one of the reasons we're as addicted as we are to the movies that Hollywood makes? We go to the movies to see whistle-blowers and gladiators and spies who risk their lives to save humanity. Almost without exception, the hero is the guy who isn't afraid, the nonconformist who bucks the system. We pay to see maverick cops who put their lives—and jobs—on the line to nab the bad guy, teachers who risk their own well-being to bring education to inner-city youth, men who court the women they love boldly and unashamedly, risking humiliation for the sake of a romantic gesture. We love to see people who aren't afraid. From Erin Brockovich to Neo in *The Matrix*, from Tom Cruise in *The Last Samurai* to James Bond, our heroes are heroic because they're imperturbable. In the case of James Bond, even his hair is imperturbable.

We are addicted to Hollywood's well of fake fearlessness, like children running into their parents' bed to take comfort from people who aren't afraid. These movies appeal to the part of us that wants to walk out of step, the part of us that wants to express our originality. Instead of doing something with those feelings, we pay ten dollars to sit passively in the dark to watch other people pretend to do something courageously.

> **We've outsourced bravery, and turned courage into a spectator sport.**

It is imperative that we begin to reclaim this virtue for ourselves.

Afraid, We Embody Our Worst Qualities

Fear always forces us to be the living embodiment of our worst qualities. Fear is ugly. People look their best when they're joyous, and they look most hideous and pathetic when they are afraid.

A friend brought a guest to our Sabbath dinner one night, hoping I could help her find a relationship. She was good-looking and professionally successful, but by the end of the first course I knew why she was having such a hard time sustaining a romance. She was the living personification of ego and arrogance, dropping names and reveling in cruel zingers about other people. She had no grace and no access to the divine within her. Even the children were inching away from her as she told yet another story about the rock stars and CEOs of her acquaintance. I didn't want to be with her for the length of the salad course; how was she ever going to find someone to spend the rest of his life with her?

It was a revelation then to look at my wife, who is gentle, generous, and feminine. She was quietly making sure that everyone's plate was full. She sat down next to a quiet and ignored guest, making him feel welcome. My wife, who finds the good in people even when I see the bad, told me after dinner that the woman in question was not nearly as conceited as she came across.

"She is simply afraid," she said. For what else are insecurities but fears writ large? Our guest had felt compelled to yell, "I matter," from the rooftops because she was so convinced that she didn't. But it was a repellent cry, deeply off-putting instead of endearing.

I realized toward the end of the evening that our guest wasn't happy with the face she was presenting either. She didn't want to be brassy and shallow. Her fears had co-opted her into becoming a person she didn't really want to be.

Our fears betray us. I had a famous author and television personality on my radio show a number of times, a man whom I had always found very intimidating. He's a brilliant thinker and debater, and I always felt that he was out of my league—until I found myself in his office, listening to him drop names for forty-five minutes. This guy, this legendary mind, was trying to impress me—or was so insecure that it didn't matter to him who his audience was. It definitely changed the way I saw him and empowered me in our further dealings. His fears diminished him in my eyes, and as I walked out, I wondered, "Am I also that pathetic?"

The bluster we use to hide our insecurities tells people that we don't believe in ourselves.

How, honestly, can we expect other people to believe in us if we don't believe in ourselves? The shrill announcement that we matter is interpreted by those who hear us as a cry of desperation. And that's when the vultures move in. Every guy who dates a woman can almost instantly gauge her level of self-esteem and will treat her accordingly. Is she easy prey who can be gotten into bed with a few compliments, or a woman of substance, deserving of serious attention? Don't we delegate the most difficult tasks in the workplace to the person who seems most confident in her ability to carry them out?

A woman came to see me not to salvage her marriage but to corroborate her decision to divorce. She complained that she had disliked her husband from the first day they married. She saw him as beneath her. "I met his parents and they were like country bumpkins, simple and unsophisticated, their house drab and unkempt. My husband has no social skills. He bores me. A woman can only love a man if he is more than her, but he is less than me. I am a woman in despair." I looked her in the eye. "You can leave this marriage, but your misery is going to follow you into your singlehood, and it will be there in your next relationship, too. Your problem is not an unworthy husband; even according to you, he does everything to try to make you happy. Rather it's your fear. You are so terrified that you're not valuable that you project that onto your husband. You thought that when you married, all your self-esteem issues would vanish. Even this great guy can't make you believe that you're worth something. Only you can fight the demon of fear and afford yourself a sense of value. But whatever you do, don't blame a loving spouse."

Insecurity Is the Inability to Say, No!

When you're afraid you don't matter, then you have to matter to everyone. Insecurity means that you can't say no. You say yes to the saleslady even though the dress you're buying is utterly unbecoming. After all, she gave a little nobody like you her time, right? However compromised you become, you say yes to the special interest group threatening to withdraw support. You say yes to the music network that wants you to make out with another pop star on national TV in order to drive up your ratings.

There is nothing more pathetic and tragic than people who try to claw their way back into the public eye after losing favor. Whether it's an aging celebrity debasing himself in a celebrity boxing match, an older man "buying" a much younger wife, or an older woman undergoing plastic surgery until she looks like E.T., it's a pitiful thing to witness. Hollywood, of course, is full of examples: the reality TV show featuring washed-up eighties stars degrading themselves with inane games was a particularly sad example.

I remember how shocked I was by the way Mikhail Gorbachev spent his retirement. He came to Oxford to speak just two years after leaving the presidency of the since-defunct Soviet Union. I had worked several years to get him there. After the fantastic lecture he gave to our students, he went from our event to open a cell phone store in the great metropolis of Milton Keynes. And remember his infamous Pizza Hut commercial? How tragic that one of the key figures of modern history, a man to whom we are all indebted for having facilitated the collapse of communism, was so insecure once he had exited the world stage that he had to parlay his fame into a career hawking fast food. Even truly great men are frightened of being poor and leaving the celebrity spotlight.

Why did Bill Clinton have sex with Monica Lewinsky? Over the course of the two years of their relationship, they had very little sex, and what there was of it, as described in the Starr Report, sounded pretty unerotic. So why did he put his position as leader of the free world, something he had worked an entire lifetime to achieve, in jeopardy? Because Bill Clinton, for all his obvious charm and brilliance, is a man driven by his insecurities. That's why he finds it nearly impossible to live outside the spotlight. To date, he has yet to overcome the fear that he doesn't matter. Despite his title and myriad achievements before he became president, his good looks, a supersmart wife, and a lovely daughter, he was all too ready to believe that he was nothing underneath it all. Monica may not have been the most beautiful girl on the block, or the smartest, but she may well have been the most devoted. She worshipped him and showed her devotion: she'd wait ten hours in a line just for a glimpse of him! The Monica Lewinskys of this world, experts in their own vulnerabilities, know all about how to win guys like Bill Clinton. Simply flatter them and boost their self-esteem. Demonstrate a herculean devotion that makes them feel important. And that approach was very seductive to a man bearing his insecurities—seductive enough that he'd jeopardize his lifelong dream and goal for some cold, humiliating sex.

Fear Makes Us Mean

Our fears and insecurities also make us cruel. When I got into radio, I was warned that it can be a pretty mean industry. Many radio programmers are famous for putting down their talent and making the on-air personalities feel as if the ax of redundancy is hovering over them at all times. It's a method of control. Although I have been fortunate enough to work with great people who value me, I have witnessed my share of backstabbing. When I asked an industry leader why he thought this happened, he said that it was because the radio business has an inferiority complex. TV is where all the real numbers are—the real audience, and the real money. Most Americans who can easily name hundreds of people on television couldn't name ten radio hosts. This second-place mentality can bring out people's nastiness. Of course, there are plenty of bastards in TV as well, just as there are in every profession. You can bet that the more nasty the person, the more insecure they are as well.

The bigger the insecurity, the meaner you become. If you're insecure, then you have no choice but to become vengeful and envious of other people, until you eventually and unscrupulously seek to undermine them. Isn't that one of the faces of fear?

> **Only people who have dedicated themselves to an attachment to the infinite—G-d, or G-dly principles—can carry themselves with complete serenity.**

Such people are always looking for mastery over themselves rather than others. Their battles are always inner battles. Can you imagine the Dalai Lama dropping a name, or engaging in bullying another monk in order to feel important? You'd be shocked if he did, because you expect that a man who is holy is also pleasant. And he is pleasant because he is bold, courageous, and unafraid. If people don't intimidate or threaten him, why would he be unkind to them? It's our fears that make us feel vulnerable enough to strike out.

Fear Robs Us of Self-Determination

Insecurity not only leaves us open to corrupting influences, but it takes away our ability to determine our own fate. This is one of the most important reasons why we can't condemn ourselves to a life lived in fear—because it means a life lived under someone else's thumb. A fearful population is less likely to speak up against injustice and more likely to roll over in the face of opposition. If we're frightened and insecure, we'll do what they want us to do, vote the way they want us to vote, buy what they tell us to buy. There's a proverb that says,

> **The moment you fear something,
> you give it power over you.**

Only by controlling our fears will we control our lives.

Many of our fears are irrational, ghosts and goblins under the bed, but these aren't always of our own invention. Sometimes we are on the receiving end of a campaign to make us afraid. Fear has always been a very effective method of control, and in fact the United States is populated by people who have become rich by manipulating us through our fears that we're too fat, too ugly, too poor, too slow, too stupid, too (insert adjective here) to matter. They know that if we're afraid, we're more easily manipulated, more malleable, more compliant. Womanizers succeed in seducing women against their will because the men know that, especially in today's culture, most women are afraid that they aren't attractive enough.

> **When you live in fear, you grant the
> manipulators instant entrée.**

Insecurity leaves us open. Not long ago I read that Abercrombie & Fitch only hires attractive young men and women to sell their clothing. The theory is that if a beautiful man or woman tells you that you look good when you come out of the dressing room, you're likely to purchase the items that won their approval, however fleeting and fake that approval is. You're intimidated by their beauty. Since you feel small and insignificant in the face of what psychologist Warren Farrell calls "genetic celebrities," you want to impress them in whatever small way you can. Even better, you want to look like them. Desperate for approval, we give these physical specimens—with big muscles and busts, but with little knowledge or wisdom—power over us.

Isn't just such a fear campaign going on in the American media today? Wear the wrong label, gain a few pounds, go bald, and no one will ever love you. Buy the wrong suit or the wrong technology, and you'll be overtaken in business. What about the supposedly objective news? Just listen to the way they tease it during prime time: There's a killer in the salad bar; what you don't know about your over-the-counter allergy medicine could kill you; around every corner, there's a maniac preparing to throw you in front of a train. The public's fear is the bait on the hook. If you don't tune in at six, that tuna salad sandwich may be the last thing you ever eat.

Certainly Hitler understood the power of intimidation and fear, perhaps better than any other person in recent memory, and used it to create the world's darkest kingdom. Everything from his bullying and demagogic public speeches to the imposing architecture of the Chancellery—everything was designed to intimidate. To get to Hitler's office, you had to walk hallways laden with banners, the length of three football fields—twice the length of the Salon of Mirrors at the Palace of Versailles—before arriving at a pair of enormous, heavy doors. It's no wonder that Chamberlain was unsuccessful in standing up to Hitler in the late thirties. Hitler had won before the negotiations had even begun. If the Allies had been able to say, "We're not impressed by your foyer, and we have no fear of your armies either," perhaps they wouldn't have sold Czechoslovakia down the river, and the Second World War and the Holocaust would have been averted. I believe that North Korea is practicing this kind of intimidation right now. Kim Jong Il is a world-class bully, just as Saddam Hussein was before him. Still the world's leaders cow before him because they are afraid of his nuclear arsenal. The most recent supplicant was the Japanese prime minister, Junichiro Koizumi, who paid a ransom to Kim for the release of Japanese hostages. Here was the leader of the world's second largest economy agreeing to be bullied by a bully.

The only answer to this kind of bullying is to stand up to it. We have to face down our fears and watch them disintegrate in front of our eyes. Only after we've gathered the courage to stand up to our fears can we finally de-fang them, realizing that we're equal to the challenge.

Fear Invites Disaster

Fear not only offers us no protection, it all too often becomes a self-fulfilling prophecy.

> **When you are motivated by fears and insecurities,**
> **they become self-fulfilling prophecies.**

There are countless examples of the way fear backfires, causing disaster in-stead of preventing it. Can you imagine anything more horrific than shooting one of your children because you think you've heard a burglar? It's an obscen-ity, and yet it happens all the time. Look at the tragedy in a Chicago nightclub in February 2003. The government had raised the security color code to or-ange, indicating a heightened state of terror alert, and the country was in a state of panic, stocking up on duct tape and plastic sheets to protect against bi-ological or chemical warfare. It's no wonder that when pepper spray was fired due to some altercation in the nightclub, hundreds of people panicked and ran toward the exits, and twenty-one of them were trampled and killed.

I once counseled a couple who were fighting constantly about the threat of the husband's infidelity. The wife's first husband had cheated on her, and she was consumed by the fear that history would repeat itself and that she would eventually be left humiliated and alone. Her new husband had eyes for no one but her, but she was making it difficult for him to stay so devoted. After a par-ticularly horrible episode in which he found himself desperately trying to cor-roborate a charge on his credit card bill (he'd had a quick drink after work with his boss), he confessed to me that he wasn't sure how much longer he could take living in a marriage that felt more and more like a police state. Instead of strengthening the union, this woman's fears were actually causing the destruc-tion of her perfectly sound marriage, the very thing she sought to prevent.

Fear Makes Us Extremists

Fear forces us to take an extreme position. The philosopher Zoroaster first introduced the concept of dualism, and this single idea has arguably done more to influence world culture than any other before or since. The ying and the yang, the black and the white, the right and the left—we live in a world that we divide into two. Dualism also supplies the fundamental difference between the Christian and Jewish religions. Whereas Christianity is, of course, a monotheistic religion, Christians believe that the universe is governed by diametrically opposed forces: G-d and the Devil. There is a constant battle between good and evil, light and darkness, heaven and hell. It's a little harder in Judaism, since Jews believe that there is only one G-d. In Judaism, which is passionately monotheistic, there are no two sides to the coin, which makes accounting for evil supremely challenging. If there's no Devil to blame, then how does evil happen? If G-d provides everything, then how can we explain evil in the world? How can we love and trust a G-d who allows terrible things to happen to the people we care about?

This is the subject of much debate among Jewish thinkers, most notably the philosopher Maimonides. Maimonides proposed reconciling the presence of evil with the existence of a merciful G-d by suggesting that evil lies in the extremes. All things are good, but too much of any good thing is evil.

Nothing is inherently evil, but existence is corrupted in extreme measures.

This makes sense, on a fundamental level. Too little or too much discipline will ruin your kids. Too little or too much jealousy will kill your marriage. Too hot or too cold a shower is profoundly unpleasant. The key is in finding a balance.

If we accept this to be true—that the mean, or middle, is good, and that evil lies in the extremes—then we see the pernicious effects of fear. I believe that fear is inherently evil, because it always forces us to embrace extremes. It takes us away from the center and pushes us to the periphery. A workaholic works the way he does because he's terrified that he's worthless if he doesn't have the position and status his job affords him, so he neglects his wife and children to work long hours at the office. His fear precludes him from achieving a healthier balance, and the result is self-destruction. Women who sleep with guys on the first date do so out of a fear that there won't be a second. Instead of allowing things to unfold gradually in the interest of finding a balance between the physical and emotional, they act out of fear and go to the physical extreme, which then sabotages the relationship. They share too much and don't hold anything back for themselves.

Evil and fear almost always coexist. Hitler and Stalin were the wickedest men of the twentieth century. Both were famously paranoid, fearing rebellion and death at the hands of subordinates. Likewise, Arab fundamentalists behind the attack on the World Trade Center and other acts of terrorism around the world are acting out of fear, pure and simple. They're afraid that their whole culture is going to be destroyed by western progress. Thinking that tradition and modernity are fundamentally in conflict, they didn't keep up with the West, so they're full of hate. Unlike more moderate Islam, which has found a balance between the modern and the traditional, the spiritual and the technological, the soul and the body, the fundamentalists have pushed out modern and intellectual influences entirely. Their extremism, founded on fear, is destroying a once-great world religion and is leading Islam into becoming synonymous with bloodletting.

We have allowed fear into our homes, our bedrooms, our workplaces. We have cultivated it in our relationships with our children. We have made it an everyday, ordinary part of our lives. And in so doing, we have allowed the pendulum to swing wildly to one extreme. Clearly, we have to make our way back to the center, to a place of moderation.

6

Busting the Myths About Fear

He mocketh at fear, and is not affrighted; neither turneth he back from the sword.

—JOB 39:22

There are very few monsters who warrant the fear we have of them.

—ANDRÉ GIDE

Humans instinctively avoid that which makes them uncomfortable. Why then would we allow ourselves to remain in a constant state of fear, when it clearly humiliates, demoralizes, and depresses us? Why would we allow ourselves to live with this cold hand around our hearts if there is a better way?

During the years I've been counseling men and women, I've heard them advance a great number of theories in favor of fear. Ironically enough, we have been conditioned to believe that fear actually serves a purpose. Instead of banishing this destroyer to the slag heap, we continue on in fear because we think it's doing something useful. The Greek playwright Aeschylus said, "There are times when fear is good. It must keep its watchful place at the heart's controls," and we believe this. Isn't it the fear of going to jail that prevents us from breaking the law? Isn't it the fear that we'll keel over that keeps us eating our leafy green vegetables? Isn't it the fear of revenge that stops us from hurting people? Isn't fear ultimately a positive driver in our lives?

This is an incredibly dangerous way to think. When we grant fear the legitimacy of serving a positive purpose, we allow it to become even more entrenched in our lives. Let's briefly expose the fear myths for the destructive fictions they are.

Myth #1: Fear Is Protective

Upon earth there is not his like, who is made without fear.

—JOB 41:33

Worry is a form of fear, and all forms of fear produce fatigue. A man who
has learned not to feel fear will find the fatigue of daily life enormously diminished.

—BERTRAND RUSSELL

There is a widespread belief in our culture that fear is somehow protective.
This belief manifests itself in worry. Americans spend an inordinate amount
of time worrying: it's practically the national hobby. We worry about everything. Jews, of course, are world-class worriers, no doubt a function of our
history of persecution. The old joke goes, How does a Jewish telegram start?
"Message to follow. Start worrying."

The mistake here is to confuse worry with action. When we sit worrying
about a problem, in some warped way we believe that we're actually address-
ing it. It's a way to alleviate the anxiety that comes from thinking that we're
powerless. If I worry about my husband cheating on me, I feel like I'm doing
something—which is easier, and feels more empowering, than simply trust-
ing someone.

People believe that if they choose to live in fear, they will be that much
more "on their guard" and end up being safe. An evolutionary biologist
would say that those human ancestors who developed fear lived to pass on
their genes to their descendants. Since I'm not a creationist and not an evo-
lutionist, I don't believe that anyway. But if you accept that theory as true, a
central question still remains: why haven't we adjusted our fear quotient to
the level of threat? It's wise to be cautious about eating new things if you're
foraging for berries and mushrooms in the forest. You don't need to exercise
that level of caution at a friend's table; caution will cause you to miss a great
meal.

When you live with the mistaken belief that fear is somehow prophylac-
tic, that belief poisons everything. I know a woman with a husband and three
children who has lived her entire life with a frown. She is never happy. At her
daughter's wedding, I asked her to smile. She responded, "I worry for my
daughter and what her new life will bring." You could see that in her warped
understanding of the universe, she thought that her frown was the umbrella
that protected her daughter against evil forces. This mother was convinced
that as long as she worried, she was doing her job as a mother in protecting
her young. It sounds irrational, but that's what fear is.

Fear is a hysterical response to an imaginary threat.

Fear doesn't make sense.

What should she have been doing? Dancing! Giving her daughter one last hug as a single woman and her first hug as a married one. Kissing and catching up with all the relatives who had traveled from so far away to see her daughter join her life with someone else's. Eating the delicious food she'd arranged. Allowing herself a moment of self-congratulation on raising this beautiful, talented, radiant bride. Instead she cheated herself out of a once-in-a-lifetime experience. How many of us rob ourselves of special moments by being anxious?

I was worried not just about her but about her daughter too! Why should her mother's concern and anxiety be something this bride had to shoulder on the happiest day of her life? Why should her blue skies be marred by the black cloud hovering over her mother? Her mother may have thought that her worry was on her daughter's behalf, but in fact, her fear was selfish.

All fear is fundamentally selfish.

Take another example. A man sits, waiting for his wife to get home from work. In his heart of hearts, he knows that she's safe. Though he really expects that she'll walk through the door at any moment, he feels that he owes it to her to worry. He believes that worrying makes him a good husband, that it shows he cares about her. And of course, he thinks that his worry can somehow protect her: if he's worried about her tires slipping on a wet road, his thoughts will magically prevent it from happening.

Later, when his wife gets home, he proudly announces that he was worried about her, and this endears him to her. Both of them have mistaken worrying about someone for missing that person, but they are not the same thing.

**When you miss someone, you're focused on her
and how her absence leaves a void in your life.
But when you're afraid for someone,
you're really worrying for yourself.**

You're focused on your own pain, because you don't want to experience tragedy or loss. Fear turns you inside yourself, away from the outside world and the people you love in it.

The husband who sits at home worrying for his wife often has a huge argument with her as soon as she walks in. Rather than rushing to hug her, he yells at her, "Where the hell were you? Didn't you know I was worried sick about you?" Then he even accuses her of selfishness. "It was so selfish of you not to call. You couldn't just pick up a phone and say you were all right?" Her cell phone may have been out of a coverage area, or maybe she was rushing around at the supermarket and didn't want to waste time. He worried, and she should have protected him from that. But no one asked him to worry. He's a great husband not when he sits and bites his fingernails but when he warmly welcomes his wife after she returns from a hard day's work.

The other problem with the concept of fear as protection is that it just doesn't work. Fear isn't protective, plain and simple. This powerful emotion has the ability to disfigure our lives and prevent us from achieving our most beloved goals, and yet it cannot keep us safe.

Worry can exacerbate an ulcer, but it can't protect your loved one. You're not doing anything. The mother of the bride isn't protecting her daughter from an unhappy marriage when she worries about her, and an anxious husband isn't empowering his wife's car with skidless tires by pacing the room awaiting her return. Instead of acting in a way that would actually add value to their relationship, by fixing the leak under the sink or starting dinner, this husband is just poisoning his own heart with fear. A man who truly misses his wife runs out to buy flowers to greet her romantically. A man who worries about his wife spends the night calling hospitals to see if she was hit by a truck—hardly the stuff of romance.

Jews may be famous for worrying, but the Jewish religion advocates that worrying should be replaced with prayer. Don't pace outside the doors of the operating theater as your husband's appendix is removed. Rather take out the book of Psalms and entreat G-d for health and deliverance. Connect to the eternal source of life, rather than wearing out the soles of your shoes. Prayer is not just a religious ritual but a psychological need that helps us stave off fear.

Fear doesn't work. You can lock your doors at night, you can stockpile your basement with canned goods and bottled water, you can buy the most expensive gas masks and anthrax alarms on the market. Each of these remedies can, in turn, be useful in its own right. But you know, in your heart of hearts, that these things will never make you completely safe. Even with the best military in the world, the toughest army rangers, the most fearsome Apache helicopters, we will not conquer terrorism overnight. There will always be evil, and there will never be domestic security so foolproof that we're guaranteed to prevent the next attack against the United States. Clearly we need something better.

We need to inoculate ourselves inwardly so that we're fit to meet any test we're presented with outwardly.

Myth #2: Fear Is the Best Motivator

> Yea, though I walk through the valley of the shadow of death, I will fear no evil: for thou art with me; thy rod and thy staff they comfort me.
>
> —PSALMS 23:4

> Nothing is more despicable than respect based on fear.
>
> —ALBERT CAMUS

In the same way that the combustion engine inevitably creates pollution, capitalism inevitably produces fear as a by-product. Everything about life in America tells you to prove yourself, constantly and endlessly. There is no such thing as unconditional love: society tells you from the moment you are born that you have to do something to deserve what you get. You have to hustle, move, shake, perform, dance for your dinner. From virtually the moment you come out of the womb, you're dealing with this feeling of inadequacy. You learn to believe that you have to deserve the love you're given, so your childhood becomes a game of "Look, Mom, no hands!"

At the same time you're also taught that there isn't enough of everything to go around. For you to succeed, someone else must fail; for you to win, someone else must lose. For you to make money in the stock market, someone else has to take a beating. All of this breeds a fundamental deprivation mentality, a cup-half-empty outlook.

If everyone is competing for the same pie, then by definition, someone's slice is going to be smaller than another's, and someone else isn't going to get any pie at all.

This is true in every aspect of life, and from the very beginning. It's true during childhood, as you compete with your siblings for the love of your parents. It's true in school, as you clamber over your classmates for the attention of your teachers and the good grades that will get you into a good college. You battle later for jobs, for more money, for professional recognition. Businesses are designed to compete in the cutthroat marketplace. Competition for a mate leads you to spend hours on your body, your hair, your clothes.

It's no wonder that, in this ultracompetitive atmosphere, there is a palpable sense of fear. Fear is the phantom that chases you, the sheepdog nipping at your heels and goading you on to bigger and better things. It keeps you working later, dieting harder, spending more. In fact, fear of failure outstrips almost every other fear. If you listen to some of the nation's most high-powered executives, the message is clear: "I would rather be horribly mangled than fail. I would rather become a fire-breathing ogre, treating subordinates like dirt, than lose my reputation on Wall Street for overachievement." The fear of being humiliated and impoverished makes business leaders work ever harder and demand ever more from their employees. It's exhausting.

There's no doubt about it. Fear can be a superbly effective motivating factor in life, and it undoubtedly serves as one of the principal engines of human advance. We don't even protest fear's prevalence in our lives. We take it for granted, because we assume it's a good driver. Yet even at its best, fear cannot be affirmative, only defensive.

**Fear is not an innovative or creative emotion,
but a fundamentally reactive one.**

It has you not running *to* any set destination but rather running *from* something profoundly alarming. Those who live in fear run not to the light, but from the darkness. Fear and the emotions it conjures are inherently limited in their productive capacity. Fear will always swallow you; it will catch and devour you. You can't outrun it.

**Fear is a guarantor of insatiability. When you're animated
by your fears, nothing is enough.**

Motivated by fear, you rob yourself of your own successes. If a parent or teacher tells you that you'll never amount to anything, and you use that to motivate yourself, then every time you find yourself confronted by what seems like an insurmountable barrier, you might find the drive to persevere in defiance. On one hand, this is a story of human triumph. On the other, it is a story of limitation and incarceration. How can you ever achieve a sense of inner peace if you're always running away from the fear that your parent or teacher was right? Who would want to live a life devoted to impressing others? Is there any dignity in that? Would there be any satisfaction in it? This is why we witness so many professionals who suffer from depression. Their professional achievement haunts them rather than satisfies them. This hurtful judgment becomes the center of your entire universe: whether you want to or not, you're dedicating every single one of your successes to another person.

If you feel that you don't matter and choose fear as your motivator, then you're always just bettering yourself in relation to your environment.

You drive a better car than someone else, you snag a wealthy wife, you win the election, but you're just keeping up with the Joneses. Your sense of self-esteem comes from outdoing others. Soon you see them not as friends but as antagonists. You lose the ability to be happy for someone else's success. You seethe with envy and jealousy when you see other people succeed. You become the kind of person who isn't interested in Martha Stewart's guilt or innocence but only in watching her fall. You will compromise all your cherished principles to stay on the treadmill, because the world is a jungle and only the fittest survive. And since you're only bettering yourself in relation to things that are transient—and those things inevitably change—you'll never really feel secure.

A woman who came to see me said that she grew up in a house without a lot of money. Her father died when she was young, which led to a great deal of insecurity in her life. She found satisfaction in marrying a well-off and essentially decent man, but the solution was only a temporary one. He fell on hard times and, depressed at his failure, started treating her poorly. Finding herself back at square one, she divorced him. The woman went on to start a successful interior design business and has become well-off in her own right.

When we met at my home, she recounted one of her favorite movie scenes. In the movie *Pretty Woman*, Julia Roberts takes Richard Gere's cash and goes shopping in the most exclusive shops on Rodeo Drive. She's still dressed like a streetwalker, so at the first boutique she tries, the snooty saleswoman won't even help her. She leaves, humiliated, and gets outfitted somewhere else. Later, now dressed to the nines, she stops back at the store to let the salespeople know the big commissions they missed out on because they underestimated her and her purchasing power.

The woman compared her own story to the movie. When she had little money, many of the people with whom she worked treated her contemptuously, she said. Now that she is able to buy anything she wants, they all envy her. She told me this story with a great sense of personal triumph. She had won in the end. This woman is not in any way a shallow person. A devoted mother of four, she is deeply charitable and profoundly nurturing. Still, the humiliation of a hard early life exacerbated the fear that she only mattered if she had money. So now she spends her life proving herself to salespeople, with her credit cards as her badges of honor.

I can well see why the revenge scene in *Pretty Woman* is so satisfying to this woman and anyone else who's ever been made fun of for having "the wrong clothes." But she can see in her own life that this strategy isn't really an effective way to alleviate fear. She's a prosperous woman now, but until she feels she never has to prove herself to anyone else, she isn't any less insecure or any less afraid; her fears are simply different now. Financial wealth can disappear at any time, as she knows. She could have a bad year, and some of what she has might be taken away from her. Besides, no matter how rich she is, to Bill Gates she is still a pauper. When wealth is the criterion you use to judge your success, every step up is shakier than the last.

This is one of the reasons I have such a hard time convincing people that fear can be eliminated. They've already tried to eliminate it, without success. Most people spend their lives trying to escape their fears—and fail! That's because they tend to go about it in exactly the wrong way. The problem isn't that fear can't be eliminated from life but that most of our attempts to do so are wrongheaded.

What most people end up doing is actually indulging their fear by catering to its causes. If the fear is that they're not important, they devote their lives to pursuing things outside themselves that attest to their importance, like memberships to the right country clubs, thereby making themselves more dependent on those things and ironically increasing their fears.

Looking for value outside yourself through the pursuit of wealth, beauty, or status is merely feeding the beast of fear that lies within. It's applying Band-Aids to fear instead of healing the wound. How can placing the locus of your sense of importance outside yourself possibly lead to a cure? Will any medicine given to someone else lead to your being healed?

Numbing the Pain of Fear with the Impulse Purchase

Of course, the vast majority of people simply escape their fears by becoming television junkies or more tragically, turning to drugs and alcohol. Afraid of rejection and tired of giving themselves the old pep talk and persevering, they stop dating and go to Blockbuster. Afraid of intimacy, they take refuge in nameless, zipless sex. Rather than getting emotionally naked in front of a trusted spouse, they simply take their clothes off in front of a stranger, which is a lot less daunting. Women who are afraid that they don't have qualities that will engage a man over the long haul are the ones who typically jump into bed as soon as they're asked. Men feel safer in bed than in a conversation, so they strip down physically instead of baring themselves emotionally, hopping from one willing partner to another. Married people are scarcely better. Afraid that their marriages are empty, most husbands and wives go to the movies on their one date night and fill the car ride with conversation about the kids and the neighbors. They rarely, if ever, confront the deeper issues of their marriage for fear that they will not be able to plug all the holes.

Afraid that our lives are empty, we also collect meaningless baubles to fill them. That's why people in the West have become addicted to the impulse purchase and spend their Sundays at monotonous shopping malls. Buying stuff makes them feel important. And it gives them something to look forward to.

One divorced woman I counseled was a true shopaholic, spending thousands of dollars every month on stuff that bored her a few weeks later. "What does shopping do for you?" I asked. She replied, "I have no man in my life. I guess it diverts me from the fear that I'll always be alone." A recent study corroborated what we always knew: that people who shop and who hoard do so out of a sense of fear. A group of test subjects were shown two films: one scary, the other happy. They were then given money and sent to a shopping mall. Those that saw the scary movie spent nearly all the money they were given. Those who saw the happy film spent nearly none.

Instead of curing the problem, escaping fear through acquisition only exacerbates it. Wealthy men become greedy instead of content. Beautiful women pursue more plastic surgery and ever more painful diets instead of appreciating themselves for their unique beauty and the grace that comes with age. In the meantime people send exactly the wrong message to the world at large: isn't a trophy wife who's only with a man for the money the ultimate sign that the money matters more than he does?

Since all the trinkets we collect are transient, people become obsessed with losing them. If you believe that you're only worth something because of your unlined face and your twenty-one-inch waist, then instead of enjoying your deepening wisdom and relationships, you're just going to be more afraid with every birthday. If you think you're only worth something because of your powerful job and corner office and impressive staff, then it's true that your self-worth can be stripped from you very easily. Fear has you wasting time and energy, traveling down the wrong path while your real goals and achievements—things that would genuinely increase your sense of self-worth—sneak out the back. It drives you to acquire more and more stuff, and all the stuff does is exacerbate the fear.

One night as my wife and I were walking a British friend back to his hotel in midtown Manhattan, our stroll took us past some of the most expensive real estate in the world, filled with the most exclusive boutiques and the fanciest restaurants. We watched two thirty-something men in beautifully tailored suits press their noses up against the window of a Mercedes dealership to admire the newly released Maybach model, sticker price $350,000.

It was a macabre scene! These men weren't running home to wives. They weren't reading children a bedtime story. They were looking through the window of a car dealership at a piece of metal. They had been working hard—till midnight!—so that they could afford expensive toys like that Mercedes. Their conversation wasn't even of aesthetic pleasure in a beautiful object but of one-upmanship, and it proved to me that these men had never grown up. When they were little boys, they looked through the toy store window at miniature cars, and now they were doing the same thing on a grander scale. They were worshipping at the throne of materialism, dreaming of the day when they could leave their fears of being nobodies behind by zooming away in their expensive, gleaming chariots.

I felt like shaking them by the shoulders and saying, "You're on a treadmill. The harder you run, the harder you'll have to run to keep up. You'll get that car, and then they'll release a new model, something bigger and shinier, and then you'll feel inadequate because you don't have it. You want that car because you feel insignificant, because you fear that you're worth nothing. That car is going to do nothing but make that insignificance more intolerable to you. You don't need it! You are significant, just because you're one of G-d's children. Go to church this Sunday. Go help raise money to send American soldiers in Iraq care packages. Take out inspiring books on history from a library. Find something else to give your life meaning. Go home to your wives and find real comfort from fear. Connect to your children and find real relief from nothingness. If you're not married, find a good woman who loves you for who you are and not the car you drive. Go to people who care about you, not what you have."

**Money should never be turned into a
currency to purchase self-esteem.**

Money is for buying *things*: shelter, food, clothing, education for your children. When you turn it into a currency to purchase self-esteem, a symbol of your success or failure as a human being, you arm it with a power it was never designed to have. It's too ephemeral to make you feel safe. Mammon is a false idol, distracting you from a real G-d.

Truth be told, those men provided a much-needed moment of clarity for me. I'm not completely invulnerable to the pull of the culture myself. As we were walking past those exclusive boutiques, I myself had wished that I could buy some nice things for my wife. We're not into $7,000 dresses, but I did wish I could regularly afford to buy her things that would highlight her beauty. Our walk had taken us past the Waldorf-Astoria, where President Bush was spending that particular night, and the sight of about a thousand armed policemen guarding one man's hotel room had made me feel insignificant indeed. Was I worth anything at all? I wasn't entirely sure I could afford a room in the hotel! Seeing these two men chasing after their self-worth through materialism came as a welcome wake-up call. I knew that I had no farther to look for a sense of self-worth than the kind-hearted, G-d-fearing woman walking next to me, someone who knows all of my faults and insecurities and who has chosen to spend her life with me anyway. Or my children, who are, thank G-d, bright and healthy and fun to be with. Or my professional work advancing spiritual awareness, helping people to appreciate G-d, heal their marriages, and participate more fully in their relationships. Or G-d Himself, who loves and watches over me, no matter what I'm driving. I know that I don't need a hunk of steel to chase away my fears of insignificance; I have things of much greater value around me so that I never have to fear at all.

For about a year I had the privilege of serving as the morning host for America's oldest black radio station. There was a period of months when my cohost, Peter Noel, had money issues. Seeing his financial pressures mounting, I asked him how he could be so calm on the air with me. "Aren't you scared?" I asked him. "It worries me sick when I can't pay my children's tuition or the mortgage. I get scared out of my mind. I freeze up," I told him. Peter looked at me, and with his trademark flair, drama, and charisma, he said to me, "Shmuley, every morning I wake up, I open my eyes and I say, 'Thank you, Jesus!' I'm just so happy to be alive. I'm not afraid of n-o-t-h-i-n-g!"

Many irreligious people would dismiss this story as typical of religious people who always use G-d as a crutch. After all, religion is the opiate of the masses, right? But Peter is not religious in a traditional sense, not a regular churchgoer, and what he meant was that fear comes from a feeling of for-lornness and abandonment. He never feels abandoned. Men such as those who were looking through that dealership window are frightened precisely because they are detached. Unconnected to anything transcendent, they are at the mercy of the elements. A blessing to them is not life or the gift of sight, it's a car that will impress their friends.

**The pull of a culture that makes us believe
that we are what we buy must be resisted
with every fiber of our being.**

The voice that whispers to us to keep up with the Joneses is the sound of emptiness and silence. This is one of the reasons that the Osama bin Ladens of this world so enjoy terrifying us. Look at the Arab world. It was once one of the centers of the cultural universe, a wellspring of intellectual activity and a place where art and science thrived. No more. Most of its citizens live in astonishing poverty, with few civil rights and little legal recourse. Of the twenty-two Arab countries, not one has a functioning democracy. Nowhere else in the world are women denied such basic rights as the right to drive a car. And yet this is the civilization that has the West on the run. Their one big area of success is that they can frighten the world's only superpower. So they continue to invest their energies into trying to frighten and bully us be-cause it makes them feel important. They love to watch us cower in fear be-cause it proves everything they think of us—that for all our big buildings, our technology, and our wealth, we are just a bunch of frivolous, frightened children, cut off from G-d, living for the next sports event, and dependent on money and luxury to give our lives meaning. When those planes crashed into the World Trade Center, the message they were sending was, "For all your giant McMansions, for all your impregnable, monster SUVs, for all your aircraft carriers and Apache helicopter gunships, we who live in caves and wear rags can still frighten you. Because G-d is on our side, we have no fear, and we make *you* cower in fear."

**Osama bin Laden wants to prove that the motto
on American money, "In G-d we trust," has been completely
swallowed by the American worship of the almighty dollar.**

Are Americans better at worshiping Mammon than they are at worshiping G-d? Our slavish devotion to stuff has made us less resistant to threats. The accumulation of money and beautiful clothes does not assuage any inner need. It's like taking a painkiller: all it does is hide the pain for a little while. It's like putting another lock on the door; it caters to the fear and doesn't change the fact that we're still trembling inside our houses. We're afraid because we're empty. Although we're tossing more and more trinkets into the void, we're not doing anything to allay the problem. We have no roots, so we are easily shaken—and if we're not careful, toppled.

It's time that we move toward the light. Follow me into something better.

7

Move Toward the Light

The LORD is my light and my salvation; whom shall I fear? the LORD is the
strength of my life; of whom shall I be afraid?

—PSALMS 27:1

Wicked men obey for fear, but the good for love.

—ARISTOTLE

You can use fear as a motivator, to drive yourself to excel at business, sports, and sexual conquests, but success born out of fear will never feel like success. There is a better solution, one that actually cures the problem instead of simply accommodating it. Whenever you're about to undertake any action, ask yourself if you're doing it because you're afraid or because you believe in the undertaking. If it's out of fear, then chances are you shouldn't be doing it at all. But if it's something that's intrinsically worthwhile, then prevail on yourself to change your motivation and undertake the action out of a sense of service rather than fear.

**The first step in conquering fear and releasing ourselves from
its stranglehold is to turn our face away from the darkness
and toward the light.**

Searching for positive rather than negative motivation is absolutely crucial in conquering fear and finding freedom. Don't be pushed by fear; be pulled by promise. What if you were to change your motivation? What if you were to better yourself in relation to things that are eternal? Then you would be judging yourself against things that can't change, things not subject to trends and fads and the vagaries of the stock market. This is always a hard argument to make. People simply don't believe me. That's because we're a short-term society.

Let's take a look at a marriage. The reason I don't cheat on my wife is not principally because I'm afraid of G-d. Although I love G-d and make every effort to obey his commandments, I sometimes do other things against His will, like engage in vanity. As far as my wife goes, well, amid her protestations that she would kill me, I believe she cares about me enough to forgive me even if I did something that foul (although she has asked me to add, once again, that she would kill me). So I don't refrain from unfaithfulness out of fear. Rather the motivation to be faithful is based on an affirmation of my marriage. Ultimately, I don't think the pleasures of a so-called fling could compare with the intimacy that a man and woman have in marriage. Adultery can be enticing and sin can be highly erotic. I even wrote an entire book on the subject called *Kosher Adultery*. But ultimately it's a letdown to have sex with someone for whom you don't feel a sense of one-flesh connectedness. If you're going to get naked and still have all your inhibitions on, well, then you're bound not to enjoy the experience fully. Unfaithfulness could never compete with the pleasures of marriage. Besides, if I had a secret from my wife, or if I were to hurt her, that act would undermine the closeness and intimacy that makes marriage the most unique relationship in which a human being will ever engage. The easy naturalness and the comforting closeness that exists between a man and his wife would be lost to us if either was to cheat. Finally, I cannot imagine that, however tantalizing illicit sex is, it can be pleasurable when you know that you are completely compromising your integrity. My positive motivation to be a decent and honest human being gives way to something even more positive—in this case, increased intimacy.

Let's say that I didn't cheat on my wife because I was afraid she'd find out and leave me, G-d forbid. What's the difference? I'm still not cheating, so the outcome is the same, right? Or is it? When you look a little closer, you realize that, in fact, when you are motivated by the fear that cheating on your wife will result in disaster, the marriage is still in jeopardy. In this scenario, you're not running toward intimacy, you're running away from the humiliation and hardship that would come from being discovered. You may not cheat, but you and your spouse certainly won't be drawn closer together. If you're faithful simply because you're afraid, your decision not to cheat doesn't beget further intimacy; it creates a little room in your mind that's cordoned off from your wife. Of course, she's going to notice that you're keeping secrets from her, that you're not as open to her as you once were, and she'll be hurt and damaged by that—even though you have technically remained faithful. You're still hiding your desire to be unfaithful. Since there's a whole part of you that you can't share with her, you'll start to feel guilty and resentful, and this will manifest itself in your behavior toward her and the family. The fear-based resolution not to cheat weakens rather than strengthens your marital union.

Fear-Based Motivation Lacks the Power to Inspire

When we're motivated by our fears, there is a difference in intention, a difference that affects the outcome. A politician might run for office because he believes that a powerful elected position will give him leverage with powerful people and raise his profile in the media and make it easier for him to date delicious young interns. Another politician runs because he honestly believes he holds commonsense answers to some of the serious problems his constituency faces and an elected position will give him a way to make a difference. Even if these two people do exactly the same things in office, there will always be a difference between them. The former will pass legislation and perhaps even be popular, but he will never inspire his people. They will not become better citizens with him at the helm. Fear-based energy is never magnetic. On the contrary, he will probably end up pandering to their interests rather than raising them up to the call of service. The other politician will inspire scores of people to be civic-minded like himself and to become more devoted and responsible citizens. Sincerity has that effect on people. Fear might be successful in the short term as a motivator, but it has a shelf life.

Examples of this wrongheaded approach backfiring are legion. You marry the wrong person out of the fear that you'll end up alone, and you end up divorced in five years—alone anyway. Why should that be surprising? You were never being pulled to a man, you were running from being stranded alone. So how did you expect to attach yourself to him? A researcher may sit all night, every night in her lab, searching for a cure for cancer. If she's motivated by the desire to find a cure, she's not proprietary about her research. She'll share her findings, and she'll find solutions faster. If she's motivated by personal gain, driven by fear and insecurity and hell-bent on winning a Nobel Prize to prove her worth, she'll dismiss the work of other labs. Without the support of others, it's only a matter of time before she crashes and burns.

The enemies she is bound to make along the way will only too happily hasten that moment. The success she craves will always remain just out of her grasp.

You are capable of transforming your motivation from being pushed by fear to being pulled by promise.

The happy, successful, and free people are those who focus on the promise of the future rather than the fear of the past. Being fear-motivated traps you in what went on before and prevents you from creating a blessed future. So you have to examine your heart, decide on your motivation, and change it from fear to love.

This book is a good example of this process. When I wrote this, I wanted the book to be a success. But why? Was it because I am afraid of being a no-body, or because I wanted to inspire people to do away with fear and have better lives? My literary agent, Robert Gottlieb, told me repeatedly that the book would not succeed unless it made people's lives better. But how could I make any of my readers' lives better if the focus was on me and my insecurities? A book that was driven by my fears would be transparent, because it would be far more about impressing rather than about helping the readers. So I had to work to shift my motivation from fear to promise, to be sure it was propelled by light rather than darkness, throughout the writing of this book.

I do not mean that you should not seek professional recognition in life. Everyone has an ego and wants to be professionally accomplished.

Ego gratification may be accommodated, but it dare not play a principal role in motivating your actions.

You can seek to be lauded for your work, but when you're consumed by insecurity and fear, you want all the praise yourself and have a real problem sharing it with others.

I once met an Australian rabbi, famous for his success in building Jewish educational facilities down under. He listed a litany of his achievements. I told him, tongue in cheek, that I thought rabbis were supposed to be humble. He responded, "Far from it. I, sir, am a braggart, pure and simple. But with a difference. When I finish listing my achievements, I shall give you opportunity of bragging as well." He made me laugh, but he also taught me a valuable lesson. The bad braggart, the one who hogs all the glory for himself, is the one who is so consumed by fearfulness that he or she cannot possibly share the spotlight with anyone else.

Isn't it through fear that we really learn these lessons? Isn't it through fear that we come to acknowledge our dependency on others? Isn't fear also positive because it teaches us our limitations? If we didn't fear an avalanche, we would go skiing in dangerous places. If quarterbacks in the NFL didn't fear concussions, they wouldn't slide into tacklers and protect their bodies. If we didn't fear being fired, we might not come to work on time. I'm not suggesting that we blithely ignore the lessons that fear has to teach us, but I do say it's time to look for a better teacher.

> **Every lesson fear can teach us would be
> better learned through love.**

One of the most powerful fear-eliminating prescriptions I can give you is this:

> **Don't run away from your fears, but find something
> to run toward—even if the ultimate result
> appears to be the same.**

Read a book, not so you have something intelligent to say at the next cocktail party you attend, but because you want to know more about the subject. Don't hunt around for another job while you're at work because you're afraid you'll get fired, but because preserving your integrity is its own reward. Go to synagogue or church not because you're afraid that G-d punishes sinners, but because there is blessing in connecting with your spiritual source. G-d is not Tony Soprano. If He were, He would not be worth worshiping anyway. So don't insult G-d by praying in order to avoid the Big Barbecue in the sky. Lead a spiritual life because you genuinely want to give thanks for your blessings and experience G-d's embrace. Do good toward others because you don't want to cause pain, not because you don't want to risk the revenge of those you have wronged. Drive safely and eat more healthfully not because you're afraid of death, but because you love life.

**Not only does the end not justify the means, but the whole
equation is backwards. The means *are* the end.**

To Have and to Be

I have made herculean efforts to implement this teaching in my own life. As
a young man, I was laden with considerable insecurity and a desire to make
an impact, and those qualities made me determined and hardworking. I
achieved a measure of professional success. I war fortunate to have written
bestselling books and win awards for preaching. And although I had a loving
wife and great kids, happiness was elusive. Who can be happy when they
spend their lives trying to impress others? I started ruminating on my need to
find a far more organic and natural motivator. I decided that I had not only to
love G-d with my deeds but to honor Him with my motivation. I determined
to transform the engine of my success from fear to love. I decided to write
articles not because I wanted to impress the readers with my wisdom, but because I wanted to share whatever I had learned about life with those who
might be struggling with the same issues. I started giving lectures not to wow
but to inspire the audience. I wanted to be a successful rabbi not in order to
make an impression, but because I thought by doing so I could bring healing.

Helping me along this path was Erich Fromm's book *To Have or to Be?*, one
of the most profound works I have ever read. I expanded on his ideas in my
book *Kosher Emotions*, in which I discuss the two different kinds of ambition.
One kind of ambition is motivated by the fear that you come into this world
as a big nothing, a giant zero. You strive to prove that you are valuable. The
problem is that if, in math, you take a zero and you add a whole bunch of
ones after it—great degree, good job, lovely spouse, respect of your peers—
the result is still nearly zero. The number 0.111111 is still rounded down to
zero. Zeroes are people who never transcend the belief that they are utterly
valueless. Beneath everything you do is a gaping emptiness that refuses to be
filled. Even once you succeed, you cannot enjoy your blessings because they
are sucked into the all-encompassing darkness.

Then there are the people who are born believing that because they are
G-d's children, they are of infinite value. They are born not zeroes but ones.
They seek professional and personal achievement in life not in order to
prove themselves, but in order to bring about the gradual unfolding of their

nature and talents. They seek to translate their G-d-given potential into something actual and life-affirming. They give love not because they are insecure but simply because it wells up inside of them. They work hard not in order to prove themselves but because they seek a healthy and productive outlet for their energies. This kind of person also adds the ones of success— good education, good job, respect from their communities—to their lives. This time the numbers add up, because there is a one, a wholesome human being, underlying it all.

There is a person who achieves things in order "to have," as Fromm would say. But there is another person who seeks not "to have" but simply "to be." While the former person is a cistern into which water must be poured constantly if it is not to go dry, the latter person is a wellspring from which an abundance of water flows naturally. The former is complicated and unhappy, the latter is simple and fulfilled.

Most people believe that, in order to achieve great things in life, you first have to be screwed up. They accept that guys like Donald Trump or Larry Ellison have built huge businesses and achieved wealth because their deeply rooted insecurities pushed them to prove themselves to the masses. Indeed, Aristotle himself said that "great men are always of a nature originally melancholy." The destructive belief that the young doctor who was told that he was stupid in class is the one who will eventually cure cancer in order to prove to his professor that he was smart all along is part of the belief system that views fear as capable of creating positive results. Even though it is arguable that the great majority of successful, rich, or famous people are motivated by their insecurities, still there are a great many hugely successful professional people who are motivated to serve. These are the ones whose success never becomes a curse to them but rather is always a blessing. They never buckle under its weight, and they usually enjoy the blessings of marriage and children along with financial prosperity and the respect of their peers. They don't create enemies, because they aren't looking to put other people down. These are the ones whose money makes them more humble, for they attribute everything to a higher cause.

As we've seen, fear is an effective short-term motivator. Sometimes I have to summon a vision of loneliness and penury to get a wealthy man to stop cheating on his wife. Invoking his growing children, his wife's fidelity to him during their sometimes difficult life together, and the promise of being a great man, a hero to her, are often not enough. The Bush administration had to keep invoking 9/11 and the war on terrorism to get us to agree to a war in Iraq. But the shame is really on us. Hundreds of thousands of innocent people in unmarked mass graves should have been enough.

By means of positive motivation you will begin to find your immunization against fear. An intimate marriage will bolster you, giving you the ammunition that you need so you can choose life and not fear. A loving and supportive family will reinforce your inner substance. True religion, as opposed to superstition, will give you a sense of connectedness to the eternal. And you will have, maybe for the first time, a genuine sense of self-worth derived from your ability to see and follow the light.

8

Tell Yourself Not to Be Afraid

For I have heard the slander of many: fear was on every side: while they took counsel together against me, they devised to take away my life.
—PSALMS 31:13

The death of fear is in doing what you fear to do.
—SEQUICHIE COMINGDEER

You should be convinced by now that fear has no place in your life. But do you also believe that fear is out of your control?

This is perhaps the biggest myth about fear. We think of fear as an involuntary reaction. And certainly that is true: when someone jumps out of the closet and scares you, there's not much you can do to prevent yourself from your body's response, which is probably to jump and scream, heart pounding. But the majority of your fears is caused by character weaknesses and insecurities that are far more deeply rooted, and it's those fears that I principally wish to address. In fact, the majority of the fear we experience is under our control. Living in fear is a choice—like eating Cheerios instead of Wheaties and vacationing in Miami instead of Cancún.

Fear is a prison of our own construction.
Its key lies in verbalizing our refusal to be cowed.

Here is how you change your motivation from fear to love. Believe it or not, a great deal of the time you can gain control over your fear by saying to yourself, "I will not be afraid. I refuse to be afraid. I will fight this tendency to fear. I will not bend." I don't mean to *think* it. I mean to verbalize it, to say it, to express it. To transform the rhythm of your racing heart into moving lips.

Fear is an emotion. It builds up on the inside and requires external release. Otherwise it stays on the inside and ices over our inner organs. That's why the very best antidote to fear is speech and action.

The more you talk about your fears, the more you tell yourself not to be afraid, and the more you take action to combat your fears (which we'll come to later), the quicker they will dissolve.

Fear Is Ice and Anger Is Fire

To be sure, there are emotions that should not be talked about or acted upon. Anger is a prime example. Anger is like a wave that builds on the inside and wants to crest on the outside. Unfortunately, if you allow it to crest with the things you say or do, it usually washes away relationships and destroys friendships. The trick with anger is to let the wave pass without riding it. If you refuse to act on your anger, it will surely subside. This is because anger, a hot emotion, is like fire. It needs to be stoked. The more fuel you add to the fire, the more it grows. Surely you've noticed that when you start growing angry about something and you're stupid enough to talk about why you're angry, rather than feeling better, you grow angrier and angrier. Every syllable serves to excite your passion. Better to wait till the tide goes down and then talk about your grievances in a thoughtful and deliberate manner.

The same is not true of fear, because fear is not fire but ice. And the stupidest thing to do in the cold is to remain immobile. You'll freeze to death. That's how people die of hypothermia. First the cold chills their blood, making them become sleepy and lethargic. Soon it stops the heart. In freezing cold you have to keep on moving. Fear is only combated through language and action.

> **Whereas you never want to add fuel to the
> fire of anger, you always want to talk and take action
> to thaw the ice of your fears.**

I have observed that while anger is primarily an exercise of the lips, fear is primarily an exercise of the mind. When you talk about your anger, it grows, and when you think about your fears, they grow.

> **Anger escalates through speech.
> Fear grows through thought.**

The more you think about the things that you're frightened of, the more afraid you become. And there is good reason. Fear, as we said earlier, is an isolating experience. To be afraid is to be cut off. Fear thrives in an environment of isolation, which is why those who live alone have a lot more fears than those who share a house with others. The most isolating thing of all is thought. You do have to think, but you should never be thinking about your fears. You should be talking about them, to others, but also to yourself. You should be telling yourself that you refuse to be afraid. And don't worry that people will think that you're crazy for talking to yourself. They're the ones who are crazy, if they're stupid enough to live with the contagion of fear.

> **Victory over fear comes about through victory
> over your thought process.**

Fear wants to get us worrying and freeze us into inaction. So the more you can stop worrying and start doing, the quicker you will conquer your fears. Thought and speech are not only entirely different, they are contradictory, with the former pulling us further into ourselves and the latter pulling us out of ourselves. Speech, being external, is akin to action. It's the things that you think, rather than the things that you say, that make you scared.

You cannot allow yourself to cave in to the bully of fear. You have to stand up to it, assert your dominance over it. You have to absorb it, rally against it, defeat it where it stands.

Go on and try it. You hear that your company is making layoffs. You get a letter in the mail and you're afraid to open it for fear that it's a pink slip. Go on. Don't think about it. Don't build this thing into far more than it is. Don't get carried away with crazy thoughts. Tell yourself, "There is nothing to be afraid of," and open the darned thing. Whatever's in that envelope is not worse than what's in your head. In your thoughts you're thinking, "Oh my gosh, I bet I've been fired. Now my kids and I will starve." Suddenly you envision yourself and your kids, scruffy and dirty, out on the streets begging people for change. Don't be ridiculous. Even if you lose your job, you're going to be fine. That is, so long as you stop thinking and start doing. Because you're active, you'll find another job.

Your daughter hasn't come home, and it's already one a.m. The phone rings. You're afraid to answer it because you're sure it's the police calling to say she's been in a horrible accident. Worse, she was found raped in a parking lot. Go on. Stop thinking and start speaking, then start doing. Tell yourself, "This is ridiculous. I refuse to be afraid. The call's going to be fine, and if it's not, I'm strong enough to deal with it." Then start doing. Pick up the phone and deal with the problem.

Never give yourself time to be afraid. Uproot the insidious thoughts of fear with the blessed words, "I refuse to be afraid." You'll see how fast your fears vanish.

Fear as a Security Blanket

Perhaps you're not being entirely honest with yourself when you claim that fear is something visited upon you, not something you yourself search out. We are, in fact, drawn to fear.

**We are drawn to fear the way we're drawn to sweets and
infidelity and other things that are bad for us.**

This is one of the ugly little truths about fear: we're not as aggressive about banishing it from our lives as we might be because it's comforting to us. It absolves us of responsibility. It's an unpleasant thing to admit, but most of us are inherently lazy. We're proof of Newton's first law: an object at rest tends to stay at rest. We want to sit on the couch and watch TV, and it's only other forces acting upon us—the need to feed our families, for instance—that get us off the couch.

As you know, fear paralyzes us. We freeze in the face of it. This paralyzing feature of fear is paradoxically comforting to us. It's a good excuse for avoiding those forces that would get us off the couch. "I'm afraid of intimacy," you think, as you dial the number for Domino's instead of going to a fund-raiser where you might meet someone. Of course, it's not a happy ending. As the night draws to a close, you're bloated with stupid entertainment and grease, lonely and desperate for real human interaction. You haven't actually gotten what you wanted at all. With all the suffering that it generates, there is something marvelously comforting about fear. It absolves you from having to act.

Fear is used as justification for stagnation.

Fear is a cocoon we snuggle into, a story we tell ourselves that allows us to take the easier road, the path of least resistance. It's a get-out-of-jail-free card that allows the baser, lazier part of us to take control. Hence, for many people fear is a panacea, offered up whenever an excuse is necessary to justify inaction.

My kids use fear as an excuse all the time. I'll tell them to go downstairs and turn off all the lights, and they'll tell me that they're scared. (The trick here is to make them more afraid of you than they are of a burglar.)

Of course, putting yourself out there can be very hard. A prominent man I know who was contemplating running for political office called me to ask for advice. "I'm scared," he told me. "I used to run around on my wife, and even though I've come clean and been a model husband for the last ten years, I'm worried about what they'll find. I don't think I can deal with the humiliation of seeing my name on the cover of every newspaper in town; I don't want to be this election's scandal du jour." I asked him if he felt that he had something to offer the people he'd be representing. I could hear the animation in his voice as he described a groundbreaking plan to improve the lousy educational system in his county. I asked him if his wife and children also felt he had something to offer and would support his bid for the job, and he said that they did. I told him that I believed he should run, that in fact, I believed that he had a moral responsibility to run. This man may indeed be letting himself and his family in for a few weeks of very unpleasant public attention, but why should that stop him if he genuinely has something to contribute? Fear, especially the fear of humiliation, isn't a good-enough reason to walk away from doing something good. In fact, it's a very good illustration of how detrimental and poisonous this particular emotion is. How sad it is that in today's slash-and-burn American political climate, good men and women are refraining from entering the political arena for fear of public disgrace.

If this man had been afraid that he would shame himself in office by doing the wrong thing in the future, that would have been another story. He was afraid of what other people might think of him—that he was unable to control his basest urges. That alone wasn't a sufficient reason not to try to use his G-d-given talents to effect some good in the world. The idea that he could never do any public good with his life because of the fear that mistakes in his past might come back to haunt him is cowardice.

Even if we cannot control the feeling of being afraid, we can—and must—choose not to retreat in the face of those fears. As I write this chapter, an American soldier in Iraq faces a court-martial for being too afraid to do his duty. The case bears mentioning because the army makes an important distinction. It does not say that it's wrong to be afraid. In fact, the manual for courts-martial says that fear is "a natural feeling of apprehension when going into battle." The crime, if it is found to be one, is in cowardly conduct—the refusal or abandonment of a performance of duty before or in the presence of the enemy as a result of fear. In other words, it's not a crime to be afraid, but it is a crime to allow those fears to color the way you act and lead you into delinquent behavior. You may not be able to control all your thoughts, but you sure can control your actions.

This is why I say that fear is a choice. To live in fear is to choose to brood over your worries and your anxieties rather than taking action that could erase or forestall them. To live in fear is to live in permanent inaction.

Viktor Frankl, a Holocaust survivor and the celebrated founder of the psychotherapeutic school of logotherapy, illustrates my point. When asked how he managed to preserve his sanity in the concentration camps when so many others lost their minds, he said that the issue came down to exercising his power of choice. The Nazis wanted to strip him of his humanity, so they put a number on his arm. They wanted to rob him of love, so they killed the members of his family. They wanted to destroy his basic human dignity, so they forced him to defecate into a bucket in the presence of his fellow inmates. They curtailed his freedom, starved him, and beat him. But they could not rob him of the core human freedom that we all possess, namely, the ability to choose how we will react to what is done to us. They couldn't take his humanity or his dignity, and they couldn't make him afraid. Despite the circumstances, he chose not to fear. This, he claimed, was the secret of how he preserved his sanity and humanity in the most challenging conditions imaginable.

When people refuse to exercise their power of choice over fear, they suffer a tremendous loss. Doesn't the definition of our humanity rest in our power to choose? It's not in our intelligence or in our emotions, both of which are also possessed by primates.

The man who becomes afraid makes a choice: he chooses slavery. He could have chosen instead to be a free man, unencumbered by fear, instead of living in servitude.

When you claim that you have no control over fear, no choice in the matter, you are dehumanizing yourself, choosing a slave mentality.

Choose Life

Don't you believe that Martin Luther King died freer than most men—black or white—who preceded him? He chose not to be afraid, not to censor his message. He sat on April 3, 1968, in a plane on the tarmac in Atlanta for hours because of a bomb scare. He arrived a few hours later in Memphis—hungry, tired, but not forlorn—and it was there that he delivered his famous mountaintop speech:

> We've got some difficult days ahead. But it doesn't matter with me now. Because I've been to the mountaintop. And I don't mind. Like anybody, I would like to live a long life. Longevity has its place. But I'm not concerned about that now. I just want to do G-d's will. And He's allowed me to go up to the mountain. And I've looked over. And I've seen the promised land. I may not get there with you. But I want you to know tonight that we, as a people, will get to the promised land. And I'm happy tonight. I'm not worried about anything. I'm not fearing any man. Mine eyes have seen the glory of the coming of the Lord.

He would be dead less than twenty-four hours later. His life may have been cut short: but he lived every moment until the very end.

**Those who live free die free. And those
who die free are free eternally.**

Our lives are cut short every moment that we live in fear. I once heard a rabbi give a eulogy. He told an apocryphal story of how, in a cemetery, there was a headstone that read, "John Smith: Died aged thirty-two. Buried aged seventy-five." Fear of life had killed this man off well before his actual death. Sure, he survived another forty years. But he certainly did not live. He was already dead because fear makes us cold and lifeless like the dead.

At the heart of Judaism is a belief in self-determination and self-redemption. You can choose to eliminate fear from your life. No one can do this for you; you have to do it for yourself. You cannot escape that choice. There are things that can help you to make that choice, things that will fortify you and support your decision, and we will continue to explore them in this book. In the final analysis, you must say to yourself that you will not be afraid and then take action against your fears.

If you're single and afraid of being alone for the rest of your life, don't sit there entertaining ugly thoughts about being found dead in your apartment by neighbors who complain about a rotting stench. Rather go and tell everyone you know that you're looking for a relationship. If you're afraid that your marriage is awful, then tell your spouse it's time the two of you went for counseling. If you're concerned about the lump you found in your breast, dismiss the horrible thoughts of mastectomy. Just go and get it checked out and deal with it. Shut your mind down of all these nasty thoughts and get moving.

My grandfather told my father, who in turn told me, that every time you say something, three things have to happen. You have to open your mouth, separate your teeth, and move your tongue. That split second gives you the time in which to decide to say something either healing or harmful. Every moment we live presents us with choices, choices that will bring either redemption or destruction to our environment. Your responsibility is to choose in the affirmative by turning your back on fear.

9

Fear Is the Hammer That Beats
Our Lives into Dust

Therefore will not we fear, though the earth be removed, and though the
mountains be carried into the midst of the sea.

—PSALMS 46:2

Fear is a darkroom where negatives develop.

—USMAN ASIF

Sometimes we seek fear out aggressively. Horror movies, an obvious example, present us with watered-down fear experiences—a way for us to laugh
at our terror and trivialize our trepidation so that we're not so scared in real
life. We also seek out fear in much more insidious ways than paying ten dollars
to see which virgin Jason or Freddy is stabbing this sequel. Aren't we frightened when we tune in every week to see "real-life drama"—the cynical cops
called in when a college student is stabbed outside her dorm, a surgeon deliv-
ering the news that the cancer has metastasized? Isn't the great pleasure of
those shows the "there but for the grace of G-d" similarities to our own lives?

I know that a lot of people watch television shows that frighten them,
shows like *ER* and *CSI*, because it feels so good when they're over. These
shows serve as reminders to love the people in our own lives. When the
credits run, you get to turn off the television with a sigh of relief, and you
appreciate your life more. You watch parents on a scripted TV drama lose
their child to a rare genetic disease, and it adds poignancy to your own
child's good-night kiss.

I find this response symptomatic of something else. Are you really so deadened to life that you're only alive when you contemplate death? Can you really only love your children and enjoy spending time with them if you're mindful that you might lose them? Kobe Bryant, one of America's foremost athletes, whose infidelities were exposed and whose freedom is threatened, realized how much he loved and needed his wife just as he was faced with the possibility of losing her. I have witnessed this same dynamic countless times in the couples I have counseled, and I have observed many couples who play a dangerous game in their relationship, pushing it right to the edge so that they can have the relief and the added frisson that comes from the near miss. The payoff is the same as that of the so-called extreme sports, in which middle-aged businessmen hurtle themselves off cliffs on snowboards. One woman, who was enduring her husband's midlife obsession with learning to fly small planes, told me that she'd rather lose him to a mistress with two wings than to one with two legs.

Fear was the real mistress here, causing him to spend time and money away from his family, chasing the feeling of being alive. To explain why Bill Clinton risked losing his presidency when he flirted with Monica Lewinsky, many pundits said that men like Clinton need to take risks to feel a rush—and the greater the risk, the greater the rush.

> **The idea that we can only feel love and life when those things are threatened is ruinous.**

It is disturbing to me that we have to risk losing something to realize how much we love it, that we're so deadened to life that we can be motivated only by death. We only need the excitement fear brings because there aren't enough wholesome reminders of love in our lives. With this model, as with a sexual fetish, we will eventually need to keep pushing our fears further and further in order to keep feeling excited. I have seen this pattern with some couples I have counseled. They provoke fights in order to enjoy the comforts of reconciliation. But this destructive pattern is the hallmark of a truly dysfunctional relationship.

> **If you need to feel that something is threatened in order to realize how much you love it, your love will always be matched by your anxieties.**

Don't get trapped in this addiction to fear. You must take the next step, the step into the light, into love, toward the thing that's positive.

In the summer of 2003 the *New York Times* and other papers reported the discovery of a cosmic dark matter, an antigravity, a mysterious force that promotes chaos and is unraveling the very fiber of the universe by making it expand much more rapidly than previously thought. Gravity is considered to be what that keeps our feet on the ground, the pull the earth exerts on objects on its surface, but it is in fact the force of attraction between all masses in the universe. So gravity is working to hold everything together, while this anti-gravity would break it apart.

**Fear is the antigravity of life that seeks
to tear everything apart.**

Fear works against the force that holds the universe together and tethers us to life. Love and honor, the connecting threads uniting all of G-d's creation, are countered by the sundering power of fear. Our only hope is to resist this dark force, the chaotic and destructive force of fear, and work instead to strengthen those things that bring us, and keep us, together.

PART TWO

TO CONQUER FEAR

10

Strengthen Your Inner Immunity

Fear took hold upon them there, and pain, as of a woman in travail.

—PSALMS 48:6

You gain strength, courage, and confidence by every experience in which you really stop to look fear in the face. You must do the thing which you think you cannot do.

—ELEANOR ROOSEVELT

Like biting your fingernails, drinking too much, or smoking, fear is a destructive habit that must be broken. Here I offer a specific blueprint. At the heart of the twenty-two practical strategies that follow is this:

If the thing that you are most afraid of is confirmation that you don't matter, then the antidote to fear is proof that you do.

If you are afraid because you have lost your footing, your sense of your place in the universe, and are therefore easily manipulated into other, more pressing fears, then you must find that footing. If you feel untethered, then you must strengthen your connections to things that anchor you. If you feel that life is fragile and ephemeral, then you must connect yourself to those things that are rock solid and eternal. You cannot be afraid when you feel that you have something to contribute, something that makes you worthy of love and respect. You cannot be afraid when you are surrounded by people who reflect your unique value back to you.

A Twofold Strategy

What I am proposing is a twofold strategy—a two-pronged attack against insidious fear. A tree can only grow tall if its roots are deep and secure. To be resilient, you need a solid, robust base, a solidity and unshakability that comes from an unyielding fundament. The first strategy is to strengthen those roots, the things that ground you, center you, and make you strong. This means that you must look for ways to strengthen the bonds between yourself and those in your life: your spouse, your children, your extended family, your community, your G-d. These things tether and support us, so we are not so easily buffeted and swayed by the winds of fear. If fear is the chaotic element that would pull the universe apart, these relationships are gravity, holding our world together.

**Fear and love are antithetical emotions,
with one always displacing the other.**

We can banish fear from our hearts by filling them with love instead. When we fill the space that fear would have occupied with lightness and life and joy and productivity and hope, we give our lives more value. The struggle to liberate ourselves from fear is really the struggle to understand and to strengthen the ties that anchor us.

**Strengthening your ever-widening circle of connections
is the best defense against fear.**

The second strategy uses that concrete foundation as a base from which to grow. You take that substantial underpinning, that position of strength, and grow out from it, attaching yourself to a bigger concept and living for a wider sense of purpose. G-d made us in His image. He gave us the power to create as well as to consume. One of the central tenets of the Jewish religion is that good deeds beget emotions, rather than the other way around. In other words, it's not because you're a good person that you give to charity: it's the act of giving to charity that makes you a good person.

**The understanding that our actions drive our emotions
is central to combating and defeating fear.**

These two strategies are symbiotic, not mutually exclusive. Strengthening your ties on earth requires that you become a bridge between heaven and earth. Simple as it may sound, there is little better ammunition against fear than an afternoon spent playing with a small child. It is an earthly pleasure, certainly, but one that also connects us to heavenly principles and ideals. What is more exhilarating than watching a young child discover as new all the things that we take for granted? What is more redeeming than being around a creature who is fundamentally innocent? What could be more glorified than to create a secure connection with the face of the future?

In the desert of fear—a vast, unforgiving landscape—there are oases that offer respite from the harsh, forbidding dryness of that desert. These oases—your family, ties to your community, the real love and support of your spouse—are what bolster you against fear. The desert is also scattered with mirages: things, like money and power and casual sex, that appear to offer some comfort from your fears but shimmer into nothingness when you actually get your hands on them, increasing your thirst instead of slaking it. As William Mulholland brought water to the desert of Los Angeles, you can increase these oases so that the distance between them is not so great. We must see resistance to fear as a prized resource, like water in the desert.

**The prescription for eliminating fear from your life
is straightforward: enrich your life.**

Fear thrives in an absence of virtue. The woman who is afraid of being mugged while jogging in Central Park is suddenly much more fearless when she dons a police uniform and guards the streets of New York. The better you feel about yourself and the more purpose-driven your life, the greater the likelihood that you will not be afraid.

You can use cheap and ephemeral external means, like taking a drug to calm your nerves or distracting yourself with a movie, but facing your fear will allow you to stop wasting your time. And what is life other than a measure of time on this earth? A natural and organic immunity to fear grows when you expose yourself to positive elements, like the love of G-d, community, and family. The elimination of fear—and many other positive benefits—will be by-products of these wholesome ingredients.

11

Principle #1:
Dedicate Your Life to
Something Higher

The LORD is on my side; I will not fear: what can man do unto me?
—PSALMS 118:6

Courage is the virtue which champions the cause of right.
—MARCUS TULLIUS CICERO

The eternal heavens and the transient earth are disconnected. Humans belong to both: you possess both a soul and a body. You can either live torn between the two, or you can choose to bridge the gap between them. How will you do this? You can choose to translate some G-dly principle into action on earth. In doing so, you become a representative of the celestial and eternal.

Isn't the fear of death really just the fear that you will leave the earth without changing it, without leaving any trace? Isn't this the major motivating factor behind the creation of great art, architecture, literature, even of children? We are looking for something permanent to leave behind us.

Say G-d came to you and said, "Cancer kills millions of people a year. I have decided to use you as the agency for its cure. I'm going to endow you with superior medical knowledge, and you will cure cancer. This is the reason for your existence; once you've found the cure, you'll die." Would you still be afraid of death, or would you embrace your glorious cause and work toward its fulfillment? Fear of death is really a fear of nothingness, of worthlessness.

People who feel that their life is dedicated to a higher cause have no fear of death: their lives on earth are consecrated to the execution of a mission.

Their lives are about the cause, not about them. The more you make your life all about you, the bigger a target you become. The man who shudders behind the high walls of his mansion does so because he knows he's a target. If he lives a more humble life and dedicates his resources more to others, he becomes far less of a target and is therefore less afraid. I know people who are so consumed with themselves that they're convinced that everybody is talking about them. They walk into a room wondering what people were just saying about them and live in the permanent fear of malicious gossip. Who asked them to bloat themselves up to be a giant target? In war, leaders tell soldiers to duck. In life, the same lesson is true. You only need to be really afraid when you grow puffed up and overblown with a sense of your own importance.

Rabbi Menachem Mendel of Lubavitch was approached by a student in his yeshiva who complained that everyone in the yeshiva was stepping on him. Rabbi Menachem Mendel responded, "Who asked you to so spread yourself out over the entire yeshiva that wherever anyone puts their foot, they're always trampling on you?"

Though I certainly fear death, my trepidation is not as intense as most people's. To be sure, I want to lead a long and satisfying life. G-d says that life is a blessing while death is a curse, and I want my existence to be blessed. I serve a purpose here on earth by being a loving father and living the life of a rabbi who tries to heal spirits and mend souls. I have attempted, however imperfectly, to inspire people to be closer to G-d, to be less judgmental of their fellow man, to strengthen their marriages, to live morally and to cherish their children. I feel that to endeavor in those fields, however imperfectly, is to make an important contribution. I know I have rescued a few marriages, and that some children's lives are much better off as a result. I hope I have done much to be a good father to my own children and to pass along the principles I have learned from my parents and from my religion. I hope that I have encouraged people to live less selfish lives, just as I have struggled to do so myself.

These things are lasting.

Our bones will dry up and turn into ash, and even the granite that marks our graves will eventually fall and be scattered. Our real headstones are the divine ideals that we caused to materialize as hard truths during our time here on earth.

When we personify something G-dlike—decency, loving kindness, compassion, a capacity for joy—we take that which is of the heavens and make it of the earth. We become a bridge between the eternal and the ephemeral.

Many people are afraid of Islamic terrorism. I would encourage them not to stop flying on airplanes but to emulate what I have sought to do. I am a well-known critic of Islamic extremism, but that has not prevented me from reaching out whenever possible to my Islamic brethren and showing decent Muslims that we in the West in general, and Jews in particular, are not their enemies but their brothers.

The cars that are sent to take me to the occasional TV appearances are often driven by Islamic immigrants from Pakistan. They immediately know that I am Jewish, and I immediately know that they are Muslim. I engage them in conversation, breaking the ice quickly, trying to show them how much we have in common and how honored we are to have honest, hardworking people like them becoming citizens in our country, which is now their country. Many of them have come over without their wives and children, either because they have too little money or because the family members could not obtain visas. I have made introductions between these drivers and prominent Jewish immigration lawyers, who have taken on their cases pro bono or at substantially reduced rates. The drivers are amazed that Jews would care about them, but the more we show decent Muslims that we are not their enemy, the more they will see Osama bin Laden and his ilk as the murderous frauds they are.

Isn't this the best way to overcome the fear of terrorism? If you're a soldier, your job is to fight and kill the murderous extremists. And if you're a civilian, like me, you can fight and win the battle for hearts and minds. Is there a better way to overcome the pangs of fear than by personifying the eternal, G-dly qualities of compassion and brotherhood, so that we don't feel like our lives are chaff easily blown by the wind?

**No living being can overcome fear without
a healthy connection to the eternal.**

When you dedicate your life to something higher, you gain perspective. Things that frighten you suddenly become much smaller and less imposing. When you're twenty thousand feet in an airplane, the houses and highways on the ground seem impossibly tiny, and the people are almost invisible. This effect always reminds me of what happens when you ally yourself with a grand cause, when you dedicate your life to something greater than yourself. People don't frighten you any longer and the loss of material things can't cause apprehension because they're way too small. You can look down at your fears and doubts as they recede and become small in your own eyes.

When you're in the center of your own world, no wonder you feel like a target! There's nothing else in your line of vision. When you step off to the side by dedicating your life to something more important, you no longer have a bull's-eye on your forehead. Martin Luther King knew that he was going to give his life for the civil rights movement, but even that didn't compromise his commitment. The movement was important, not his life. And his life gained significance through its attachment to the movement.

Become the Representative of Something Greater than Yourself

A few years ago, on the way home from a lecture in the Netherlands, I stopped in Iceland for two days to see the wonders of that majestic island. After walking around Reykjavík in the evening, I was heading to my hotel when two Palestinian men cornered me on the street. The last thing they expected to see on the streets of Iceland was a rabbi with a yarmulke, and the last thing I expected to see was two Palestinian men. They were menacing, mocking me, and one said to me, "You dirty Israeli. You murder our people. How dare you come to this country?" And he pushed me against a wall.

Although I am writing a book about overcoming fear, I do not consider myself to be particularly courageous. But when I am accosted for my Jewishness (something that has happened too often, especially on the streets of Europe), I am a lion. These were two huge guys, intent on humiliating and maybe hurting me. I didn't back off an inch. I straightened myself up and said, "You know nothing about me. How dare you threaten me! First of all, if you lay another finger on me, I'll call the police and get you arrested. Second, I'm not Israeli, but I am Jewish and proud. Third, I have never harmed your people and I see your people as the children of G-d, just like my own. Finally, it's this kind of disgusting behavior on the part of people claiming to represent the Arab cause that leads to immeasurable suffering for your people. If you want to have a civilized conversation with me about this issue, fine. Otherwise, move out of my way."

And with that the one who pushed me apologized. "I'm sorry. You're right. But there are a lot of Jews who justify the murder of my people." "Well, maybe there are," I said to him, "but I certainly don't know any. We Jews believe that the Arabs are our brothers, even if we're currently in a terrible argument." We said good night to each other in a manner that might even pass as genuine warmth, and I walked on.

I'm not a terribly imposing figure; had they wanted to, those two guys could have easily beaten me to a pulp. In the face of possible physical violence, how did I find the courage to stand up for myself? I felt I was representing Judaism, something larger than myself. I wasn't the target of their hatred, my faith was, and I have spent my whole life defending and preserving that faith. My commitment to Judaism requires that I defend it even when it's not comfortable for me to do so, and it's easy to be courageous when you're defending something glorious. I can tell you as honestly as I can recall it, I did not experience an iota of fear.

This story, while of course it does not compare with real shows of courage on the part of, say, American soldiers in Iraq, encapsulates many basic truths about bravery and its consequences. My commitment to something bigger than myself, my Judaism, gave me the courage to push past a significant physical threat. There is also the impression that my courage made on those men. They surely knew that they could have made mincemeat out of me in about five seconds, but they were intimidated by my refusal to be bullied and so, taken aback, they retreated.

And my act of courage inspired them to their own act of bravery—an apology. I have found in my counseling sessions that getting people to apologize to one another is one of the hardest things in the world. A husband and wife come to me, embroiled in a fight that's been going on for weeks. I tell them to drop it and apologize to one another. Have you noticed that all people are lawyers when it comes to why their spouses are in the wrong? Invariably, instead of apologies, the oral arguments start. What these couples don't understand is that I'm not interested in arguing the merits of the case. "You're probably both right," I tell them. "Apologize anyway. It's better to be wrong and still stay married than to be right and get divorced." I'm asking them to make the leap of faith that an act of courage requires. They rarely do it. They're too frightened that if they give in this time, they'll be taken advantage of next time.

Nothing substantive, by an outside reckoning, was decided during my midnight encounter with those two men in Reykjavík. No one left the incident with changed opinions: they, no doubt, still think that Israelis are imperialists who are squatting on Arab land, and I still think that their people have resorted to terrorism because they see democratic and prosperous Israel as an affront to Arab pride. But we were able to behave courageously toward one another despite those differences, and that is something very great indeed.

People today seem to be the most aimless of any since this country was founded. We are desperately in need of a higher cause that can take away our fear. The success of Tom Brokaw's best seller *The Greatest Generation* had a great deal to do with a certain nostalgia on our part for a time when people believed in the Big Issues—truth, justice, liberty, and patriotism—and were unafraid to fight for them. The people who fought in World War II knew how to put the "we" before the "I."

But these fundamental principles aren't dead. Returning to a working relationship with them is our ticket out of the state of fear we find ourselves in today.

Connecting our lives to a higher purpose immunizes us against fear and endows us with the courage to be brave.

Finding those things about which I can be passionate has been easy for me. I am Jewish. I thrill to the cause of my people, and I believe passionately in the brotherhood of all humankind. I believe in inspiring people to be closer to G-d, more appreciative of His blessings, and better people. As a child of divorce, I know that happy marriages are the cornerstone of a healthy civilization, and I do what I can to improve my own marriage and those of people who seek my counsel. I believe in being a decent person and lending others dignity, and I struggle to live by these convictions. I do not do these things specifically to combat fear, but one result of living a decent and moral life is a dissolution of fear. There are many question marks in life. But one thing that is certain is that standing up for your convictions always requires courage. Even writing this book to help others overcome their own fears has served as one of those higher goals and helped me dissipate my own fear.

Notice that the first thing we learn about Moses, when he becomes a man, is not that he was spiritual, G-dly, or wise, but that he was bold, brave, and courageous, prepared to risk his own skin to save innocent people from being beaten:

> One day, after Moses had grown up, he went out to his people and saw their forced labor. He saw an Egyptian beating a Hebrew, one of his kinsfolk. He looked this way and that, and seeing no one, he killed the Egyptian and hid him in the sand (Exodus 11:12).

Courage was what most qualified Moses to be the leader of G-d's chosen people. You can't stand up to Pharaoh if you're afraid of him and his henchmen. What granted Moses such extraordinary courage, to stand up to the might of Pharaoh, was his belief in the cause of justice, and his connection to a higher authority.

When I was doing my radio show with Peter Noel, I regularly had to summon the courage to state my beliefs to an audience who might have felt slighted by what I was saying. To be sure, I have long been very close to the African-American community. I greatly admire the commitment to faith, family, and children in the African-American community and have been deeply troubled by the deconstruction of the black family in recent times, with approximately 65 percent of African-American children being born out of wedlock. Children need the nurturing influence of a mother and the strong hand of a father if they are to grow up with both love and discipline. Needless to say, coming from a white Jew on a black station, this statement could sound judgmental and condescending. When I discussed the subject, the phones would light up with people calling me everything just short of racist.

There were mornings when I didn't feel up to the invective. Sometimes people's comments were very painful to me, but I always tried to push myself to remain true to my convictions at all times. I have always fought for the family and I will do so whether those families are black or white. Sometimes I had to give myself a pep talk, remind myself why I had been given this unique platform. My sincere admiration for the black community came through. The radio show was an opportunity for me to continue my own work of healing myself and healing the world. I was on the air to speak the truth from the vantage point of a man who grew up in a broken home and to encourage honest, open communication between blacks and whites. It helped to think of myself this way. I wasn't just a guy who could be punctured by other people's angry arrows. I was a man with a mission. After a few months I won over most of my listeners, and I was treated like family. Sure, they often disagreed with my views, but they respected my authenticity and my refusal to pander. The time I spent doing that show was one of the greatest and most rewarding experiences of my life.

12

Principle #2:
Believe in Your Destiny

Be not afraid of sudden fear, neither of the desolation of the wicked, when
it cometh.

—PROVERBS 3:25

Destiny is not a matter of chance; it is a matter of choice.

—WILLIAM JENNINGS BRYAN

D o you believe that you were born with a special destiny? Or do you believe that your life is an accident? Fear loves to prey on accidents. Indeed, one of the things we most fear *is* accidents.

**The sense of destiny that comes with belief in a
divinely inspired plan is a potent weapon
in the arsenal against fear.**

Believing in destiny, being sure that you were created to accomplish some
great thing—and "great" does not have to mean playing on a world stage—
immunizes you against fear, because it means that you are above being affected by the elements. Some thug may mug you and take your money, but

he cannot take your life, try as he might, because you were born for some important role that you have not yet fulfilled. G-d, and G-d alone, has power over your future, not some evil miscreant.

Here is where religion plays such a vital role in combating fear.

Religion shrinks those things that loom large in your nightmares down to their actual size.

If your faith inspires you to believe in your personal destiny, then you can never be afraid of terrorists. Wicked people with machine guns are not powerful enough to subvert the divine plan. If you believe in a divine regulator, you know that G-d has a plan for you. If your religion reminds you of G-d's power as you gaze out upon the vastness of the ocean, then it will help you to put a job interview into perspective. If your religion gives you insight into G-d's infinite wisdom while you're contemplating the infinity of space, then you're less likely to be freaked out by your bank statement. If you feel awe when you contemplate the miracle of your children, then you're less likely to feel awe and intimidation in the presence of a television personality.

A famous Hasidic scholar came to Brooklyn after World War II. He had been in a concentration camp and had lost most of his family in the Holocaust. Those who were left were in the United States; they took him in and got him settled, then told him they were going to take him to see the tall buildings of Manhattan. "It's the most amazing place in the world," they said, sure he'd be impressed. "You won't be able to believe your eyes. The buildings reach the sky." When they got there, he looked up at the tremendous skyscrapers and said, "This city is nothing but the excrement of the angel Michael."

The idea that the material world is made from angelic waste is a complex Kabbalistic concept that may sound bizarre at first, but this scholar's message was more than clear. If you're on the ground looking up, the Empire State Building is impressive indeed. But if you're attached to G-d and you're now looking down, they're not very impressive at all. This Hasid was saying, "I live a life of the spirit and see a different reality. And compared with the grandeur of the human soul, everything else seems unimpressive. These buildings will be ruins in a thousand years, but G-d's glory is eternal. I'm up here, looking down, and from my perspective, those buildings don't look very big to me at all."

> **If all you see is the earth, then size matters. If you're committed to the view from the ground, then you're going to be intimidated.**

That girl is prettier than you are; that guy is richer. You should be impressed; they're in a different league.

> **If you ally yourself with the infinite and choose the perspective of the mountaintop, then the little bumps that make someone's hill bigger than someone else's—money, fame, physical beauty, even intelligence—become indiscernible.**

And those things that connect us to God serve as reminders of that perspective. Rabbi Joseph Isaac Schneerson headed the Chabad Hasidic community in Stalinist Russia and was imprisoned for teaching Judaism. Threatened with a pistol by an officer of the NKVD, the forerunners of the KGB, and warned that he would be placed in front of a firing squad for the charge of treason, the great rebbe looked his tormentor contemptuously in the eye and said, "Toys like those guns only frighten people with many gods and one world. But I who have only one G-d and two worlds live with a permanent sense of destiny that even you cannot obstruct. I am not afraid of you at all. So put away your silly toy." He continued to show utter fearlessness throughout his incarceration and was eventually released. He is today credited with having literally saved Judaism in the former Soviet Union, and as a mark of my esteem for his courage, I named my youngest child after him.

Believe in Your Destiny

I recognize that much of my readership is not that religious. Does that mean that you are destined to live in fear for the rest of your lives? Certainly not. The key here is a belief in this sense of destiny. And I mean destiny, not fate. The Greeks believed in the awesome and tragic power of fate, from which no human can escape. That's why so many Greek plays are tragedies—plays that promote and encourage gloom and fear. The Greeks made man feel that he was but a powerless pawn, at the mercy of the gods, a small player on a stage that dwarfs him and makes him insignificant.

The Bible, on the other hand, believes in destiny. The word *destiny* is etymologically related to the word *destination*.

**Destiny is a belief that our lives are all headed
to a glorious place.**

In contrast to fate, destiny empowers rather than weakens. In the Bible man is part of the grand cosmic drama and plays a central role. Fate says that the events of your life are written in the stars and that there is no way to escape the doom that awaits you. Destiny says that your whole life is headed toward a specific destination—the wide spaces—and that you will live to fulfill that destiny. If you believe in destiny, you're not just cosmic chaff, blown about by the winds of outrageous fortune. You're immune to the elements, rather than subject to forces outside your control.

We don't have to be tested to reconnect to destiny. A parent feels a sense of destiny. When your child is born, suddenly you know that you have a purpose: to be around every day to nurse this kid to adulthood and to dance at his or her wedding to some deserving woman or man. You feel a sense of destiny when you are able to help a friend in a bad situation or a stranger in need. In other words, we acquire a sense of destiny when we think of our lives not in terms of self-fulfillment and inward meditation but in terms of service.

**In order to conquer your own apprehension,
get in touch with your own destiny,
using the idea of service as a key.**

Many soldiers relate how, when shot or injured in battle, they closed their eyes and thought of their wives who loved them and awaited them at home. And this gave them the conviction that they would not die on a lonely, far-off battlefield. They were destined to return to take care of the women who loved them. They were born for a purpose that they were not about to fail.

What is destiny if not a sense of purpose? Viktor Frankl said that all mental illness and depression resulted from the sense that there was no meaning to one's life, that it had no purpose. He founded the psychological school of logotherapy, which argued it wasn't dark sexual forces (Freud) or the yearning for power (Adler) that motivated human action, but rather the search for purpose.

I have long noted a curious fact that demonstrates the natural human compulsion to find purpose. A friend of ours spent thousands of dollars on a brand-new kitchen. Two weeks later a fire in the kitchen destroyed the whole room. The insurance company came forward to reinstall the identical kitchen. Although our friend loved pink—the color of the renovation—she insisted that the reconstruction, just two weeks later, be a cream color. Changing the color was her way of saying that she could not accept that, after all the effort she had put into building that new kitchen, it had burned down pointlessly. She wouldn't just duplicate the original. By changing the color, she gave the misfortune purpose. She could not just duplicate her effort. "See, it wasn't for nothing. I got this great new color out of it."

The same is true with most things we lose. When people have their car stolen, they rarely ever buy the same car again. Not because they are traumatized by the loss, but because they have to give the event meaning. "Having it stolen has allowed me to replace it with something better." Humans love taking accidents and giving them purpose. And they insist on taking capricious circumstances and affording them meaning.

> **Humans are best described not as creatures of habit but as creatures of purpose.**

All our fears result from the sense that life has no ultimate purpose, that it can be snuffed out with impunity at any given moment. When we reduce our lives to nothing more than a capricious collection of cells brought about by an evolutionary accident, when we no longer believe in our own sense of destiny, we leave ourselves susceptible to the ravages of fear. Nature abhors a vacuum. When there is no meaning in our lives, fear rushes in to fill the empty pit.

Develop Your Gifts

If we reconnect with our destiny, we immunize ourselves against fear. When you believe that you are destined to do certain things, you make it so. I was put by G-d on this earth to accomplish certain goals, and I know that I have not yet fulfilled all of them. Only I can blow it. No drunken motorist can take away my life's promise—only my own distraction or laziness or conceit.

As long as I believe that I will not go until I have fulfilled my destiny, that belief renders me immune to fear and resistant to fate. This attitude is much, much easier to adopt than it seems.

Ask yourself two simple questions:
What do you believe is most wrong with this world?
How can you use your unique gifts to address that wrong?

Everyone believes that an area of the world is deficient in some way, and everyone is blessed with a unique gift. The secret to rediscovering your sense of purpose, and through it your sense of destiny, is to bring those two together in the form of positive action. You may believe that the world is cruel and judgmental. If so, make it your purpose to put yourself in other people's shoes before you ever pass judgment. Or you may think that the world treats people unequally. Then dedicate your life to treating all people—regardless of circumstance—with respect.

A husband and wife came to see me. She hated him. She felt unfulfilled in an empty marriage. She complained he was simple and uncouth. She hated his manners. To my surprise, the husband agreed with her. He admitted that she had married beneath herself and that he wasn't her intellectual equal. Is there anything more pathetic than a man who considers himself an idiot? He said in our counseling sessions that he lived with the permanent fear of inadequacy. I asked him if he had any special talent. He was a "simple" schoolteacher, he told me. "But I have a real capacity to listen. To make kids feel important. To take their concerns seriously. I am a comforter." I responded, "A comforter is a beautiful thing, and it's exactly what your angry and disappointed wife most needs. Sadly, you think you're a comforter in the sense of being a couch, a lifeless object with no personality. Is it any wonder that since you think you have little virtue or purpose, you are afraid that you're nothing?"

Maybe you believe that your unique gift is to build the strong, loving family that your parents were unable to provide for you. Maybe your gift is in bringing people together and opening dialogue where there once was none. Maybe your gift is in making beautiful things or in inspiring people who feel lifeless. As long as you're consciously using that gift on a daily basis, you don't have to quit your job or move to a commune. You can start small by telling your children that you love them.

An Oxford student who had won the Rhodes scholarship was terrified after he arrived at the university that he would not live up to the hype that had greeted the prestigious award. He sweated before every exam and moped around looking unhappy. I asked him what he most hated about the university, and he said, "I guess that it makes me feel like I only matter if I excel, like it's my brain rather than my being that counts." "Then become the exact opposite of that. If you're afraid that you only matter because you won the Rhodes, help create a world where that idea doesn't apply." He went well beyond what I recommended. He became one of those unusual people who drop notes to friends constantly, for their birthdays, their mother's birthdays. He even wrote to his friends the day before their major exams wishing them the best. And in so doing he became far less afraid. He was living his destiny—to change the world from cold- to warmhearted. From him I learned to try to send my friends around the world warm e-mails to tell them I've been thinking of them.

The more self-absorbed you are, the more afraid you are.

**The smaller you make yourself and the more
you allow yourself to be part of a greater plan,
the smaller a target you become.**

Children's fears center around their belief that they are the center of the universe. They don't yet understand that they're part of a grander whole. It makes perfect sense to them that the monster in the mask would come to their bedroom of all the bedrooms in the house, after choosing their house, on their street, in their town, in their state. When you fail to see yourself as part of a greater plan, you're doing exactly the same thing. You are at the center of that circle, but when you turn your awareness outward and see yourself as contributing to something greater, you are acknowledging that there is a plan for your life. You're not untethered, floating around without an anchor: you are part of something much bigger. And that is the single best comfort measure that I can possibly imagine.

The Rewards of Service

You only have to look to people who live without fear to know that you cannot be afraid when you feel that you have something to contribute, something that makes you worthy of love and respect. In the army there are plenty of soldiers who are afraid but very few officers, because the officers realize that the troops look to them for leadership. That sense of destiny and purpose renders them far less susceptible to the emotion of fear.

**When you devote yourself to a higher cause,
to the service of a concept or an idea that is G-dly
and eternal, you then begin to matter.**

Even if no one has ever heard of you, you matter. Even if no movie will ever be made about your life, no epic poem written, no statue erected, no twenty-one gun salute fired, you matter.

Someone will replace the current half-naked pop diva of the month, guaranteed. Come back to Planet Earth in the year 2100 and you will not find her mentioned in the *Encyclopaedia Britannica*. Someone will come along with a better hook, bigger breasts, a firmer tush—and no one will miss her when she drops back into anonymity either. If you have dedicated yourself to a cause bigger and better than yourself, something more lasting than the cover of a weekly magazine, something more meaningful than money, then you will be missed, I guarantee it.

**If you embrace this concept of service
within your community, your family, and on a
larger scale, you will have made an ineradicable,
ineffaceable impact on the world.**

We will return to this concept again in the pages that follow, but take a moment to ask yourself now, "What is my essential gift, and how can I use that gift to heal the world?"

13

Principle #3:
Become a Leader

The fear of man bringeth a snare: but whoso putteth his trust in the LORD shall
be safe.

—PROVERBS 29:25

Keep your fears to yourself but share your courage with others.

—ROBERT LOUIS STEVENSON

T he concept of service, of dedicating your life to other people so that
you're not such an enormous target, is one of the most effective vaccina-
tions you have against the insidious disease of fear. When you assume a leadership position, your focus changes. Fear turns you inside yourself,
leadership forces your gaze outward so that you can guide others. The man-
tle of leadership itself confers boldness and fearlessness, because it puts us
back in touch with our own sense of destiny.

This sense of destiny can arise from service in times of extreme heroism.
Richard Picciotto, a New York City fire chief, was evacuating survivors inside the North Tower of the World Trade Center on September 11 when the
South Tower collapsed. He and his men realized they had to escape before
their building fell as well. With unparalleled bravery, he led his men and
twenty injured civilians down the flights of stairs while the building suddenly
collapsed all around them. When I interviewed him about his miraculous escape on my radio show, I asked him how he had survived. He told me that the

people around him needed him. How could he let them down? He had to survive and rescue them.

It's time to cultivate leadership again as a necessity rather than a luxury of life. We should be cultivating a nation of leaders rather than followers.

Today Americans are delegators, not participants. "Vote for me, and I'll take care of it," our politicians say—and then only half of us can even motivate ourselves to get to the polling booths. We're not an active part of the struggle. There's little concept of national service. So of course we're afraid!

Share the Burden—and the Benefits!

John F. Kennedy's Inaugural Address is famous for the line, "Ask not what your country can do for you; ask what you can do for your country." The speech is a leader's call to service, asking for patience and participation in the struggle ahead. "Now the trumpet summons us again—not as a call to bear arms, though arms we need; not as a call to battle, though embattled we are; but a call to bear the burden of a long twilight struggle, year in and year out, rejoicing in hope, patient in tribulation, a struggle against the common enemies of man: tyranny, poverty, disease, and war itself."

Right now a group of warriors defends the American people. They aren't afraid: they're on the front lines; they're participating; they're doing something about the threat. They get paid mediocre salaries to have bullets whiz by their heads in places like Kandahar and Najaf, but they have something the rest of us can only envy. Even in the belly of the beast, their fear does not stop them from fulfilling their duty.

The rest of us are sitting around watching football games on Sunday, inane sitcoms on weekdays, grotesque reality TV in between. We're not meaningfully involved. We're divorced from the principles for which these battles are being fought. If we were to grab the reins by organizing a community effort to support the soldiers in Iraq, for instance, or raising money to support victims of terror in embattled democracies like Israel, we would all become leaders, and we would all benefit from the fearlessness that leadership confers.

You are a leader to somebody, and we can all find ways to exercise leadership in our own lives. It's not an accident that religious institutions have so many lay leadership positions. At any church or synagogue there's a youth group leader, a choir leader, a prayer group leader, someone who coordinates charity efforts for the elderly in the community, the person responsible for organizing child care during services, someone who keeps the community calendar, someone who manages the building fund, someone who runs the women's auxiliary, someone who organizes hospital visitation—the list goes on and on and on. This system gives everyone the opportunity to share in responsibility and in the strength and honor that leadership confers.

In his book *His Holiness*, author Carl Bernstein of Watergate fame relates that Pope John Paul II, w,hen first called to the seat of St. Peter, wrote a letter to the secretary of the Soviet Communist Party saying that he would resign the papacy to join the front lines of the Solidarity movement in Poland if Russian tanks invaded his homeland to crush the pro-democracy movement. With that letter he arguably saved Poland and initiated the ultimate decline of the Soviet Union.

Our Fearless Leaders

An attitude of fearlessness is one of the major responsibilities of someone in a position of power, and promoting that attitude of fearlessness to those who follow is an essential ingredient of leadership. When your goal is to inspire fearlessness in others, there is no substitute for going and doing yourself. "Example is always more efficacious than precept," as Dr. Johnson said. That's why Lincoln insisted on traveling to the Confederate capital of Richmond just hours after its capture by Union troops and while there was still a hornet's nest of Confederate snipers. Throughout the war he went out of his way to demonstrate fearlessness, and he wasn't about to stop when the war entered its final stages.

Too many politicians use their powerful positions to promote fear instead of dispelling it. Even when Washington, DC, came close to capture by the South after the battle of Bull Run, Lincoln refused to consider evacuating the capital, just as Churchill refused to leave London during the Battle of Britain. President George W. Bush did not back down from his gallant mission to bring democracy to the oppressed people of the Arab countries, even as he became the most hated man in the world for doing so. Instead of using their positions to promote fear, the way so many other politicians and media have been known to do, these great men used their platforms to diffuse it.

**True leaders do not create followers but leaders. And there is
no better way to inspire leadership in your subordinates than
to teach them to be fearless.**

Most Americans are familiar with Franklin Delano Roosevelt's inaugural speech in which he said that the only thing Americans had to fear was fear itself. Far fewer are familiar with his famous "Four Freedoms" speech, delivered to Congress on the sixth of January, 1941:

> In the future days, which we seek to make secure, we look forward to a world founded upon four essential human freedoms. The first is freedom of speech and expression—everywhere in the world. The second is freedom of every person to worship God in his own way—everywhere in the world. The third is freedom from want—which, translated into world terms, means economic understandings which will secure to every nation a healthy peacetime life for its inhabitants—everywhere in the world. The fourth is freedom from fear.

What an incredible statement on the part of a world leader, that every human being has a right to live completely and utterly without fear, and that such a right is as important as the right to freedom of speech, freedom of religion, and the means of life. Since a determined leader showed such remarkable courage, it should come as no surprise that FDR was able to muster an entire nation's courage to fight the Nazis.

We all share this responsibility equally. A rabbi must stand up and counsel his congregants to stand strong in the face of anti-Semitism. A priest must counsel his flock to avoid the trap of conforming with an increasingly secular world. An executive should bravely show his employees that despite the difficulty of the last quarter, the company is strong and will prevail.

In fact, taking an active role is key in beating back terror. Laurence Gonzalez, the author of *Deep Survival: Who Lives, Who Dies, and Why*, interviewed thrill seekers—extreme sports enthusiasts, test pilots, and others who take extreme risks—and discovered that a majority of people who survive life-threatening incidents dedicate their survival to someone else. "My mother will never get over it if I die out here." In this way they become rescuers, not just survivors.

14

Principle #4:
Face Your Fear

Say ye not, A confederacy, to all them to whom this people shall say, A confederacy; neither fear ye their fear, nor be afraid.

—ISAIAH 8:12

You cannot run away from a weakness; you must some time fight it out or perish; and if that be so, why not now, and where you stand?

—ROBERT LOUIS STEVENSON

As with most bad habits, the first step in learning to live without fear is understanding the depth of your addiction. How afraid are you? How much of what you do is governed by fear? I'd like to invite you to do what I've done since I began writing this book—to live with a heightened awareness of fear.

You will be disturbed by what you discover. The amount of fear in our lives is staggering. Once you identify the fears that largely govern your life, it's time to admit to yourself that you live in a pound, that you have vanquished your humanity and chosen instead to be a caged animal.

It's time to summon the resolve to be free. I have many times verbalized to myself, "I will not live in fear. I refuse to be afraid." In the book of Psalms, King David proclaims, "I shall not die, for I shall live, and I shall proclaim the glory of G-d." These beautiful words have been in my mind as I have proclaimed my freedom from a life lived in fear.

I will not die that cold horrible death of having my uniqueness snuffed out because I am afraid of being out of step.

I will not die the silent death of being afraid to articulate views that are unpopular.

I will not die the death of loneliness by being afraid to love and afraid to get hurt.

I will not commit figurative suicide by leaving my potential underdeveloped because I am afraid to take risks.

I will not die the pitiable death of destroying my life because I am afraid to take criticism.

I will not die the painful death of watching my health waste away because I am afraid to hear what the doctor might say at a checkup.

I will not die a national death by being afraid to stand up to evil and save my country from being overrun by tyrants.

I will not die the lamentable death of becoming a prisoner of my insecurities and living a life that is designed to impress others rather than pursuing justice and righteousness.

I will not be suffocated by the horrible death of self-absorption and self-ishness, brought about by the fear that sharing with others will diminish who I am.

The Declaration of Independence, authored by Thomas Jefferson, is a declaration of fearlessness. What the American colonists were saying was, *"We are not afraid.* We're not afraid of you anymore, George III, you oppressor of the people. We're not afraid of dying by your bayonets, and we're not afraid of fighting to expel your soldiers. We will never again allow ourselves to live under tyranny and without dignity."

We too have to make a declaration of independence from our fear, a declaration that we will not submit to the tyranny of fear ever again.

I determined to try to rid my life of all fear when I discovered just how corrupting an influence fear is. In fact, it is precisely those things that bring us the most pride and joy that turn out to be the leading causes of our fear. We love our children, but for many, that love is accompanied by very real terror that something will happen to their children. We take pride in our successes—a cultivated garden, a book we've written—but we're afraid as well. What if there's an insect infestation or an early frost? What if our books won't sell or they're panned by the critics, or both? The real tragedy, of course, is that fear is so unpleasant, so debilitating, that we learn to resent those things that make us afraid.

Fear turns life's blessings into burdens.

Before I show you how to replace the fear in your life with much more productive, effective, and creative emotions, I need you to make the following commitment. I want you to promise that over the course of this book, you will commit yourself to confronting your fears. Say it aloud: "It is time to turn around and confront the things that frighten me, so that I can move beyond them."

Learning to confront your fears puts you back into the driver's seat of life.

Courage allows us to conquer our fears, as opposed to being conquered by them. It is only in confronting our fears that we learn the depth and breadth of our own capabilities. Teaching children to dive is almost entirely a case of encouraging them to believe that they can do it. They have to be shown the way. The first time, you may have to hold a young child's hand as she walks out onto the end of the diving board. You may have to tread water below the board to catch her the first time she jumps. But by the end of the day, she'll be flinging herself off with abandon, and you'll have to bribe her to come out of the pool.

It's one thing for children to be afraid; in this case, the fear is innate, a manifestation of a healthy survival instinct. Surely it's better that they don't throw themselves into bodies of water without any trepidation at all. But eventually they have to learn that they can do it. Children are inherently driven to participate, however cautiously. By nature they want to learn, to experience, to live. Where is our incentive as a nation? When the media is encouraging us to buy duct tape and hide under the bed, where is our encouragement to take the next difficult step? When fear is as firmly ensconced as it is in our society, what are the social forces that will push us out of our cocoons?

You will have to issue—and answer—these challenges to fear by yourself. You have to train yourself to believe that you will ultimately be OK. It's like a vaccination: you have to expose yourself to the disease in order to build up your body's natural defenses.

**When you confront your fear, you realize that many
of your criteria for being afraid are false.**

Learning to do anything involves overcoming fear. Learning the technical aspects of skiing is 10 percent of the challenge. The other 90 percent is overcoming the fear that you'll die once you start moving. When you get down to the bottom of the mountain—a slope that looked like Everest from the top—you realize that it was just a gently graded bunny slope after all. You experience an amazing feeling of accomplishment, a renewed sense of confidence in yourself and your abilities, and a commitment to take your skills to the next level.

Know What You're Up Against

For me the most chilling moment in Michael Moore's Academy Award–winning documentary, *Bowling for Columbine*, was when he asked Charlton Heston if he'd ever been the victim of a crime. The answer was no. The man is in his eighties, sitting in a gated community, protected by the best security money can buy, and he's also got to surround himself with firearms "for protection"—despite the fact that, by his own admission, nothing bad has ever happened to him. Now, I'm not a liberal, and neither am I a fan of Michael Moore. I was especially opposed to his slanderous portrayal of President Bush in *Fahrenheit 9/11*. But the great Jewish thinker Maimonides always said, "Accept truth regardless of its source." Michael Moore was absolutely right in his film about our irrational obsession with fear. I believe in the right of citizens to bear arms, and I also believe in the necessity of responsible gun laws. In the end it is the largely unfounded fear of crime that leads to so many mistaken shootings.

When we examine the facts, we find reasons to be concerned and to be ever vigilant, but never to fear. The rise in Arab fundamentalism is tragic and dangerous. So were the Crusades and the Inquisition, and they were defeated just as the terrorists will be. Saddam Hussein was the Hitler and Stalin of his time. He is now rotting in jail, just as Hitler and Stalin are in their graves while the horror of their deeds will live on in the history books.

**A careful study of the facts yields one important conclusion:
there is no reason to be afraid, because ultimately good
always triumphs over evil.**

There are many casualties along the way to triumph, and we lament every
one, especially if it's someone we love, but fearing evil will only make it
stronger. Believing instead in evil's eventual defeat will hasten that day.

That doesn't mean you shouldn't be vigilant against terrorism. When I argue against fear, I am not blithely suggesting that you leave your doors un-
locked. One of the strongest weapons you have against terror of any kind is
to feel that you are prepared and have protected yourself adequately. If the
best way to combat fear is to do something, then you must protect yourself as
best you can against the things that threaten you.

**Fear is based on conjecture and ignorance.
The more information you obtain, the less afraid you become.**

Caution grows weaker in the light of rational inquiry; fear is completely dis-
armed by it. Almost all fears fade when they're dragged out of the darkness—
and the very act of confronting them allows you to do this. Whenever I hear
a strange noise at night, I nearly always go down to discover what it was. I
know that usually it is nothing, but I go down purposely in order to confront
my fear. If I sit in the bedroom, my imagination gets the better of me, and I
can imagine ghosts, robbers, or something truly frightening—mice! When I
confront my fear, I am empowered and in control.

In response to the economic slowdown, a television commercial showed a
man running away from his brokerage statement. It's not really funny: I've
spoken to any number of people who genuinely can't face the financial reversal they've suffered during the last few years. Indeed, I have run many times
myself. Unfortunately, running away doesn't make it better. In fact, running
away from the feeling of dread you get when you see the envelope magnifies
those fears instead of allaying them. The unopened envelope looms larger
and larger in your nightmares, and your poor investments keep losing money
as the months pass. The solution, of course, is to confront your fears and
then do something about them. If you can take a deep breath, pour yourself
a small drink, and sit down with the statement, you put yourself back in the

driver's seat. It's often not easy. You sometimes have to force yourself to walk over to the envelope, convince yourself you're going to do it, close your eyes, and just open it.

In confronting fear, the initial steps are always the hardest.

After you get over that hump, the job becomes easier. You can figure out the exact state of your financial affairs and call your broker in order to come up with a plan to stop the damage before it gets any worse. You'll notice that a miraculous thing happens: you feel less afraid. You won't spend the month tossing and turning, wondering how bad it's gotten. You'll feel liberated, as if a weight has been lifted from your shoulders. You'll feel proud of yourself— the kind of pride that follows every victory and personal triumph—and you'll be fortified to find a way to do better next year. Next month, when you see that familiar return address, you'll open the statement with fortitude, not apprehension, because you know that you've taken steps to remedy the situation. Besides, is a shabby piece of paper going to make you afraid? You've taken control, and that means you don't have to live at the mercy of an unopened envelope.

Beating fear involves converting an unconscious process to a conscious one and an irrational disposition to a rational one.

Don't let your thoughts and fears run away with you. Grab them with the hand of your mind. Hold them in your palm and examine each and every one. Pay attention to those moments when you feel fear's icy-cold grip tighten around your throat and pledge to yourself today that you will not permit a single one of these fears to stand unchallenged. You're going to drag them out into the harsh light of day, and you're going to make an action plan for eliminating them from your life. If your insecurities are causing you to procrastinate about making a phone call ("He doesn't want to hear from someone like me," or, "I know that all I'm going to get is bad news"), you're going to make that call today. If you're terrified of your credit card debt, promise yourself that you will sit down and figure out how much you owe. If you're afraid of the water, sign up for beginner swimming classes at the Y. Fear stops here and now.

Principle #5:
Keep Hope Alive

Fear, and the pit, and the snare, are upon thee, O inhabitant of the earth.

—ISAIAH 24:17

Fear is the faith that it won't work out.

—UNKNOWN

Over the course of writing this book, I had a series of conversations with a woman whose greatest fear is that something bad will happen to someone she cares about—her parents, her in-laws, her husband, or her child. This is one of the major fears we cope with in our lives, and I talked often with my friend to get to the bottom of it. One day I said, "What do you think you'd do if, G-d forbid, something did happen to the baby or to your husband?" She said, "I wouldn't survive it. I wouldn't be able to go on. It would kill me—or I'd kill myself."

These conversations helped me to clarify an aspect of the nature of fear. For her, the real fear was that there was nothing on the other side of that horrific event. It was terminal, unendurable: the end, game over, no more quarters. I think this is true about all of our fears. As I said earlier, fear pushes us to extremes.

When we're afraid, we automatically move to the doomsday scenario.

Fear is about "the end." It annihilates you, kills you off, finishes you. I have seen this response again and again when talking to people who are caught in the grip of a terrible fear. A pregnant friend of my wife's called our house, nearly hysterical. And early blood test had indicated that her baby might have Down syndrome, and she was scheduled for an amniocentesis in the morning. Debbie, my wife, asked me to speak to her, to see if I could comfort her in some way. It was as I had suspected. She had taken the fear path, going to the endgame without passing go.

I encouraged her to stop worrying about the test and instead to focus on positive thoughts, but she was too far gone. So I took another tack. What, I asked her, would happen if she stepped back instead and explored all the scenarios the circumstance presented? One possible scenario was that she could have a child with Down's, G-d forbid. Was that really unsurvivable? I encouraged her to explore that possibility. Did she really think she would love a child with a birth defect any less passionately than she would a "normal" child? As the father of seven, I felt very confident reassuring her that she wouldn't. She suddenly remembered reading a deeply impassioned and intelligent article in the *New York Times Magazine* by disability rights activist Harriet McBryde Johnson. We talked for a little while about the hundreds of thousands—maybe even millions—of disabled people in America who are right now living productive and happy lives.

As soon as she could see to the other side, even though the scenario she was exploring certainly wasn't the best possible outcome, she felt better. When she had been stuck in that moment of panic, she hadn't been able to see the light; her fears had extinguished the positive possibilities. That's what fear does: it eclipses all that is good and positive. It shuts off all the light in your life and plunges the whole world into darkness instead.

I am not suggesting that in every circumstance it's healthy to confront the worst possible scenario. My wife's friend would have been better off clearing her mind of anxiety about the procedure the next morning and leaving any thought of a possible disability for the day when the test results came back. It's much healthier to live in hope than to live in dread. We spend too much time dwelling on all the possible negative combinations and permutations. But this woman needed to know that even in the worst-case scenario, the situation was survivable. I suggested that she bring a rational dimension to fear so that her imagination did not create endgame scenarios. Incidentally, the results came back negative: the child is happy and well.

The antidote to the doomsday mentality is hope, faith, and fearlessness—all those things that destroy the possibility of a worst-case scenario.

When fear grips your heart, you have to remember to keep looking to the other side. You have to keep hope in your heart. When there is hope, an emphasis on the positive, and courage, there is no worst-case scenario.

What we're really afraid of, in those terrible moments of anticipation, is that we're somehow not up to the job of coping with the worst-case scenario. We don't believe that we have the internal strength to stand up to the test. In other words—and this is an absolutely crucial point—we are never really frightened by those things outside of ourselves.

We really fear not that something bad will happen, but rather that we won't be able to cope with it if it does. In other words, it's not events that we fear. We fear ourselves and our own weakness.

You don't believe that you'll survive whatever it is that you're afraid of—getting fired, discovering the infidelity of a spouse, or especially suffering the death of someone you love. You won't be able to weather the disruption; you'll fail when you try to assimilate it into your life. You think that the news will crush you like an empty soda can, that you'll shrivel up into nothingness, that you'll be permanently exposed for the frightened, helpless weakling you are.

Fear is always about our thought that we will not be able to rise to the occasion, that we will not be able to deal with an external threat.

In war a man is afraid of death but not as much as he's afraid of his own reaction: will he run or will he fight? If you listen, a woman who's scared about her biopsy results is as afraid that she won't be able to muster the courage to fight back, to go through the chemotherapy with dignity, as she is that cancer will kill her.

On my radio show I was host to Sherri Mandell, a woman who had suffered the tragic loss of her thirteen-year-old son in Israel in a gruesome terrorist attack. The boy was hiking with his friend when two Palestinian terrorists crushed their heads with boulders. Mandell had written a book about the incident called *The Blessing of a Broken Heart* and had started a summer camp called Camp Koby for children who have lost a family member to an act of terrorism. Every year about six hundred kids—her own surviving children included—come to the camp to be with others who have lost loved ones to terror. I asked her if she had thought about the danger of living in a settlement on the West Bank. She answered that she had felt very guilty in the months immediately after Koby's death, wondering why she hadn't moved her family somewhere safer. She had felt strongly at the time that it was important to show her children fearlessness. "Koby lived fully for the thirteen years he was with us, something a lot of American parents can't say of their own children."

When the segment was over, I was left to think about this woman. She had not allowed her grief and fear to annihilate her. She knew, because she had experienced the very worst thing a parent can experience, that the worst thing didn't necessarily mean the end. The death of her son, infinitely and indescribably tragic as it was, did not annihilate her, just as the attempted extermination of the Jewish people in the Holocaust did not annihilate them either. There are still other children who need her—in her family and outside it. There is still a marriage, someone else who can comfort and who needs comforting. There are still other people who care about her, who need care as well. There is a memory to be respected, and there is still hope to be had.

In fact, even this terrible tragedy held the seeds of a new beginning—something wonderful, something designed to alleviate suffering. There is a Jewish saying that G-d never challenges any human being with a test he or she cannot withstand. Our resistance to fear must emanate from a deep-seated belief that we are up to the challenge, whatever that challenge may be. We have to keep hope alive, always. Where the bright rays of hope shine, the darkness of fear must recede.

16

Principle #6:
Redefine Vigilance

And it shall come to pass, that he who fleeth from the noise of the fear shall fall into the pit; and he that cometh up out of the midst of the pit shall be taken in the snare: for the windows from on high are open, and the foundations of the earth do shake.

—ISAIAH 24:18

Do not look back in anger, or forward in fear, but around in awareness.

—JAMES THURBER

One of the stickiest forms of resistance that I've come up against during the course of writing this book is the idea that fear makes us cautious and therefore safer. When I counsel fearlessness, I am often accused of being reckless. We are a fundamentally cautious rather than courageous society.

Caution is an intelligent response to a real threat, a risk management technique, while fear is a hysterical response to an imagined one.

When I drive, I wear my seatbelt, and I make sure the kids wear theirs as well. This isn't a response to fear; it's a simple calculation. I'm not shaking with fear at the thought of an accident every time I put on that seatbelt. I'm simply responding to these facts: road accidents do happen, seatbelts prevent fatalities, and it takes minimal effort to secure the seatbelt. The risk/benefit ratio is so strongly in favor of the seatbelt that only a fool wouldn't put one on. A soldier going off into the heat of battle is wise to wear a bulletproof vest. There is a likelihood that he will be shot at, so it is prudent to take precautions. A woman going out on a blind date is right to travel to the rendezvous with her own car and to meet the guy somewhere public. These are sensible safety measures that are motivated by a simple calculation of the risks.

There is a marked difference between this kind of behavior and what we saw in Washington, DC, when the snipers John Allen Muhammad and Lee Malvo were holding the city hostage through fear. After someone was shot at a gas station, people were getting out of their cars to insert the nozzle into their gas tanks, getting back into the car while the gas pumped, and getting back out to finish the job. Hundreds of thousands of children were being kept home from school.

The randomness of the sniper's murderous acts might well strike terror into anyone's heart, and I have nothing but sympathy for the victims and for their families. But sitting in the front seat of a car while your tank fills is, I believe, a typical fear response—hysterical and irrational. Realistically, how much more protected are you when you're sitting in the front seat? Someone can just as easily shoot you through the glass. And what was the real risk anyway? The truth is that you were far more likely to get killed in a car accident on your way to get gas—or to be injured in a household accident before you'd even left the house!—than you were to be shot by the snipers, two gunmen in a metropolitan area of more than five million people. If you're more likely to get hit by lightning walking down the street than staying inside, does that mean that you're going to stay inside forever?

The Washington area's response to the horrible sniper episode was hysterical and not in any way commensurate with the level of threat posed. I happened to have had a meeting at a local radio affiliate at the height of the crisis. Into the meeting walked a female friend who works at the station. She was late, distracted, a downright mess. We all asked her what was wrong. "I don't know," she said. "I can't eat, I can't sleep. I can't even think. What keeps on running through my mind is that there is some crazy guy out there who at any moment can blow my head off." A lot of people reacted the way she did. But it was irrational! What if she had walked into the meeting and said, "I saw on TV that a man choked on his food yesterday and died. Now I can't eat." Everyone around her would have told her that she was behaving hysterically. And yet a lot more people died of mundane things like that during the rampage of the snipers than were felled by bullets.

**Caution is a response to a threat;
fear is a response to an impulse.**

Getting back into that car at the gas pump is the equivalent of wearing an amulet or keeping a rabbit's foot on your key chain. These are not actual safety measures; they just make you feel better. You can see how short-term the benefits of fear always are. Do you really feel better? Or do your actions actually increase your fear by making you feel enslaved by it?

An Intelligent Response

Fear flourishes in the dark spaces: like a twisted, unnatural plant, it grows out of proportion in the shadows. It is your duty to flood the area with the brilliant light of wisdom, rationality, and intelligence. You have to make those calculations that expose your fears for the irrational superstitions that they are. This principle is applicable to every single area of your lives: your professional fears, your relationship fears, your financial fears—all of them. It is only in the bright light of intelligent analysis that you can see what safety precautions are required.

You have to learn to triage the rational from the irrational so that you can proceed sensibly, protect yourself from the things you do control—and let go of the things you don't.

It's easy to get stuck in precaution mode, especially where children are concerned. My friend Miriam recently hired a woman to take care of her young children so that she could return to work. Fran, the woman she hired, could not have been better suited to the job. The mother of three adult children, she was also a retired pediatric nurse and came with excellent, unreserved recommendations from her last job. What's more, Fran was a good fit for Miriam's kids: she hit it off with them right away, and they invariably came back from their days with her bursting with fun and good cheer. And yet, during a conversation with Miriam about our children, it turned out that she was plagued with doubts and fears. What if Fran wasn't actually as good as she looked? What if she had lied on her résumé?

No one expects you to hand over your children blithely to a stranger. Miriam had done her homework and hired the best person for the job. She'd checked Fran's references and seen with her own eyes that her children were well taken care of and stimulated appropriately. I pointed out to her that Fran's medical background made her infinitely more qualified than Miriam herself to handle a medical emergency and reminded her that children benefit from different types of adult stimulation and interaction. I showed her that she had exhaustively covered all the bases and told her that she now needed to concentrate her attention elsewhere. Miriam needs to redefine her concept of vigilance.

**We have to take reasonable precautions, and then
we have to get on with our lives.**

I am fortunate enough to live, thank G-d, in a relatively safe community, where the incidence of trouble is low. Crimes, when they happen, tend to be against property. So I allow my children to go down to the ice cream store, a few suburban blocks from our home, without parental supervision. As far as I'm concerned, it is much more dangerous to teach them to be afraid of their neighbors than it is to let them go for a walk alone, and as a father I constantly look for ways to teach my children never to fear anyone but G-d.

I do charge my eldest daughter with the responsibility of looking after her siblings. I do remind everyone to wait for the traffic light to change to green and to look both ways before crossing the street. Those are reasonable and essential safety precautions. Once I have done those things, I don't sit and gnaw at my fingernails until I see them coming down the driveway with their sundaes, unless they're bringing me one. Once I have isolated the practical things I can do to allay my anxiety about their safety, I do those things— and then I must move on.

The execution of practical safeguards allows me to carry on with my life. Sure, sometimes I worry. Like every father, husband, and son out there, I'm not completely immune to concern. But to be honest, I don't worry a lot. Knowing that I have done what I can to protect those whom I love allows me to take a tremendous step forward, out of the shadow cast by my fears. Miriam, are you listening?

17

Principle #7:
Replace Caution with Courage

Say to them that are of a fearful heart, Be strong, fear not: behold, your
G-d will come with vengeance, even G-d with a recompense; he will come
and save you.

—ISAIAH 35:4

Courage leads to heaven; fear to death.

—SENECA

ear is the single largest obstacle standing between us and what we want. Bravery may melt that roadblock, but bravery is a commodity in short supply these days. Courage is no longer cultivated as a virtue in this country. Instead it is a quality most Westerners have allowed to atrophy. Just look at how Spain caved in to terrorists after the horrific March 11 attack on Madrid. When they voted the prime minister out of office, I wondered, "If Churchill were alive, what brilliant speech would he have given about the Spanish actions?" We have replaced courage with caution. We are a profoundly cautious generation. Now, I'm all for caution, but I believe that vigilance should accompany—not replace—acts of courage.

**Caution is a supplement to, not a
replacement for, courage.**

American history is filled with acts of astonishing bravery. Patrick Henry looked tyranny in the face and said, "Give me liberty or give me death." William Prescott, an American officer at the Battle of Bunker Hill in the Revolutionary War, famously commanded his soldiers, "Don't fire until you see the whites of their eyes." When it looked as if he had been defeated in a desperate naval engagement, the Revolutionary War hero John Paul Jones was called upon by a British captain to surrender. His legendary response was "I have not yet begun to fight." With his garrison completely encircled in Bastogne during the Battle of the Bulge in the Second World War, Brigadier General Anthony McAuliffe was visited by German envoys who called for his surrender. His immortal reply: "Nuts!"

The very founding of the country was an act as audacious as you could wish to see: a ragtag group of rebels, fighting for the freedom to speak and write and worship freely, took on the world's largest superpower and won! Out of nothing, they built a country that in less than two hundred years would become the foremost power in the history of the world, greater by far than even Rome at its height.

In 1956 John F. Kennedy published his Pulitzer Prize–winning book, *Profiles in Courage*, about United States senators who took courageous stands despite political and social pressure to do otherwise. It is a book about integrity, and it was a popular as well as a critical success. It was also a key ingredient in Kennedy's successful bid for the presidency, which he won despite his youth and Catholicism. As late as the sixties, then, courage was a quality still held in great esteem.

No longer. We have allowed this most precious of natural resources to dissipate. The most courageous nation in the world has become one of the most cautious. Could it be that the heirs of Washington, Jefferson, Lincoln, Teddy Roosevelt, and Martin Luther King Jr. have become a nation of cowards?

First, we have to define the term. Merriam-Webster defines *courage* as the "mental or moral strength to venture, persevere, and withstand danger, fear, or difficulty." We get our first clue in that definition. Of course contemporary America isn't as courageous as it was. To exhibit courage, we must experience danger and difficulty. We're extremely fortunate to be living in one of the most prosperous economic periods in human history. The postwar boom of the fifties gave birth to a time of unprecedented wealth, and this economic prosperity has resulted in unprecedented freedoms, but a dangerous dependency has grown as well.

A Hasidic story illustrates the point. An extremely rich man invites a homeless man, the poorest of the poor, to his house for dinner. When the food arrives, the rich man eats with pinky raised, wiping his lips daintily after every bite, while the starving man throws himself at the food like an animal, crumbs flying, until not a roll is left on the table. This continues, course after course. The question that follows the story is this: who is more attached to the food? The answer is the rich man. The starving man is so hungry that he's not swallowing between bites, but if you tell him to go back to his cardboard box and his mickey of Night Train, he'll go. He's lived without the sumptuous banquet before, and he can do it again. Easy come, easy go, thanks for having me, and back to reality. Try to take that food away from the rich man, and you'll be talking to the cops and his lawyers for the next five years. He doesn't need the food, but he's attached to it: he needs to know that it's his.

Embedded in the definition of courage is the concept of risk, the possibility of loss or injury.

There's nothing inherently wrong with prosperity, but becoming unhealthily attached to things that don't matter is inwardly corrupting, and that is the predicament we find ourselves in today. We're attached to our Xboxes and our SUVs and our Big Gulps. Americans are spoiled. As with fruit left out too long, part of us is rotten. We take our good fortune for granted, and we are allowing our initiative, our passion, our ability to persevere to fall away. We're becoming lazy and stupid, wasting our lives in front of TVs while a select and honorable few defend our freedom, which for many of us, sadly, comes down to the luxuries to which we have become addicted. There is an undeniable and growing disparity between the founding ideals of this country and the life of the average American. Is this really why Washington crossed the Delaware? So fifty million people could become brain-dead all at once watching *American Idol*? Is this what Pershing and Patton fought for? To grant every American the right to become couch potatoes while watching the stupidest and most brain-numbing TV shows ever devised by man?

The primary difference I see between the United States and Israel is in the response to terrorist acts on home territory. If Palestinians were blowing themselves up on buses in America, buses would be empty. The Israelis realize that they have a duty to keep boarding those buses, to demonstrate—to themselves, to their enemies, and to the rest of the world—that they have not been immobilized by their fear. They don't just want to survive. They want to live.

There is a rabbinical legend that has the ministering angels coming before G-d and asking, "Tell us about this Messiah figure. Why is he so special? When he eventually comes, what will make him distinct?" And G-d replies simply, "The Messiah is one who will stand straight."

> Most of us in life develop, over time,
> a curvature of the spine. Fear bends us out of shape.
> But the Messiah will stand straight. He will know
> no fear. And the capacity to be brave is the
> Messianic spark that lurks within each of us.

Force Yourself to Make Decisions

The courage to stand tall is what defines greatness, no matter in what arena. Great businesspeople, great lovers, great warriors all have one thing in common: they are bold and unafraid, courageous enough to take risks. Americans today have become bean counters, trapped in an endless cycle of data collection, immobilized by our fears, too scared to take significant strides.

Alistair is a businessman friend of mine who has made a lot of money. He recently explained to me the secret of his success: "A lot of guys are afraid to invest, afraid of making decisions, afraid of making mistakes and losing money. But I've discovered that if you can overcome fear and make decisions—even if they're the wrong decisions—you're a lot better off. Since you've cultivated the art of decision making, you can quickly get out of a bad place if you make a mistake. Unlike other people who lose money in the market and don't know when to get out, I decide instantly that the position is bad and I'm out." Making decisions, forcing yourself to take action, is the antidote to being paralyzed by fear.

> Procrastination is a sign not just of laziness
> but of cowardice.

Indeed, the fear of making decisions is one of contemporary life's greatest problems. So we delay and delay and calcify as a result. Our fearfulness is standing in our way. How often do we lose something of real value because we're "not sure yet"? My friend Jonah had been through a messy divorce. He had been dating a good woman for two years, but he wouldn't ask her to marry him. They wanted the same things in life, and they were very much in love, but he was consumed by fear, afraid that he might again make a mistake. I heard all his excuses: "I've been burned before, all of my friends are in terrible marriages, look at the national divorce rate, I can't go through it again." He was stuck. This wasn't someone coolly weighing the pros and cons of a decision. It was someone hopelessly revving his wheels without making any progress.

I told him that all the contemplation in the world would never help him overcome his fears. "Only by getting on that knee, throwing caution to the wind, and believing in love are you going to overcome your fear of being hurt." His girlfriend wasn't a stranger! They'd built a solid, honest relationship. It was time for him to overcome his fear by taking the plunge.

How many of us are stuck like Jonah? We've adopted a national policy of timidity, and *risk* has become a four-letter word. I recently read an article in the *New Yorker* about the actor Christopher Reeve, who was paralyzed from the neck down during a horseback riding accident in 1995. He has dedicated his life since the accident to an aggressive program of physical rehabilitation and has used his considerable fame to help make scientific research on spinal cord injury possible. In the article he described his frustration with what he sees as the careerist, conservative world of scientific funding and research, and the snail's pace at which it progresses as a result. "Research should not be reckless," he says, but he does countenance fearlessness, "adding courage to the equation."

Too often in this culture, boldness reads as recklessness. You can call it whatever you want, but I prefer to think of it as an aggressive, stalwart belief in the future. Consider Washington crossing the Delaware. The British had humiliated him in New York and New Jersey, and he was in full retreat. His soldiers, the few thousand who hadn't been killed or captured and hadn't deserted, were starving and shoeless. Washington knew that a victory was his only hope of salvaging the morale of his troops. So out of the blue, he launched a daring raid across the frozen Delaware River and caught the British by surprise at the Battle of Trenton on the day after Christmas in 1776.

Was it a reckless act to launch that raid? Perhaps. But so what? Was it not reckless of Churchill to imperil the entire British Empire by continuing the fight against Hitler when everyone else had been defeated? Many modern revisionist historians argue that it was, and some say that Churchill rashly and stubbornly squandered Britain's manpower and resources in the fight against Hitler, not to mention eventually losing its colonies in the aftermath of the war. Well, let them live under Hitler—cautiously. Aren't there better questions we can ask than whether or not something was rash? For example, what might have been lost if the risk had not been taken?

I was mesmerized by the story of Aron Ralston, the hiker in southwestern Utah who amputated his own arm below the elbow in 2003 in order to free himself from the rock that had fallen on him. Certainly what happened to this man was a tragedy. For safety's sake he shouldn't have gone out hiking alone without leaving information about his whereabouts with friends, and with no way of communicating in case of emergency. That wasn't courageous but thoughtless; it would have taken no effort to tell someone where he was going.

Although I would not wish his fate on anyone, part of me can't help but admire him. You see, just a few weeks after losing his hand, he started hiking again. He showed that he refused to be emotionally scarred by his past. Would he be more alive now if he had stayed safely ensconced in front of the TV? Is his quality of life—even now without a hand—really worse than that of someone who thinks playing Playstation 2 and eating Cinnabons is a wholesome way to spend a weekend? For every person who dies in the wilderness, hundreds of thousands die from an unhealthy lifestyle consisting of fast foods and no exercise. Thousands more believe that life consists of awaiting the latest Hollywood film. They are completely dead inside, hopeless automatons with no energy, no initiative, no spirit of adventure at all. Ralston went hiking and rock climbing again as soon as his doctors gave him the okay. He acted stupidly, and he paid a terrible price, but that does not change his undeniably heroic nature. He is a man who lives without fear.

As a Jew, I am a member of a people who have long shown irrational courage and ferocious independence, refusing simply to disappear by assimilating into the nations of the world. We have struggled throughout our history against mighty armies that could easily crush us, just to preserve our religion and monotheistic beliefs. Julia Balbilla was a Greek princess who served as lady in waiting to the Empress Sabina, the wife of the Roman emperor Hadrian. When the cruel Hadrian sought to build a new pagan temple on the site of the ruined Holy Temple of the Jews in Jerusalem in the year 132, the Jews erupted in revolt against the mightiest empire on earth. This was the second time in seventy years that the Jews had revolted. As Gibbon wrote, there was no precedent for any nation believing it could alone defeat the might of Rome. Still, the Jews would not allow themselves to be severed from their G-d without a fight. They were simply not afraid. Here is what Julia wrote of the war in May of the year 132 CE:

> The Jews have long been a troublesome people, endlessly resisting the subjugation which might protect them; even among themselves they brawl and intrigue. They will foment trouble until they destroy themselves, not just their temple, my brother once said. Yet, no one could

ignore them—they were always clamoring for their space, irresistibly individual and uncompromising. My grandfather—a man of the cast of Hadrian—determined to lead the Jews away from their strange customs and he failed. My noble father sought an allegiance in marriage with their most beautiful princess, Drusilla, and he too failed. Still, we who are monuments to expediency look across to them and wonder what it must be like to be so proud. There is something magnificent in the obduracy of the Judeans, their utter inability to learn from the past. Again and again, they refuse to play their part in this secure, Roman world. Ours is an empire united by advantage. The Jews think otherwise.

Courage may make us irrational, but it is the source of all human greatness.

Need also redefines risk. As Abigail Adams said, "Great necessities call out great virtues." In that same *New Yorker* article, Christopher Reeve describes the disparity between the extremely cautious risk profile of a scientist afraid of the potential consequences of a setback and the much higher risk profile of someone who sees experimental treatments as his only hope for eventual movement. It's not for lack of volunteers that experimental treatments don't move to human trials. If you have to strain to lift a single finger, you'll do anything that might help, no matter how serious the potential downside. "Let's face it," he says, "nothing of any significance has ever been achieved without reasonable risk." It's true: risk involves potential sacrifice. The concept of sacrifice is central in the Jewish tradition. Abraham, of course, is called upon by G-d to sacrifice his beloved son Isaac, as a test of his willingness. The very word *sacrifice* means that you offer something precious up for the sake of something else; it connotes readiness to give something up, to lose something, for the sake of something greater.

I talk to American Jews who refuse to go to Israel on the grounds that it's too dangerous. I think about boatloads of Jews being turned away from safer shores during the Second World War, Jews who went straight back to Europe and the gas chambers, and I think, "Israel is too dangerous?" I feel quite sure that the eighty thousand Ethiopian Jews who were brought to Israel during two major operations in the 1980s, Jews who might otherwise be dead from starvation and persecution, Jews who have since proliferated and prospered, would not agree with that assessment.

We cannot be courageous without the
willingness to sacrifice.

At Sabbath dinner during the war in Iraq, I thought many times about how fortunate we were not to have our food rationed. Can you imagine not being able to get as much meat and milk and butter for our children as they need? Can you even imagine our government asking us to give up these staples? But the British went years without them during the Second World War as part of the war effort, an effort undertaken by every man, woman, and child in the country. And they didn't complain because they believed in their national mission.

To most Americans, sacrifice means cutting carbs. Instead of going without, we chose instead to complain about the amount of money the war in Iraq was costing us. If you watch baseball, you know that the seventh-inning stretch used to be accompanied by the organist playing "Take Me Out to the Ball Game." Since September 11 we now sing "God Bless America." At the World Series in 2003, I listened as the announcer in his plummy accent directed our attention to center field, so that we could honor the brave men and women "fighting to defend our way of life." It struck me that I didn't know what that meant. They were fighting for our way of life? Brave men were laying down their lives so that we could watch baseball? Brave women were being picked off by snipers so that we could have a thousand cable channels? Our way of life in America all too often means scratching our crotches and belching in front of yet another reality TV show. Were men and women dying in a desert half a world away to support my right to a deluxe refrigerator with an ice maker?

I find our attitude toward the war in Iraq telling. During World War II, Churchill's legendary BBC broadcasts were intended to celebrate the ordinary British citizen for his or her contribution to the war effort. The British people, unified, were taking on the murderous Luftwaffe. Churchill called upon them to be courageous, as they lived underground with their children, as their houses were bombed nightly into rubble. He did not pander to their worst inclinations but inspired them to greater feats of everyday courage by asking them to be brave.

Our response is completely different. Can you imagine everyday Americans today, not members of the military, "fighting them on the beaches"? When we say that the men and women fighting in Iraq are "defending our way of life," we're effectively saying that they're sacrificing so that we don't have to.

When was the last time you really called upon yourself to be brave?

18

Principle #8:
Embrace the Superrational

Fear thou not; for I am with thee: be not dismayed; for I am thy G-d: I will
strengthen thee; yea, I will help thee; yea, I will uphold thee with the right
hand of my righteousness.

—ISAIAH 41:10

What's courage but having faith instead of fear?

—MICHAEL J. FOX

Caution is a rational response to a potentially dangerous situation. When you discover that a threat is credible, you take precautions to protect yourself as best you can. Fear, on the other hand, is an irrational response to an imaginary threat. Are these our only options in the face of danger? Is a measured response as good as it gets? There is a crucial third possibility: courage.

**If cowardice is irrational, and caution rational,
then courage is superrational.**

When we look at true acts of courage, they often violate the constraints of the purely logical, the fixed principles by which our lives are bound. I am greatly inspired by acts of military courage in defeating totalitarian aggression. When I was rabbi at Oxford, I had the pleasure of hosting as speakers some of Israel's great heroes at its most desperate hour, the Yom Kippur War. On October 6, 1973, on the day of Yom Kippur, the holiest of the Jewish calendar, Egypt and Syria launched a surprise and murderous attack against the tiny state of Israel. The country's soldiers were mostly in synagogue and vastly outnumbered. At the Suez Canal, approximately 500 Israeli soldiers were charged with holding off more than 80,000 Egyptians, and in the Golan Heights, 140 Israeli tanks faced 1,400 Syrian ones. After devastating initial setbacks that even Defense Minister Moshe Dayan feared marked the "destruction of the Third Temple," Israel not only defended itself but pushed the invaders back deep into Syria and Egypt.

A battle like this, against those odds, can only be won if those fighting it demonstrate astonishing courage and heroism, and indeed, there are hundreds of inspirational stories that emerged from that war. Almost all of them share one common denominator: by definition, they transcend logic.

Consider, for instance, Moshe Levy, who commanded two armored personnel carriers going to the Suez Canal. The Egyptians had landed about fifty commandos armed with shoulder-launched antitank missiles on a hill in order to prevent the Israelis from reaching and crossing the canal. Levy stopped his vehicle and opened the hatch to get out. As he climbed up, the fin of a shoulder-launched missile cut off his right arm. His men pulled him back into the tank. The next missile hit the track of the carrier. The first missile, the one that took his arm, was high, the second was low; even in his agony, Levy calculated that the next one would be a direct hit, destroying the vehicle and killing his men. He'd lost so much blood, he figured that he was dead either way. All that was left was to save his men. He grabbed his machine gun and a couple of grenades, pulled himself out of the tank, and ran—one-armed, bleeding profusely, and delirious—up the hill to where the Egyptians were hunkered down.

The Egyptians in the machine-gun nest must have been so shocked by the sight of him that they didn't know what to do: a ghost was attacking them! How could this man be alive, let alone launching a lone offensive? He was shot several times on his way up the hill, but he threw the grenades into the bunker before laying himself down to die. Instead the men whose lives he saved carried him to safety. He won Israel's highest military honor, the Gibor Yisrael (Hero of Israel) Prize. He now runs a successful security company in the United States and returns often to Israel. Before the war, he was an artist who painted with his right hand. He has since trained himself to paint with his left.

There's nothing logical about this story: there's no reason in the world that Moshe Levy should have been successful in what almost anyone else would have thought was a fool's errand, and it's even more surprising that he survived. A coward wouldn't have been there in the first place, and a cautious man would never have left the tank. One armless, severely injured soldier against scores of heavily armed commandos? That's not just reckless, it's suicide! It took a courageous man, a man with his trust in the superrational, a man who understood that the Middle East's lone democracy was fighting for its life against totalitarian aggression, to destroy those Egyptians and to save the lives of the Israeli soldiers in his battalion.

Isn't it clear that there was a higher law at work in this case, one that superseded simple mathematics and military strategy? That law says that those Egyptian soldiers, for all their superior numbers and firepower, were starting at a disadvantage as soon as they woke up in the morning. Under this higher law, Moshe Levy's attack was not a battle between a single, badly injured man and an entire battalion, but a battle between good and evil. Contrary to the evidence, the Egyptians were actually outnumbered, because Levy was representing democracy and light—and those things will always win out over the dark side.

Righteousness will always win, although we may need to sacrifice in order to make it so.

The Heights of Courage

Military history is filled with superrational stories like this one: acts of astounding courage winning out against insupportable odds. One thing is clear: the superrational renders fear completely irrelevant; this kind of courage gives you the key to a domain where fear cannot reach. Was Moshe Levy afraid as he ran up that hill? Maybe he was—but it didn't stop him from saving his men. In fact, I can imagine no better definition of courage than the ability to act bravely and with dignity despite your fears. Isn't this what courage is all about?

In the same war Avigdor Kahalani, a company tank commander whom I would later befriend, found himself and his twenty tanks confronting approximately four hundred Syrian tanks. Kahalani knew that there was nothing standing between him and the rest of the north of Israel. If his company were destroyed, the north of Israel and its population centers would be lost. With a courage that is the stuff of movies, he vowed to hold the line. In what is now known in Israel as the Valley of Tears, he led one of the largest tank battles in history. His dying platoon knocked out hundreds of Syrian tanks and saved the country, even though his own tank was hit several times and the heat inside made the interior unlivable. As long as his tank could still fire, he would not give up the fight. When the war was over, the commanding general of the entire northern region got on the radio to tell him, "Kahalani, you have saved Israel." A few moments later he was informed that his younger brother, who had married just days before the war, had been killed in combat.

Kahalani, who later served as Israel's minister of internal security, is unassuming, a soft-spoken family man with a quick smile. This is a man, just like you and me, an ordinary man who when called up, scaled "the heights of courage," as he titled his book.

Superrational courage is certainly not limited to the military; let's look at a more pedestrian example. A short, bald man sees a beautiful woman in a bar and wants to talk to her to ask her out on a date. He knows that on the scale of physical attractiveness we so slavishly follow in this country, she's a nine, and he's a five, tops. In this situation, most of the time, the guy won't even approach her. Haven't you been watching *Average Joe* and *Blind Date? Dismissed? Extreme Dating? ElimiDate?* "Nines" don't date "fives." Since the consequences are foretold, and there's no way she's going to say yes, why even attempt it?

This is a typical fear response; it's irrational, and it causes paralysis. What's the worst thing that could happen? Let's say he introduces himself, and she suddenly remembers that she has something to tell her friend across the room. He's afraid his friends will make fun of him, or that everyone in the room will see him disrespected. At the end of the day, so what? If she's rude about it, he's better off not knowing her. It's not a pleasant moment, but his head won't explode either. Our man can't see this. His lack of confidence sucks him into a fear vortex.

Another possible response might be caution, a more rational response to be sure. Our five knows that he's below her on the objective attractiveness scale, but he thinks he can level the playing field. He enumerates his good qualities to himself: he's got a good job, he's wearing his best tie. He'll make his pickup line funny; women like a man who can make them laugh, and that's got to be worth a point or two. He sensibly arms himself before he goes over to talk to her. He's not so fearful that he's going to lose the opportunity to talk to her, but he's not going to jump in like a maniac either.

The third response is superrational, throwing caution to the wind. It's a Moshe Levy–style true leap of faith, an act of courage. The guy says to himself, "I believe in myself. I believe that I was put on earth to love a woman fully, and I believe that I have qualities that will enrich some lucky woman's life beyond measure. I reject false notions of a human grading scale, and I refuse to feel inferior to any man. I believe in love, in a great love that has nothing to do with stupid cultural limitations. I don't make calculations based on waistband size, and I'm not going to give her the opportunity to make them either." (Now I, of course, hope that this man defines a woman as a "nine" by her being as beautiful on the inside as she is on the outside.)

In this way he transcends the laws of nature by tapping into their source, the divine code that inspired them. He's not bound by rules or limits; he supersedes them, bending them to his will. He's not interested in the mean, reductive, and petty machinations of a grading scale that tells him he's worthless because his hair happens to be falling out; he's looking to something higher. Logic isn't a factor anymore: he's transcending logic, overcoming human limitations, and throwing his lot in with the universe's intangibles. I'm going to tell you right now, this man has the greatest chance at success, no matter whether Ms. Nine (beautiful on the outside but especially on the inside) gives him the time of day or not. She is most likely to talk to Bachelor #3; he's going to get her attention because he demands her attention. Even if she doesn't respond, he's won, because he hasn't allowed fear to curtail his ability to live his life fully. He has shown courage, and that makes him truly alive.

True courage makes for true heroism, and history is filled with examples, because it is the superrational response that makes history. Think about Franklin Delano Roosevelt's response during the Great Depression. An economist would have predicted (and many did) that the country would be in an economic slump for a long time. But FDR told Americans (in so many words), "Put your trust in me, not the rules. Forget about the rules. We'll break them; we'll make new ones." And he put millions of people to work, turning the economy around and creating astonishing national treasures like the Blue Ridge Parkway, which would not have existed without his superrational vision.

In the Bible, G-d promises Abraham that he will have children. In those days people followed astrology, and Abraham, who was childless, had seen in the stars that he would remain childless. The Bible relates that G-d took him out under the stars and said, "Do you see how many stars there are in the sky? That's how many children you will have." A rabbinical legend has it that G-d took Abraham not *under* but *over* the stars and said to him, "You are unlike the others. You transcend fate. You live above the stars." Abraham had worshipped G-d as a young boy, even though the man-god Nimrod tried to kill him for it. His devotion to the superrational made him different, raised him above astrological predictions.

The superrational requires that we take a leap of faith. When you drive along the Palisades Parkway in New Jersey, the majestic Manhattan skyline is so close that you feel you can almost reach out and touch it. On a foggy day the skyline disappears completely. We know that this means not that Manhattan has disappeared, just that it's temporarily obscured. We have to trust in something our eyes cannot necessarily see.

An allegiance to a higher truth requires the same kind of faith. I am intimately familiar with the kind of faith required to fight back against unwholesome influences. The culture is polluted, and I believe humans deserve and want something better than reality TV's *The Swan*, wherein women disfigure themselves cosmetically in order to transform themselves from ugly ducklings into the perfect feminine specimen. Where is my evidence? It's certainly not in the Nielsen ratings. If I were debating a television executive, he'd point to the astronomical ratings and say, "Shmuley, if Americans aren't into being degraded, why did sixty million of them tune in to see which slut was going home with that rich guy when they could have been doing something more wholesome, like playing with their kids?"

Despite what must seem like clear evidence that he would be right, I remain unshaken. I have faith in my fellow man, and I know that we want something better, that after repeated exposure to this garbage we'll eventually regurgitate it en masse. That executive can take his Nielsen ratings; I believe in a higher reality—and in doing so, I am actually creating a world in which that higher reality is truth.

19

Principle #9:
Create Your Own Reality

For I the LORD thy G-d will hold thy right hand, saying unto thee, Fear not; I will help thee.

—ISAIAH 41:13

Nothing is impossible to a willing heart.

—JOHN HEYWOOD

Courage, or a superrational response to fear, is within the reach of all of us, but it requires that we appeal to the very best part in ourselves, a part that too often goes neglected. There is a saying from the Talmud that at the wedding of his only child, a man will even dance with his enemy. I like to call this "the mountaintop"—those moments of special clarity in our lives when we're able to put aside pettiness and trivial distractions and answer instead the call from the better angels of our nature.

We are, of course, all able to tap into that superrational part of us when we wish. Think of the decision to have children. People willingly put away all the pleasures of their unencumbered lives—the discretionary income, the late nights out, the afternoons spent reading novels and seeing friends—in exchange for years of diaper changes and playdate pickups and plays put on by fourth-graders. And yet people not only do it but look forward to it. You won't find too many parents out there who will tell you they regret the decision. Having children is a sacrifice, but only in the sense that it means giving up superficial things for something that is much better, discarding the trivial in favor of the eternal.

You have to choose the superrational, though: like fearlessness, courage is a choice you have to make. To return to my example, it now seems that in the modern world, professional couples are waiting longer to have children and having fewer of them when they do. They're afraid of losing their big clients, their gym-hard bodies, their sex lives. Even this—the most powerful drive we possess, to reproduce in our own image—is overshadowed by external, material concerns.

When you opt for washboard abs over the joy of bringing another life into the world, when you choose junk food and junk TV over being romantic with your spouse, when you select selfish pleasures as opposed to G-dly ideals, you're acting out of fear, and your fears will cheat you every time. They will drive you to make the wrong choices, choices that leave your life empty, without guiding principles—choices that guarantee you more fear in the long run, not less.

Making the Right Choices— for the Right Reasons

I want to run to the light, not away from the darkness.

When you're running away, you don't know where you're going to end up. When you run toward something, you're the author of your own life, the creator of your own destiny.

When we rediscover our ability to be courageous, when we believe in the superrational and we act despite our fears—when we fight back, even though the conclusion seems foregone—we're doing something very powerful: we are beginning the process of creating our own reality.

This is a central tenet in Judaism. It is said, for instance, that Abraham invented G-d. He didn't, of course, but he made Him known and spread the knowledge of His existence. Without Abraham, people would have thanked the sun for their survival. Abraham "invented" G-d by hearing Him. In the Jewish religion we follow the lunar calendar. Yet, there's no such thing as a truly fixed calendar, or the first day of the month. This is why the holidays are in flux. This is the way it worked in the time of the Temple: the moon disappears for a few hours every month, and when it reappears, witnesses testify before the high court that they have seen it "reborn." In other words, people take an active role in the creation of time.

Judaism also makes a distinction between two different kinds of history, the causal and the covenantal. Causal history is straightforward. The events of yesterday inspire and cause the events of today. Everything is linked in a causal relationship. You smoke, you get lung cancer. Your husband cheats on you, you walk out. Osama bin Laden attacks the United States, we rain fire and brimstone upon him from the skies. Causal history is the understanding that what precedes an event is what gives rise to what happens next. History is propelled from behind.

Rabbi Joseph Soloveitchik calls another kind of history "covenantal." In this sort of history, it is not the events of yesterday that are responsible for the proceedings of tomorrow. On the contrary, it is the promises of tomorrow that cause and inspire the events of today.

Covenantal history is not being pushed by the events of yesterday, but being pulled by the promise of tomorrow.

When I was a confused Bar Mitzvah boy of thirteen, shaken by my parents' divorce and doing poorly at school, I had the unusual honor of a private audience with the world's foremost Jewish spiritual leader, the Lubavitcher rebbe. The rebbe read the letter I presented him and then, with a deep sea of compassion sparkling in his blue eyes, he blessed me to grow in time to be "a light to the Jewish people and a light to all the world." What the rebbe did with this blessing was change the history of my life. My parents' divorce had left me bitter and bewildered. By giving me a vision of what my future could be, the rebbe was saying, "Your life is governed not by the events of yesterday but by the promise of tomorrow. You are going to do something glorious with your life. I am going to give you a goal to which you will work, and that will automatically erase the hurt of your youth. You have a bright future rather than a scarred past. Rather than be consumed by your own darkness, you're going to give others light." I left feeling that I would be healed, and ever since I have attempted to fulfill the blessing's promise.

The Importance of a Promise

G-d and humans enter into certain promises to one another, and these promises, no matter how outlandish and unrealistic their satisfaction may seem, will be kept. That's the power of a covenant, and that's the force of covenantal history. The pact is binding, regardless of whatever obstacles may lie in the way of keeping it. This is the story of the state of Israel. G-d promised the Jewish people that they would one day return to this land. As impossible as it must have seemed over the thousands of years of persecution, the promise eventually came to fruition. Since they were promised that it would be so, the Jewish people worked to make it so. The flame of that promise was something that even the crematoria of Auschwitz could not extinguish. Just three years after losing half their number to the gas chambers, the Jews returned and set up a democratic Jewish state, even though lesser calamities have caused far more powerful nations to fall.

I do believe in the power of a promise to create a new reality. A promise is like a grappling hook thrown into the future, and by working toward it, we allow it to come true. In 1969 Joe Namath famously "guaranteed," while lounging around a Miami swimming pool, that the New York Jets would win Super Bowl III. Everyone was stunned. Oddsmakers everywhere gave the Colts an eighteen-point advantage, and even Namath's coach, Weeb Eubanks, was upset. The Jets not only won 16–7 but dominated the game from start to finish. Namath was named MVP, having completed seventeen of twenty-eight passes for 206 yards. Even a late-game touchdown pass from the legendary Johnny Unitas couldn't save the Colts from this stunning upset. The country was awed and shocked. Some asked, "How could this have happened?" But how could it not? Broadway Joe had made a promise.

One of my wife's friends found a lump in her breast, and she had to wait ten agonizing days for the results of the biopsy. Everyone around her was in a frenzied state of terror, while she remained preternaturally calm. My wife asked her how she was maintaining such composure in the face of what could be devastating news, and her answer was covenantal history in action. She said, "I made a promise to my children in their cradles that I would take care of them until they were grown, and I'm not going to renege on that promise. If I have cancer, I will beat it." Causal history would have her look at the statistics; covenantal history made her promise to her children supreme, above and beyond some article in a medical journal.

> **Causal history leads to acceptance, resignation, and defeat. Covenantal history leads to engagement, struggle, and triumph.**

The biopsy, thank G-d, came back normal, but she would have lived up to her promise, no matter what the results.

Depend on Your Own Resources

I believe that you can harness the power of covenantal history, creating your own realities, by boldly making promises about the future that you intend to keep. This type of history requires a greater leap of faith than the causal kind, for sure, but the rewards are thrilling. You've heard stories that border on the outrageous—people who survive natural disasters against all odds, people who use their last five dollars to begin building massive business empires. But what is resourcefulness, if not the ability to create your own reality?

Let's say that two salespeople go out to similar territories, selling the same product. One of them comes back with fifty closed sales, the other two. Sure, sometimes you hit bad luck. But most of the time, the successful salesperson is simply the one who has created a reality in which people need to buy the product he's selling.

There is an enormous correlation between the people I know who are the most resourceful and those who are least afraid. These are the people who say, with complete conviction, "No problem. We'll get through this. I'll do what I have to, and I'll make it work somehow." They know they're rock solid and that they'll survive no matter what life throws at them. I saw this recently, when a couple I know were crippled financially in the recent economic downturn. The man had lost his job, their investments were worthless, and they were going to lose their house to the bank. He was terrified and unable to see over to the other side of the current difficulty.

His wife, on the other hand, fell back on her natural resourcefulness. "We have each other and the kids, and I won't let us starve, I promise you. If I have to take a job as a waitress, I'll do it. If I have to clean other people's houses, I'll do it. We'll economize at home, and we'll see if our friends and families can help us through this rough patch. I'll make this work, I promise." He believed her. I believed her. She created opportunities where he saw none. It was clear to both of us that this was not the kind of person who was going to let something stupid like a financial reversal destroy her family. Since she always felt as if she had a fallback position, since she felt that there was always something else she could do, she was never going to feel as afraid as he did. Admiral William Crowe, who served both as chairman of the Joint Chiefs of Staff as well as American ambassador to Britain, came and lectured to our students at Oxford and told them never to fear hard times: "In times like these, it's important to remember that there have always been times like these."

> **As long as you have confidence in your own resourcefulness, you cannot be afraid.**

Americans are lucky, but our good fortune has led to a certain apathy. We stand by helplessly, watching our lives crumble, instead of taking an active role as creator in the direction they take. For obvious reasons this is a path that leads us directly into fear: since we don't *exercise* any creative control over our own lives, we don't feel that we *have* any.

> **Let your first act of courage be to throw a grappling hook into the future. Make an impossible promise to yourself—and keep it.**

20

Principle #10:
Fight Back Against the Darkness

Hearken unto me, ye that know righteousness, the people in whose heart is my law; fear ye not the reproach of men, neither be ye afraid of their revilings.
—ISAIAH 51:7

We must accept finite disappointment, but we must never lose infinite hope.
—DR. MARTIN LUTHER KING JR.

An editor and friend with whom I've worked a number of times called me in great distress. His mother, who had beaten cancer before, had gone back to the doctor and received the news that she had six weeks to live. He was terrified and grief-stricken, and he wanted me to help him accept the prognosis.

Mindful of the importance of creating our own realities, I said that he must not, under any circumstances, accept the doctor's time line. Rather than accepting his mother's death, I told him to plead with G-d for her life. If Abraham could do that for the wicked inhabitants of Sodom and Gomorrah, surely we can do the same for the good people whom we love. "Pray like you've never prayed before," I told him. Man is not created by G-d for blind obedience. Rather we must always fight for what's right, and it is never right for a man or a woman to die too young. "Tell your mother that there's no such thing as six weeks, that she is going to live long beyond that. Tell her you're going to be with her every inch of the way." As you already see, I was advocating a covenantal approach.

"But," he said, "what if it doesn't work? What if she does die in six weeks? Then all this 'fighting back' has just been an evasion of reality, right?"

I said, "No. When you spend those six weeks struggling for life, even if they end in death, you will have changed reality. By giving her six weeks of real, vigorous, engaged life instead of a hopeless, fear-filled countdown, you will have changed the situation from one riddled with trepidation to one shot through with hope." The doctor wanted to kill her off in his office. The six weeks he promised her wasn't six weeks of life but a six-week deathwatch. He effectively said to her, "You're the living dead. There's no hope. Go home and die now." He could have said something very different. He could have said to her, "Medicine would say that you have a few weeks to live. But medicine has been wrong countless times before. So don't say good-bye to your loved ones, but gather them around you and take this time to appreciate your blessings."

It's the Jewish nature as well to struggle and fight: the name *Israel* means "He who wrestles with G-d." We do not blithely accept injustice, plagues, or hardship; we question and call G-d onto the carpet and protest his inscrutable will, when it is necessary. It's not over until it's over, and until it's over, it's our job to fight back with every fiber in our being.

> **When you fight back, you are aggressively staking a claim to life. Every moment spent focusing on life is another victory over death.**

Doesn't this immunize us against fear? As long as there's an ounce of fight left in us, we need never be afraid.

Say It Out Loud

As I told you earlier, there is tremendous power in articulating to yourself, "I will not be afraid." It is, in fact, the first stage in heating ourselves up and thawing the frozen winter of fear. I mean say it out loud. When you say something, you help make it so. Promise it to yourself, "I will not be afraid. I will not be defeated by this. I shall not die for I shall live." Give yourself an honest goal to which to aspire.

Your boss calls you in and terminates your job; you walk out not with a bowed head but with gritted teeth, and you tell yourself, "I will not be afraid. I know I'll get something else, something better." Your doctor tells you to come in, because the test results are back, and he won't discuss them with you over the phone. When you get off the phone, verbalize to yourself, "I will not be afraid. I will be fine. And whatever it is I have to do to be healthy, I'll fight that battle." Whenever life hits you with a fearful challenge that you do not believe yourself capable of surmounting, you must tell yourself that you are not weak but strong. "I know that I have what it takes within me. I will not be afraid."

You're probably thinking, "What kind of advice is that, to say, 'I am not afraid?' It's a tautology, not a solution. It's like telling an overweight person that they need to stop eating so much and begin exercising more: it may be true, but it's not the kind of advice people pay for."

But you know what? It *is* the kind of advice that works. The people who successfully lose and keep weight off are people who have the discipline to change their habits. I have used this technique in my own life, in those moments when panic threatened to flood out good sense and sanity. I can offer no other testimonial than this one: it's effective. Aside from panic, almost any kind of action in the face of fear is rewarding.

I was talking the other day to Jan, a woman I had known in Australia. She was complaining about her teenaged son and the terrible friends he has. Her son, she said, had started sneaking out of the house and lying to her. I listened patiently for a while, but I couldn't shake the suspicion that the source of her son's misbehavior was on the other end of the phone. Jan's elderly parents had recently taken sick, and she'd been spending an inordinate amount of time with them. Their precarious health had made her very afraid that they would die, and this fear had seeped out into the rest of her life. She had become morbid, preoccupied with death, and this state of mind had led her to circumscribe her son's freedom. I felt sure that she was taking all the oxygen in their home and forcing it through the lung of fear, and everything was toxic as a result.

I explained, as gently as I could, that I thought her own depression and anxiety were behind her son's evasive behavior. "You've always been so sunny and bright," I said. "Your fear is causing you to betray your true self—and it's infecting your relationship with your son." There was a stunned silence at the other end, and I was worried for a moment that she would just hang up the phone. But she recognized a truth in what I was saying and asked me what she could do to make the situation better.

I told her to let her fears go and to talk to her son, even if she could only sustain that fearless state for a matter of minutes. "I don't know whether or not your parents are going to die. Some say that it's an inevitability, but that attitude in your case seems to be the problem. In your mind they're dead already," I told her. "You have to enjoy them while they're alive, not in a countdown to their death. Do you want to spend your whole life terrified of an inevitability? Whatever happens, you'll deal with it then. In the meantime, clear the path of your fears so that you can have real relationships, especially with your children." I later received an e-mail from Jan's son telling me that she had apologized to him for being so unavailable in every aspect aside from making rules. It was the first real communication the two of them had had in many months. Jan still struggles with her fear. The war is not won, by any means, but she has made significant advances, simply by telling herself not to be afraid.

You need not be cowed by evil but instead must show complete and utter contempt for it. You can meet whatever challenge you're faced with.

There is no single solution: you can't snap your fingers, or bob your head like Samantha in *Bewitched*. If you are a person who struggles with fear—like a person who struggles with his weight—your struggle will be daily and sometimes difficult. Jefferson said that "the tree of liberty must be refreshed from time to time with the blood of patriots and tyrants," and we know that anything worth fighting for is worth fighting for all the time. You have to say to yourself, "Fear has no place here. I will go out and do my duty. I am going to raise my children with joy and optimism; I am going to see the good in people; I am going to love being in relationships, even if they sometimes cause me pain. I am going to prevail against the deadening emotion of fear."

21

Principle #11:
Do Something

In righteousness shalt thou be established: thou shalt be far from oppression;
for thou shalt not fear: and from terror; for it shall not come near thee.
—ISAIAH 54:14

Inaction breeds doubt and fear. Action breeds confidence and courage. If
you want to conquer fear, do not sit home and think about it. Go out and get
busy.
—DALE CARNEGIE

In the Temple in ancient Jerusalem, when one of the priests would slaughter an animal for the altar, he would capture its blood in a gold container and stir it. Blood, when it's not moving, quickly congeals. So it is with fear. When we're not moving, fear grips and freezes us. It is a profound immobilizer.

Sometimes fighting back against terror is as simple as just doing something. There is simply no underestimating the importance of action in the fight against fear.

Fear, like its brother depression, is a dead, inanimate emotion. Fear transforms us from the animate to the inanimate, from the organic to the inorganic, from being alive to wishing we were dead. It roots us in place, robbing us of our life force, our ability to act and to do.

I am telling you that you can do this: you can shake off your fears; you can delay them; you can outwit them; you can postpone them until a more appropriate time. When the government raises the terror alert from orange to red, fine, be more cautious. But don't change your daily habits. Get on and do, do, do. Get on that bus; board that train. Put up with the pain-in-the-butt security at the airport, unbuckle your pants and take off your shoes, but get on that plane. Be alert for suspicious packages left on the subway, but once you've taken a quick look around, get back to reading your newspaper and forget about it. Nothing's going to happen. Even if it does, do you want to spend your life like a psychotic with flying saucers for eyes, like someone who hasn't slept in years because he's convinced that every noise he hears is a maniac about to murder him?

You read that there's been a jailbreak in your neighborhood and a killer is on the loose. So what? Take that walk to the neighborhood grocery store anyway. You want to walk where there are lights rather than in dark streets; that probably makes sense. Aside from that modification, don't change your habits. Never live in fear.

**While life and love are about sensation,
fear and dread are about cessation.**

We stop feeling, because we are frozen and desensitized. A major study in Scotland recently concluded that the single best treatment for depression is activity—doing something. Activity is also the single best cure for our fear and the passivity resulting from it. If you take one thing away from this book, let it be this:

Positive, external action eliminates fear.

If you stand still in a cold pool, you'll freeze, but as soon as you start swimming, your limbs warm themselves—and you forget that you were ever cold. When you're frozen in fear, you're always its captive. When you start to move, when you start to do, you're fighting fear on its home turf.

Talk About It

My friend Stephanie was badly affected by the news that a casual acquaintance had been struck down by a brain aneurism, leaving him incapable of speech or independent movement. The event had made her very frightened that something terrible would happen to someone she loved, and she was finding that fear debilitating. She was fixated on the tragedy, and she couldn't concentrate on anything in her own life. When I asked her what she'd done about it, her answer was nothing. I knew she'd feel better if she'd do something about her fear instead of letting it bring her whole life to a halt. If she could get in touch with the joy inherent in life, I knew she'd be less fixated on its loss.

I think she knew this, because she mentioned her fears to me in the course of a conversation about something else entirely. Talking about it was a good first step. When I talk about "doing" as a countermeasure to fear, I don't mean to suggest that your action has to be a grand gesture. In fact, even the simple action of speaking honestly about your fears, as Stephanie did with me, is a useful start.

Sometimes conversation is a necessary bridge between paralysis and action.

Confiding her fears was Stephanie's own way of acting: it enabled her, as her fear had not, to do something to make the problem better.

Talking is only the first step, and as I had suspected, when she started to act, my friend's dread largely fell away. She needed to participate in life instead of wasting time worrying that it would be snuffed out. She wrote a check to an institute that studies the brain, making the donation in her acquaintance's name. She had made some healthy and delicious soup for the man's wife and children to eat as they sat by his sickbed, and the gesture lifted the weight from her own shoulders. She took her own children to the zoo to remind herself how much of life is a celebration. This was how she began to transcend her own fears.

Another acquaintance of mine served in the first Gulf War. There was talk that Saddam Hussein would gas the soldiers with chemically armed Scud missiles. I asked him if he had ever been afraid. "Only while we were waiting around, doing nothing," he told me. "The air campaign went on for a month and we sat there, in the deserts of Saudi Arabia, waiting the beginning of the land war, doing nothing. Waiting there like a sitting duck made me afraid. But once we started to move, I had no fear."

My cousin told me a similar story. A sniper in the Israeli Army, he was summoned from his family's Passover Seder in April 2002 to go to Jenin after the infamous Passover massacre in which nearly thirty Israelis, mostly Russian immigrants who had already suffered under communism, had been blown to smithereens by Palestinian suicide bombers using weapons-grade explosives. His family was terrified for him when they were told that he was to assault a huge terrorist stronghold. He was only twenty years old. He told me that he himself was not frightened until they got to their destination and had to wait for three hours before the assault. "That was the only time I was frightened. When you're in combat, you have no time to be afraid, but while we waited, we were sitting ducks." He claims it was the only time he was ever afraid in the three years he was a soldier in the Israeli Army.

But it's not only when terrorists are threatening that fear makes you into an easy target.

> **Fear is the permanent terrorist that lurks, waiting to strike at any moment, but it can only catch you when you are immobile.**

We have to start to move.

I counsel many unhappy wives, and some of them are afraid that their husbands are having affairs. Many of them have been confronted with evidence that their husbands are playing around, but they have chosen to stay in denial about it, because knowing means that they have to do something.

My advice to a woman in denial is "Do something." Of course, she's terribly hurt when her worst fears are confirmed, but she's also empowered. Instead of sitting around and wallowing in self-pity, the woman becomes a lioness, defending her marriage. Instead of waiting for her husband to call because he's "working late," she starts dictating the terms. Instead of allowing him to treat her like a sucker, she's suddenly sitting him down and reading him the riot act, demanding that the affair stop and that he join her in counseling. She's acting, instead of being acted upon—and that makes all the difference.

A man who was at our home for dinner one night during the heightened terror alert was telling us all the reasons why another terrorist strike in New York City was inevitable. His concern about this future attack was robbing him of all the joy in his life, so I told him what I tell everyone who's afraid: go do something. Read about Iraq's history, I said. Educate yourself about Arab fundamentalism. Throw a dinner party. Go buy Chinese takeout and deliver it to the guys at the local firehouse. Pick up a book and read it to your kids. Call your grandmother. Visit a homebound elderly stranger. Take a single mom's kids to the museum and give her the afternoon off. Stop wallowing and start doing something.

His response was interesting. He said that busyness such as I was proposing was a type of denial, a way to sidetrack yourself so you didn't have time to worry about the bigger picture. He said that I was trying to distract him with escapism.

I have news for him: Osama bin Laden is the distraction. In reality, he's a fake, a phony, a fraud.

**Osama bin Laden is a mirage of our own making.
We took an extremely evil yet ordinary man
and elevated him into myth.**

He hit us in the solar plexus a few times and we transformed him into Muhammad Ali—and ourselves into Woody Allen. We aggrandized him as a mythical figure who can strike with impunity and belittled ourselves as neurotic basket cases who can only sit around and wet our pants. Only we can give that wicked loser power over us by giving him too much attention, by flattering him with our fears. The longer he stays on our minds, the stronger he becomes, but only we can empower him. To be sure, we must be vigilant, have a strong and dedicated Department of Homeland Security, and do our best to guard our borders against killers. After that we have to go home to our kids and learn to live and laugh again.

I'm not trying to distract my friend. I'm trying to bring his attention back to the things that matter, the things that give him a purpose in life. I'm telling him: *this* is your life—your family, your friends, the good works you do in the community—not the fear that your head cold is really a first sign of anthrax poisoning. Far from encouraging him to escape, I'm trying to bring him back to reality. Fear is something that's absorbed, and the less time you have to absorb it, the more protected you are from it. The people who are the least fearful are the people who are out there doing something worthwhile. Why does doing something work to allay our fears? Earlier I explained that fear is a freezing agent, congealing our blood and ossifying our limbs. The best way to stop from freezing over is to flex and exercise, in this case flexing our capacity for courage and exercising our ability to be audacious. But there is a further consideration.

**Actions pull you outside yourself, away from your fears,
and into a realm where you can
do something about them.**

Actions are more real than thoughts. They pull us away from troubling fantasies into the world of hard reality. Fear, like depression, causes us to curl up. It draws us into ourselves. We become numb to the outside world. It makes us selfish; it paralyzes us; it tangles our feet and gets in our way. Moving our focus outward is our most powerful weapon to combat this insidious threat.

The Danger of "Zoning In"

The culture as a whole, however, seems to be going in the opposite direction. Probably the biggest divide between eastern-influenced New Age spirituality and the Judeo-Christian tradition is that eastern religions are focused around a withdrawal from the world. You meditate, you retreat to the woods or the desert, you abstain from food and sex and the pleasures of the flesh and retreat inside yourself to contemplate a conceptual world. You find all the answers on the inside instead of seeking purpose on the outside.

In the Judeo-Christian tradition, the focus is in the other direction: outward. You go to church; you give to charity; you pray to a G-d outside yourself. G-d is found through good acts, which in turn lead to good character. Rather than finding the inner "I," you connect with the outer "thou."

It's not difficult to see why concepts from eastern religions have spread like wildfire throughout this country. Material engagement—lavish parties, elaborate country homes, our enormous cars—haven't solved our problems, so the secret to happiness must be to renounce those things, right? The thinking is that if we only go outside ourselves to do something selfish, then withdrawing inside ourselves must be the right thing to do when we want to be spiritual.

> **Since activity is what we do when we conquer,
> we mistakenly believe that passivity must be
> the way we transcend.**

I believe that zoning out has gotten us into this mess. You're stressed out, so you turn on the boob tube. Your relationship isn't working, so you take your spouse to sit in a dark movie theater and watch other people's made-up lives for two hours. You throw endless amounts of money at the problem of "finding yourself"—yoga retreats, spa weekends, seminars—and all you're doing is driving your focus more and more inside yourself. I think we're heading in the wrong direction, and I think that direction is exacerbating our fears. As a culture we're too meditative.

Meditation has no *intrinsic* value; it is valuable only insofar as it guides outward actions.

Meditation at best is a means to an end and never an end in itself. Since the major impact we're going to make in our lives lies in the outer rather than the inner world, the only purpose in exploring the inner world is to make that leap to the outer. It's like taking three steps backward to kick a soccer ball. The only purpose of that movement is to kick the ball farther; otherwise you're just moving in the wrong direction.

Anything else, as spiritual as it may sound, is purely selfish. If you're more interested in personal growth than in improving the lot of others, then you are still a self-absorbed jerk, even if you're an enlightened jerk. If you're more focused on becoming a better person than on making the world a better place, you have forgotten that no man is an island. If we are going to beat fear, we have to change our orientation. To fight fear, we have to be confidently outwardly oriented, struggling and engaged with the world. In other words, the problem is not with engagement, it's in the things with which we have chosen to engage. We feel empty when we spend our leisure time aspiring to emptiness, whether we're drooling in front of the TV or deliberately chasing after it in a yoga class.

G-d can—and should—be found in our businesses and our bedrooms and at our dinner tables, not in a mountaintop cave somewhere. It is essential that we learn to shift our attention from our own internal concerns to those things that take us outside ourselves, things like charity, parenting, and prayer. Even exercise, which gets us moving, gets our blood pumping and our endorphins raging, is a positive form of engagement.

Engaging life on the outside helps us conquer our fears on the inside. The slow grind of action creates the friction which melts away fear.

I'm not suggesting running from our fears by engaging in mindless frenetic activity. Rather I'm suggesting carrying on with purposeful and fulfilling action despite our fear, by not allowing it to render us passive.

22

Principle #12:
Kill Your Television

Go not forth into the field, nor walk by the way; for the sword of the enemy and fear is on every side.

—JEREMIAH 6:25

You can discover what your enemy fears most by observing the means he uses to frighten you.

—ERIC HOFFER

This is not a book about the celebrity culture or the damage you inflict upon yourself when you allow it to overtake your life. I have written extensively on the pernicious and corrosive effects of celebrity obsession in a previous book, *The Private Adam: Becoming a Hero in a Selfish Age*. But I would like to mention celebrity worship in this book, because there is unquestionably an intersection between the explosion of this phenomenon and the escalation of fear we feel.

I don't think anyone would argue about the supremacy of the entertainment industry and the celebrities it manufactures in the United States today. There's no question that movies, television, music—and the gossip that surrounds the stars who appear in these media—far outstrip politics, religion, even sports, in terms of what the average American knows. I would assume that for every American who can identify a photograph of John Ashcroft there are three who can recognize Britney Spears.

The degree to which this celebrity culture has insinuated itself into our lives is staggering. What we fail to recognize is how detrimental this insinuation is. I am flabbergasted by articles I read, for example a recent one about the final season of the hit sitcom *Friends*. A woman is quoted as saying, "I don't know what I'll do when it goes off the air. These people are more real to me than my own friends." Another one offered, "I feel like I've grown up with these people."

If your significant relationships—your friendships, your infatuations—are taking place with characters on television, you're in deep trouble. This is a fundamentally draining relationship. You care about these people and receive exactly nothing in return. Imagine if this were true about one of your real friendships! You give someone a significant amount of your time and energy, and they are incapable of returning that emotional connection with anything more than patter. They can't comfort you after a loss, or compliment you on a job well done, or inspire you to see another day: they're not even real!

What's more, your "relationship" with the characters on *Friends* is taking up time you could be using to have a meaningful conversation with a real friend or your spouse or your child. These are the relationships that will support you in times of trouble and fear, not one-sided half relationships you've struck up with actors in a box.

At Oxford I took a risk by publishing my book *Kosher Sex*. I did so because ever since my parents' divorce I have wanted to contribute something to enhance the institution of marriage. After the book became an international bestseller, I was honored that thousands of couples from around the world wrote to tell me that the book had helped, and in some cases saved, their marriages. Many traditionalists found it scandalous that I had published a book by that title, and I was excoriated in speeches and newspaper articles around the world. It's no fun having your name dragged through the dirt, I can assure you, and it made me very afraid. I woke up every morning with a pain in the pit of my stomach, wondering who would attack me next.

In the midst of this torrent of abuse, a group of friends, many of whom served as governors of my student organization, the Oxford L'Chaim Society, visited me at home. I had counseled some of them in their own marriages. They said to me, "We just want you to know that we're with you, standing right behind you. We believe that religion can and should address these all-important issues, and you're not going to go through this alone." Their support provided me with infinite comfort against the fear I was feeling. Thank G-d I had those relationships to fall back on during that very difficult time. I learned an important lesson from the experience:

Fear is always an isolating experience.
To be afraid is to fear that you will be abandoned,
that you are destined to endure your suffering alone.

Fear is magnified through loneliness, and who is lonelier than a generation who connects more with TV, movies, magazines, and the Internet than with real people? We can't carry the burden of disappointment and pain that life metes out on a daily basis without finding a healthy outlet in the form of an intimate emotional partnership. Yet we consistently allow our celebrity addictions to supplant the possibility of those partnerships.

We run the risk of making these celebrities into gods. In many cases they are talented, but so are you. Their talents just happen to be ones that are rewarded by the culture. If your talent is for something I would consider truly valuable—helping people without expecting anything in return, for example, or being really good at giving your children self-esteem—then I would say your talent has a greater value than that of someone whose main ability is to entertain.

Detached as we are from G-d and estranged from lofty pursuits, we have invented new gods here on earth.

Once people were awed by the heavenly stars; today they
prostrate themselves before movie stars.

Once man pondered the secrets of the universe. Today he seeks to uncover the enigma of Marlon Brando.

The thing that confuses me about the celebrity culture is that it seems to run so contrary to the spirit of America. When we make celebrities into gods, aren't we contradicting the principles upon which this country was founded? Any dingbat with a cell phone can call up a talk radio program and get on the air to curse out the president of the United States. Every single day people are saying, "He may be the president, but he's just a man. We put him in office, and we can take him out." Isn't this fantastic? The most powerful man in the world answers to the guy who's fixing my sink—not the other way around. That is the true definition of democracy. So what are we doing bowing down before Jennifer Aniston?

This worship too is a function of fear. We are so concerned with the or-dinariness of our own lives that we have to grab at the coattails of those who we think live glamorous lives—people who really matter, according to us. A woman thinks to herself, "My life is unimportant. What do I do that's excit-ing anyway? Homework with the kids? The dishes? I don't matter. My mar-riage doesn't matter. But that celebrity couple? Now *they* matter. I wonder how their romance is doing." And she runs to read *People*. Absorbed in the life of a celebrity, living vicariously through the idol of the moment, she no longer feels afraid.

Celebrity seems to offer the solution to our greatest fear: that we're not important. For me, among the many comforts offered by religion, the feel-ing of accessibility to G-d at any moment unimpeded by a feeling of unwor-thiness is perhaps the most profound. A religious person makes the decision not to be awed by anyone but G-d. Feeling inferior to others is the hallmark of fear and invites manipulation. It also leads otherwise intelligent people to take seriously the uninformed opinions of clueless celebrities.

> **A religious person makes the decision not to be awed by anyone but G-d.**

It's not that I don't find inspiration from people, but I dare not be awed or cowed by them. I read biographies of great men and women because I find them inspiring and informative, and I have been honored to spend time with some of the great statesmen and thinkers of our day. Exposure to great men and women should lead only to a positive development in our own lives. It should motivate us to develop more of our own potential. When I read about a great philanthropist, I am moved to increase my own acts of charity. When I read about a tremendous intellect, it inspires me to learn more, and more deeply. When I hear the words of a great orator, I am spurred to greater ex-cellence before my own audiences.

All Madonna can inspire us to do is to wear—and think—less. "But she's a role model for young businesswomen," people say. There are plenty of women out there who have made very good livings without taking their clothes off, mainstreaming sadomasochism, and mocking homosexuals by making out with another woman on stage for the publicity on an awards show.

We make celebrities into idols, and then we are afraid of our own gods. Instead of humbly assuming the benefits—and responsibilities—that come with notoriety, our celebrities instead have contempt for us. As a result, no real relationship or communication is possible, even among themselves. It's a system that's based on fear and one-upmanship: She's thin, and you're not. He has big muscles, and you don't. She can dance like a woman possessed, and you can't. We become small in our own eyes, and of course, that makes us small in theirs. That can only increase our fear of inadequacy with all its tributary trepidations.

In the presence of someone powerful or famous, you're suddenly struck dumb. It's not that we have nothing to say, it's rather that we're too afraid to speak. What could we possibly have to say that would make these celebrities want to listen to us? They're so special, and we're, well, so ordinary.

This is a self-fulfilling prophecy. If you behave like you're a loser hanger-on, of course you're going to be dismissed, just as you dismiss yourself. At Oxford I used to bring world-renowned people to lecture to my organization: presidents, famous thinkers, and film stars, and I noticed something:

The essence of success in life is never to be intimidated by any human being.

There were essentially two kinds of students who came to the events to meet our famous speakers. The first were the awestruck students, the crawlers and sycophants who acted as if they were blinded by the light. They offered fawning, monosyllabic comments that made them appear stupid, shallow, and boring. "Wow, it's such an honor to meet you. I can't believe this is happening. This is amazing." Fear robs us of color and vitality, rendering us emotionless and lifeless. Who wants to hang out with a petrified robot? Then there were the students who truly were not impressed. "OK, so you're Mikhail Gorbachev. But you're just a person." Such a student would greet the guest, "It's a pleasure to meet you President Gorbachev. What did you think about Professor Brown's biography of you and his insistence that you alone were not responsible for perestroika? Did you agree with his assessment?" It's not that these students were disrespectful. They weren't. Rather, they gave respect commensurate with what an accomplished human being deserved. Inevitably, it was these latter students who connected with the guests and often established long-term friendships.

And the greatest irony of all: our gods are terrified too. It always amuses me. The more macho the superstar—the more stuff he blows up onscreen, the more bad guys he single-handedly nukes at the movies—the more bodyguards he surrounds himself with in real life. The security, the dark windows in their SUVs, the walls around their homes—all these things are expressions not just of their contempt for their fans but of their own fear. The celebri-tocracy is not a system that works well for anyone, even the stars.

Celebrities' own fear quotient increases as they get wealthier and more powerful. The more successful they become, the more isolated they become—and the more isolated, the more fearful. What could possibly be more terrifying than surrounding yourself with people who may or may not only be hanging out with you because they want something? Celebrity without a foundation that solidly anchors you is like an untethered helium balloon. As with the rest of us, if celebrities don't ground themselves with the essential ingredients of a normal life—strong ties with family, community, friends, and ultimately G-d—they self-immolate.

Celebrities live in the perpetual fear of being forgotten. They start off their public lives wanting to be noticed: our attention confers existence. They scour the newspapers for any mention of their names. They only exist when we tell them they exist, but they end up hidden away behind their tall walls because, after a time, they begin to hate their fans. What could possibly be more frightening than feeling that your entire value as a human being is based on your popularity with a notoriously fickle and changeable public? And would you want to hang out with people who determine your self-worth? Of course not. On the contrary, you would develop a subliminal feeling of contempt for them in order to even the score. That's why so many celebrities actually loathe their public. They refuse to sign autographs. And they sure as hell would never be caught dead living in their fans' neighbor-hoods. They're almost saying, "Do you have any idea who I am? How dare you decide if I'm important!" Yet celebrities cannot escape the undeniable fact that, given the very nature of celebrity, stars empower us to determine their fate to a huge degree. "She looks fat in that disgusting dress," we sniff as we page through US Weekly. They see us as jailers, for we control the level of their self-esteem. Would you want to spend time with a person who controlled how you felt about yourself? It's a tragedy, but one of their own making. Nobody forced them to put their reason for living in someone else's hands. They hate their fame, but without it they're nothing. They'll do almost anything in order to stay in the public eye. All the attention feels good, but the public will lose interest if you don't do something fast to top your original stunt. What's next? Our fingers are on the clicker.

Many celebrities are so riddled with fear that they eventually self-destruct. They end up quivering, pathetic messes like Elvis, downing hundreds of pills just to quiet the demons. Like Marilyn Monroe or Janis Joplin, also dead of overdoses. Or like Michael Jackson, tragically disfigured. How sad. How pathetic. And what a waste. More important, how tragic and heart-breaking for those of us stupid enough to follow them off the precipice.

Doesn't the intense popularity of reality TV prove that everyone in America wants to be famous? Reality TV is celebrity at any cost. You can be famous instantly (and for about fifteen minutes, as Warhol said), and you don't have to create anything or know anything or do anything harder than eat a couple of bugs or bury yourself in feces.

I'm not surprised that so many people hunger for celebrity, because it seems to offer the solution to our greatest fear: that we don't matter. In our shallow estimation, if paparazzi run around taking our pictures when we're picking up our dry cleaning, and Learjets wait to whisk us from city to city, then we definitely matter. Obscurity, on the other hand, is confirmation that we don't. Remember the question that philosophers used to ask: if a tree falls in the woods, and nobody hears it, did it actually fall? Today we would ask: if someone leads an honorable life, yet nobody has heard of him, does he truly exist?

> **We are overwhelmed by the fear of obscurity,**
> **valuelessness, and meaninglessness,**
> **and celebrity seems to be the instant fix.**

It says, "You're special, as long as people know who you are—even if you haven't actually accomplished anything." What a brilliant antidote to the problem of fear.

This empty solution only feeds the fear beast, however, making it grow stronger and stronger. Although the celebrity culture isn't the only thing wearing away at our internal fortifications, it is a telling symptom. We have allowed trivia to supplant real knowledge. We have allowed superficial relationships to supersede ones of real value. And we have allowed half-naked, overpaid women to unseat our true G-d. This rise in the celebrity culture is one of the principal reasons that we have such a weakened immunity to fear. It distracts us from the things that really matter.

If you are serious about eliminating fear from your life, I would exhort you to turn off your televisions and to turn your attention to the very real people in your life deserving of your attention. Make music something that plays in the background as you dance with your wife, not something piped in through headphones to replace the sounds of your family life. When choosing a magazine, ask yourself: Do you really need a long-lens shot of Cameron Diaz furniture shopping in Beverly Hills? Or would you benefit more from a newsmagazine that will help you to understand why India and Pakistan have been at each other's throats? Isn't it the big issues that matter?

Doesn't this obsession with celebrity degrade you? And by getting a life, you'll be surprised: you'll also be living in much less fear. When you wean yourself from the celebrity habit, your immunity to fear grows substantially in its absence. Your whole life is no longer "Wow, look what I'm not," but rather "Great, look what I *am*."

23

Principle #13:
Choose Righteousness

And I will set up shepherds over them which shall feed them: and they shall
fear no more, nor be dismayed, neither shall they be lacking, saith the LORD.

—JEREMIAH 23:4

Keep conscience clear, then never fear.

—BENJAMIN FRANKLIN

Now that you have decided to turn your head away from those whose fame comes from their provocative behavior, I'd ask you instead to consider people whose courage comes from their faithfulness to their convictions.

Isn't saintliness always accompanied by courage? What if Mother Teresa had refrained from treating the sick of Calcutta for fear of contracting leprosy? What if the Dalai Lama had meekly submitted before the invading Chinese forces in Tibet? What if Rabbi Joseph Schneerson of Lubavitch had not repeatedly risked his life to keep Jewish life in Russia alive against the terror tactics of Stalin?

Righteousness is the loftiest antidote to fear.

A lack of fear is an inevitable outgrowth of a wholesome life of righteousness. What are you afraid of when you have nothing to hide? If you have repudiated the corrosiveness and destructiveness of the world we live in, if you have turned your full attention to that which is good and G-dly, what power can fear have over you? If a politician has always been faithful to his wife, need he fear being exposed as an adulterer? If you have always carefully paid your taxes, need you fear an IRS audit? If you have invested a huge amount of time into loving and supervising your children, need you fear that they'll grow up to be drug-taking bums? In the most practical way, righteousness and blamelessness are the antidotes to fear.

> **The righteous are unafraid because they are always attached to G-d. Connected to the eternal source of life, they are unafraid of being six feet under.**

Even in the grave their attachment is eternal.

Few of us are unafraid of death. I would postulate that the fear of death is actually a fear of the failure to live life to our own satisfaction. People who feel that they have lived their lives fully spend a lot less time worrying about death than those who have spent their time on earth chasing trivialities. This seems to be true right up until the end. If you have a great relationship with your wife and children and are working to make the world a better place, you don't fear death, because you haven't squandered your life.

> **Since the root cause of all fear is a feeling of insignificance, fear is greatly exacerbated when you feel you've wasted the gift of life.**

Don't you want to be truly alive while you're alive?

People who live only for themselves are absolutely terrified of death. They're decaying even as they're breathing. Since nothing is important except themselves, they spend their time trying to save themselves. In the final years of their lives, they're either scrambling to make amends, like a teenager cramming for an exam, or they abandon all hope and give up completely.

Follow Your Moral Compass

A righteous life defeats and defangs the worst-case scenario. Fear comes from not being sure of your moral direction. As horrible as it is to lose one's life, it is even more horrible to lose one's integrity. Without integrity, you're leading a life you can't be proud of. We become afraid when we feel that we have compromised our convictions, that our moral foundation has been loosened. This is when I am most afraid, when I feel that I'll betray myself by failing to live a noble life or by losing my attachment to G-d.

In one of the Bible's most famous stories, Jacob and Esau, the only sons of Isaac and Rebecca, are identical twins but complete opposites. Jacob is studious, gentle, and good. Esau, the firstborn, is a brutish lout, an aggressive archer who enjoys dominating others. Seeing his severe flaws, Rebecca decides that Esau cannot be trusted with the blessing of the firstborn, and she encourages Jacob to trick his blind father into believing that he is Esau and taking the firstborn blessing for himself. When Jacob succeeds at his task, the furious Esau vows to murder his brother, so Jacob flees. More than twenty years later, Jacob is on his way back home with his four wives and his twelve children. To reach his parents he must go through his brother, who is on the march to meet him with four hundred men. Jacob is afraid, and he prays to G-d: "Deliver me, please, from the hand of my brother, from the hand of Esau, for I am afraid of him; he may come and kill us all, the mothers with the children." (Genesis 32:11)

I have always struggled with this story. Jacob is one of the boldest biblical heroes, so why is he afraid? Just after this prayer, he wrestles and triumphs over an angel, earning the name Israel—"he who wrestles with G-d"— but he's afraid of his thuggish brother? As I approach my fortieth birthday—Judaism says you get wise at forty—I understand the story. Jacob is scared because he's not sure he has behaved righteously in stealing the blessing from Esau. His fear is a direct result of the uncertainty he feels about his actions. He's wondering, "Did I do the right thing?" and his lack of moral certitude makes him fearful. Perhaps his brother, for all his flaws, is a better man than he. He worries that he will not be able to rise to whatever challenge Esau presents—because he thinks he may have taken what rightfully belonged to his brother.

Jacob's critics portray him as an unscrupulous schemer who tricked his brother into selling him his birthright in exchange for a bowl of soup. In my friend Rabbi Harold Kushner's eyes, Jacob was a man prepared "to get what he wanted by whatever means it took." I disagree. Jacob is the first hero in the Bible forced to struggle with his ideals in the practical world. Abraham, the father of monotheism, discovered the kernel of an idea, the seed of faith, which needed isolation to grow. And so he separated himself. He prayed for the people of Sodom and Gomorrah but would not live with them. Isaac, who could not mix with the corrupt elements because he was brought up on G-d's altar, led a similarly insular life. Both were separate from the rest of the world—righteous men, but men whose contributions to the world were personal before they could be made universal.

As the Bible tells it, Jacob was the first man who was challenged with having to translate an ideal into something real, a philosophical thought into a practical mode of living. Perched between heaven and earth, his was a life of struggle between the nefarious forces of the world and the divine tradition he was charged to uphold. Characterized by the Bible as "a wholesome man who sits in tents," he wanted to be an enlightened man of learning, inhabiting the world of theory, leaving the corrupt world to its own oblivion, but he was not that lucky.

Jacob was born with a violent and conniving twin brother, Esau, who planned to run off with the family silver. Later Jacob was tricked by his father-in-law into seven extra years of work, and he continued to live in fear of Esau's exterminating him and all his family. His daughter was raped, and his ten elder sons kidnapped their youngest sibling, Joseph, and led their father to believe that he was dead. Yet through all of this, Jacob did not once throw off the cloak of ethical obligation. He walked the razor-thin line between morality and necessity, facing life's challenges without relinquishing his obligation to decency. The ancient rabbis teach that Jacob was careful with his language when he pretended to be his brother, trying to use the least possible trickery to get the job done. He went as far as he had to, but no further. Jacob was not happy with what he had to do, but he understood that the world is inhabited by forces of good and evil and that evil must be defeated.

What would Jacob's critics have had him do? Cede the world to the brutish and violent Esau so as to remain above the fray? That would be moral cowardice and false piety. Heroism is not saving your skin and letting everyone else perish.

Abraham and Isaac were more of the heavens than of the earth, more angels than men. Jacob was a homegrown, earthly hero. Although he had to struggle his whole life, he and his children were entrusted with establishing the Jewish nation as a lasting entity, bringing G-d into the real world of commerce, politics, and everyday life. This nation is not known as the children of Abraham or Isaac but as the children of *Israel*, the name given to Jacob. Jacob understood that if you do not prevail in the struggles of life, it is often a loss not just for yourself but for all humanity. He never withdrew from the battle with darkness, but his involvement with the rough and tumble of life made him question his own righteousness and left him, like the rest of us mortals, susceptible to fear.

**If righteousness and justice guide our decisions,
then we need never be afraid.**

This is an intensely personal subject for me, and one that I learned very young, out of necessity. At the age of fourteen, I left my Jewish day school and traveled three thousand miles from home in order to attend yeshiva. I had not been raised in a religious home, but I had just met the Lubavitcher rebbe and decided that I wanted to be a rabbi. My parents were strongly opposed to my decision. Attending yeshiva meant living far away from my family at a very young age. What if they were right, and it was a mistake? But I was bolstered, even in times of real fear, by the knowledge that I was doing the right thing in strengthening my attachment to G-d and in seeking a more religious life. My choice could not have been wrong: it was the righteous one. Certain about my direction in life, I was not afraid.

I was afraid again when I asked Debbie to marry me. Was I marrying so young out of loneliness? After all, I was only twenty-one. Wasn't it possible that someone better, with whom I had more in common, might come along? Debbie and I were total opposites in every regard. What if my motivations were wrong? What if I was marrying so young out of a desire to rectify my parents' divorce? But I looked at my wife-to-be and knew that I would not find a woman with more goodness. Her character and morals were sterling, the dignity she accorded others exemplary, and I knew that I would always cherish and respect her. She was the kindest young woman I had met, and I knew that being with her would inspire me to be a better and more understanding person. To this day, sixteen years later, although I love many things about my wife, that is what I most admire about her. She runs an open home, filled with guests. She is always available to her husband and children. She is unstintingly courteous to all she meets, and she has made me a better man. Righteousness dictated my decision to marry her, and though my fear did not instantly vanish, I knew that it could be vanquished.

If moral righteousness is the guideline you use to make decisions, then you have nothing to fear. These decisions are always right.

In an age of wishy-washiness and uncertainty, acting on principle is extraordinarily refreshing. The formula is simple: if you do no wrong, you have nothing to fear.

24

Principle #14:
Have Contempt for Evil

For thus saith the LORD; We have heard a voice of trembling, of fear, and not of peace.

—JEREMIAH 30:5

We will not be driven by fear into an age of unreason if we remember that we are not descended from fearful men, not from men who feared to write, to speak, to associate and to defend causes which were, for the moment, unpopular.

—EDWARD R. MURROW

Righteousness gives us the strength to be courageous, even in the face of danger or painful opposition. The righteous are not only fearless in the face of evil, they are contemptuous of it. While we see evil as something that can harm us, they see it for what it is: an aberration in creation, a void of goodness, a dark space that must be filled with light.

**Evil motivates the righteous to combat
rather than paralyzes them.**

A fearful woman sees drug activity on her block and triple-locks her door, refusing to let her children out after dark. A righteous woman organizes against the dealers, mobilizing her church group to patrol the neighborhood and forcing the attention of the police. It's the difference between going to jail for civil disobedience or a political cause and going to jail for committing a crime. In the first scenario, you are bolstered by your alliance with justice. In the other, you are spiritually incarcerated by the knowledge that you have betrayed yourself and acted ignobly. Going to jail for a free Tibet or your right to practice your religion is not easy. Though the experience may be painful, fear and shame do not play a part. On the contrary, you wear your imprisonment like a badge of honor. You're elevated by your alliance with something greater than yourself, something moral.

The courage to stick to your guns is a big part of righteousness. As Abraham Lincoln said,

---

**"Be sure you put your feet in the right place,
then stand firm."**

I am always disappointed when I see people I respect show indecision or cowardice in the face of opposition, especially when they are representing a cause that requires strength.

In the summer of 2003, the Palestine Solidarity Movement, a student group that openly condones terrorism and suicide bombings against Israel and openly calls for its destruction, announced that it was going to stage a conference at Rutgers, New Jersey's largest state university. John Bennett, a Republican leader, sent a letter to the Democratic governor, Jim McGreevey, calling the organization abominable and asking the governor to cancel the conference, saying he was "strongly opposed to taxpayer dollars being used to help spread their message of hate."

Governor McGreevey had the president of Rutgers issue a statement that said, "The governor and I agreed that the best way to counter deplorable arguments is more discussion, not less, and that the appropriate place for this kind of discourse is the university." Imagine for a moment that the Ku Klux Klan planned a conference at Ole Miss where they would openly call for black children to be burned in their churches. Every black leader in the country—and hopefully white as well—would be on a plane within hours to protest this atrocity in person. Imagine for a moment that an Islamic organization sought to stage a conference at which they would openly call for the murder of American soldiers in Iraq. Would any governor who allowed such a conference have survived in office? This is how the Jewish community reacted to Governor McGreevey's decision. The Rutgers

Hillel announced that it accepted the governor's decision because "legal precedent favors free speech in this context." To me, this is not free speech but incitement! Calling for children to be blown up on buses is not an exercise of First Amendment rights but a call to murder. Hillel later invited McGreevey to be one of its speakers at a pro-Israel rally. (To be fair to the governor, he later had the courage to call me and discuss the issue after I had been public critical of him, and my respect for him rose as a result of his fearlessness in politely confronting a critic.)

Many in minority populations consider this kind of conciliation as a way to get along, a way to survive without drawing negative attention on ourselves. We're afraid to make waves. Jews, especially, are often fearful: a long history of persecution and violence has conditioned us not to make too much noise or demand too much. We often make the mistake of feeling like guests in other people's countries.

Lying down and refusing to fight gets us nothing either—except more persecution. Look at how the black community has changed. After three hundred and fifty years of slavery and persecution, under the leadership of Martin Luther King Jr. African-Americans declared they would never again be afraid. They agitated for their rights and demanded equality and respect. Fifty years ago, politicians ran on segregationist platforms and won. But today Trent Lott, who praised the formerly segregationist senator Strom Thurmond at his birthday party, paid for it with his leadership position. The black community is right: their cause fighting racial prejudice is just, and there is nothing to lose when you are allied with righteousness.

No Deals with the Devil

I am reminded of the fight between Churchill and Roosevelt during the Second World War. From 1943 on, Roosevelt was demanding unconditional surrender from Germany. Churchill thought that this stance would only make the Germans fight harder and longer, but Roosevelt knew that the struggle was a moral war, not just a military one. Hitler and the Nazis were the darkness. They were evil, and the Allies were good. Any conciliation would represent an unacceptable deal with the devil.

**If you are going to conquer fear where it lives,
you can't broker a deal with darkness;
you can't negotiate a treaty with the devil.**

You have to vanquish it completely. When you sit down at a table with it, you elevate it to your level instead of showing complete contempt for it. Only when Israel started making concessions to its Arab neighbors was its security compromised along with its international standing. The only thing that Israel has gained from its many land-for-peace deals is more terrorism and more international condemnation. The lesson: when you're in the right, you can't make concessions, or people will no longer believe that you are in the right. On the contrary, let your righteous position free you from fear, stand fast, and hold your position.

Standing your ground in the face of opposition changes your enemy's perception of you as well. When you are afraid, you have "victim" written all over you. When you are prepared to stand up and fight for your convictions, people can sense your invisible shield, and they will often back off.

Living in fear is like taking a dip in shark-infested waters while you're bleeding from a massive cut: it's practically an invitation to attack. When I was at Oxford, many of the Orthodox students would remove their yarmulkes on campus. Again and again I'd hear that they were afraid of drawing anti-Semitic attention to themselves, an unfortunate but perhaps understandable posture of European Jews after centuries of persecution. I believe fear draws anti-Semitic attention, not the yarmulke. Fear transmutes this head covering from a symbol of piety and community to one of shame, and it becomes a self-fulfilling prophecy.

By contrast, Avraham Netzach was a Hasidic Jew who spent twenty years in Stalin's gulags for opening Jewish schools after they had been banned. In the maze of Soviet prisons where he spent much of his life and had his health ruined, he earned the moniker of *Subbota*, or "Sabbath," from the Russian authorities, because of his refusal to work on the Sabbath. As a result of his refusal he was severely beaten, stripped naked and tied to a wooden pole and left outside in the subzero temperatures every Sabbath, but the jailers could not break him. In his book of the same name, *Subbota*, he tells how the Soviet authorities finally decided to rid themselves of him by putting him into a den filled with men convicted of violent crimes, including murder. They thought for sure that the meek scholar wouldn't last for more than few days in this brutish lair. When Netzach was thrown into the enclosure by his Russian guards, he quickly identified the leader of the group as the man sitting closest to the fire, surrounded by his lieutenants. Walking fearlessly over to him, he grabbed him by the collar and threw him out of his place. When the thug's men walked over to retaliate, he looked them squarely in the eye and said, "The first person to get close will be the one whom I punish most." Now, of course, this saintly Hasidic Jew had never hurt a fly, but he understood that the appearance of fearlessness was necessary if he was to win their respect.

Bullies always seem to be fearless, that is until you confront them, after which they inevitably back down. Underneath it all, they're cowards. They're so insecure, so hollow, that they can only feel good about themselves by seeing other people squirm. Hitler never once visited a city in Germany that had been bombed. The coward couldn't face it. His people were being shelled, fighting for their lives, and he lived in a bunker like a rat. Finally, he took the ultimate path of the coward and killed himself.

Saddam Hussein murdered more than a million people and talked a tough game. He was ultimately found hiding out in rat hole with packaged underwear. Surrounded by six hundred American soldiers, he didn't go down fighting: he offered to "negotiate." You have to stand up for yourself against the bullies. Better to risk a beating than to live in resignation and fear.

25

Principle #15:
Recognize Holiness

Therefore fear thou not, O my servant Jacob, saith the LORD; neither be dismayed, O Israel: for, lo, I will save thee from afar, and thy seed from the land of their captivity; and Jacob shall return, and shall be in rest, and be quiet, and none shall make him afraid.

—JEREMIAH 30:10

It is not death that a man should fear, but he should fear never beginning to live.

—MARCUS AURELIUS

I've heard young people say that it's easy to feel that you have a sense of purpose when you're fighting the great evils of your time, but they feel there's no such worthy cause today. I would argue that there is much to be said for finding the higher purpose—the holiness, if you will—in our everyday lives as well.

A couple came to me, asking for help with their troubled marriage. They spent a lot of time fighting about money. They were upper-middle-class, but the husband was very cheap and refused to spend money on his wife or their baby daughter. She, in turn, had an ugly temper and degraded him constantly in their interactions, so he spent a lot of time trying to get away from her. Their sex life was dead, and he said that he didn't even like touching his wife casually. The situation came to a head when their daughter began wetting the bed again at age seven, and the problem was attributed to the stress in the house.

As I listened to the list of woes afflicting their relationship, I had a thought. "We have two choices here," I said. "We can address the items on this list separately: your cheapness, your abusive tongue, your lack of a sex life. Or we can address all these things—and, I'd wager, some problems you haven't even told me about—in one fell swoop." My diagnosis? All the holiness had gone from their marriage. If these two people could find a way to reinstate holiness in their union, then all their problems would be fixed. I turned to the specifics: "Your bedroom is a holy place. It's the place where a man and a wife make love, the place where their affection for each other materializes in a physical form. It's the place where children are conceived, where the miracle of life begins. What's a television doing in your bedroom? Your bedroom should be a shrine, dedicated to love and intimacy. Would you watch ESPN in a church? Is it fair that your wife has to compete, in her own bedroom, against *Real Sex* on HBO? Get the television out of your bedroom and put the holiness back into it."

We went through the other items in this manner. "Synagogues need money to buy Torah scrolls and to pay for the upkeep of the building. If you see your wife and child as holy then how can you then rob them of their dignity by skimping on necessities? And you would never, ever call a priest a f——ng a——hole, would you? Of course you wouldn't; the very idea is shocking. And yet you call your husband that all the time. Before you scream profanity at him, you might want to remind yourself that he, like you, is one of G-d's children."

Imagine what might happen if we brought this idea of sanctity to the world at large. Imagine what great things could be wrought if only we'd choose the positive over the negative! I think we've got a holiness dearth in our culture, and it's exacerbating our fears. I said earlier that one of the hallmarks of fear is a feeling of abandonment, a feeling of having to confront a threat entirely on your own.

Because we have lost our holiness, we do not find G-d anymore in our daily interactions, and we feel fearful and abandoned.

That's one of Osama bin Laden's biggest arguments against the West. The fact that he can scare us so easily proves that we are utterly unconnected to G-d.

Holiness means finding G-d wherever you look.

You look at your wife, and instead of seeing lumpy thighs and drooping breasts, you see the glory of the divine countenance, and you are drawn to her. You see a mountain, and instead of feeling small and lowly, you are filled with awe. You see a homeless man on the street, and instead of seeing a parasite who smells, you cross the street to help a child of G-d in need. If we could find G-d in every interaction, wouldn't that negate our fears?

Holiness isn't only associated with religion. Think of the Lincoln Memorial in Washington, DC. People automatically drop their voices to a whisper when they enter, as if they're in a church. They step carefully, taking the time to admire the statuary and to read the great man's speeches engraved into the walls. It's a place that feels holy, a fitting place for Abraham Lincoln's memory to be enshrined for eternity. I have often stood with goose bumps in that shrine that honors the memory of our greatest president and felt shivers running down my spine as I have read the words: "In this Temple, as in the hearts of the people for whom he saved the Union, the memory of Abraham Lincoln is enshrined forever." The new hall in the National Archives where the Declaration of Independence, Constitution, and Bill of Rights are held evokes the same awe. People walk in silently and are visibly moved as they depart—as indeed they should be. These documents are the foundation of our country's ability to uphold the dignity and sanctity of hundreds of millions of people. There's no litter at the Vietnam Memorial; people instinctively know better. You don't throw trash at a shrine. Why are these structures any more holy than our bedrooms, which should be temples of love and family togetherness? Why do we treat celebrities as if they're godlike, and our spouses as if they're beneath our contempt?

Allying ourselves with a higher cause helps us to combat our fears, because it affords a sense of destiny and purpose. The higher cause may be closer than you think.

**Strengthening our ties to the eternal
reinvests the everyday with holiness.**

If we're more attuned to the holiness in other people, we will treat others with dignity and respect. We will be more likely to defy dictators who systematically murder or starve their countrymen.

One of the major arguments against secularism is the tendency it has to excuse evil. From time immemorial, philosophers have debated what the primary determinant of religious faith is. How do we know when someone's religious conviction is sincere? Some say faith is evidenced by a love of G-d's creatures, but I have met legions of confirmed atheists who are sincere humanitarians and lovers of the human family. Others argue that the proof of faith is martyrdom and a readiness to lay down one's life for G-d. Yet suicide bombers—who are as distant from G-d as Hugh Hefner is from fidelity—die for their "G-d" every day of the week. Others argue that faith is judged principally by ritual observance, but we all know religious people who are devout church- or synagogue-goers who are not always ethical in business.

Which brings us to this conclusion:

The most accurate standard for judging people's attachment to G-d is the extent to which they hate evil and fight against those who oppress the innocent.

Secular humanists can be good people, but they usually find some way of excusing the actions of a Chairman Mao or a Marshal Stalin. A man as enlightened as George Bernard Shaw called Hitler a great man.

The truly religious hate murderers because people who kill are the archenemies of the G-d who created life. They despise the heartless because the cold-blooded are the opponents of the G-d who created love.

A person who is sincerely attached to G-d will manifest his or her faith in loathing cruelty and abhorring mercilessness. Those who are detached from G-d are usually fearful in the face of evil.

If you don't hate Kim Jong Il, who is starving his people; if you don't loathe the Klan for killing innocent black children; if you are not filled with odium at the *muttawa'a*, the Saudi religious police who in March 2002 allowed fifteen high school girls to burn to death rather than be allowed to escape without their head coverings, you may still be decent, but you have a very weak relationship with G-d.

The book of Proverbs declares, "The fear of the Lord is to hate evil," and King David declared regarding the pitiless, "I have hated them with a deep loathing; they are as enemies to me."

**Reclaiming a sense of holiness in our lives rescues
us from fear not only because it makes us conscious
of how G-d accompanies us through all our travails, but
also because it teaches us to have contempt for evil.**

If you see your marriage as holy, you won't jeopardize it through flirtations with people who are not your spouse. If there were more holiness in our culture, perhaps we wouldn't need to portray women as pathetic and money-grubbing in TV shows like *Joe Millionaire* and *For Love or Money*. If you saw more holiness in your children and encouraged them to see it in themselves, maybe one out of every four high schoolers wouldn't have an STD. If you do these things, you reinforce everything in your life that supports you in your fight against fear. By reinvesting in holiness, you close the chinks in your armor.

Mend Your Broken Windowpanes

Rudolph Giuliani became famous for implementing the "broken window" theory of small crime in New York City. The theory goes like this: if you let a broken window sit unrepaired, people will assume that the building is uncared for, and they'll break more, eventually moving into the building to set up a drug operation. If you let small crimes go unpunished, the crimes will continue, getting more serious as they go. Holiness has leaked out of our lives, and we, like abandoned buildings, are broadcasting our lack of self-esteem far and wide.

**If you feel that your life is ordinary—that there's
no divine spark animating it, nothing making it
special and unique—then it becomes something
that doesn't deserve your reverence.**

It's here that fear seeps in: who will revere your life if you don't?

If you're in touch with the holy, the sense that you're an integral part of something bigger and that G-d is omnipresent, you can't have low self-esteem. Holiness means that you know G-d is where you are. Without that feeling, you're like a branch cut off from a tree: it's inevitable that you'll eventually wither and die. You can't have holiness unless you live a holy life, one dedicated to higher principles than junk food and junk culture.

**We have to bring a sense of awe back into
our everyday lives, and we have to live lives
that are worthy of that sense of wonder.**

From that sense of holiness will come confidence. I once went to see a lecture by a young man whose original research had catapulted him to the top of his field. He was clearly nervous throughout the glowing introduction he was given, and the first words out of his mouth were, "I'm not really sure why this would be interesting to anyone, but here goes." He stumbled through his lecture, which he delivered with the same lack of self-confidence. I felt very bad for him. After his lackluster start, the energy of the room turned against him. He wasn't sure what he was doing there, so we weren't either.

We are a society consumed and tortured by our insecurities, which are nothing but fears writ large. We have to get out from under them somehow, and the power of behaving as if you are not afraid simply cannot be underestimated. Don't worry if you don't actually feel that way, because habit, as Aristotle said, eventually becomes second nature. Job interviewers say that the number one thing they look for in a candidate is confidence. When you walk into a job interview with your head held high, sit down as if you belong there, and treat your conversation with your future boss as if he's your peer, you send a very powerful and positive message that you have a right to be there. "I already fit in," you're saying. "I belong here. We need each other."

Acting as if this is true makes it so. We underestimate how powerful we are in the creation of our own reality. Scientists have demonstrated that the mere act of smiling—even if it's insincere—releases endorphins and stimulates other physiological changes that make you feel happy and suppress the fear response. Of course, this creates a feedback loop. You smile, you feel happier doing it, other people treat you better, and ultimately you *are* happy.

**You create a positive inner reality
through positive external action.**

The same thing is true about confidence. There is tremendous power in behaving as if you are confident. Of course, it's essential to differentiate between confidence and arrogance.

Confidence, a belief in your essential capacity to contribute, is a liberation from the shackles of the ego, whereas arrogance is a sign that you're enslaved to it.

Abraham Lincoln had confidence. Reviled by millions in the North as well as the South, he nevertheless clung to his ideals. After a succession of defeats in the political arena and on the battlefield, and after four horrible, cruel years in the White House, he found the temerity to hang on, sustained as he was by the knowledge that preserving the Union was just and ending slavery was righteous. Consider instead General George B. McClellan, a highly decorated officer and the commander of the Union Army of the Potomac. Afraid of losing his reputation for gallantry, he became immobilized by fear. He was so terrified of losing face that he lost the nerve to attack and spent most of his time complaining to Lincoln that he didn't have enough troops, even though his usually outnumbered those of Robert E. Lee by three to one.

True confidence comes from self-knowledge, the secure feeling of knowing that you're on this earth for a purpose, and in this room because it advances that purpose in some way. "I'm here to do something important; it's written in the stars." If that lecturer had felt strongly that he had a message to deliver, wouldn't his presentation of himself have been different? Instead of approaching us as a supplicant, he would have taken the attitude, "I have something important to share with you. Thank you for giving me the opportunity; I know you'll benefit from what I have to say." You have to know that you're bringing something of value. Fear subsides in someone who is confident that he has a gift that must be shared.

This is true whether you're on a job interview, on a date, giving a speech—and it should be true when you're walking down the street. You're not developing this kind of self-confidence for other people.

One of the most psychologically insightful passages in the Bible is in the book of Numbers. Moses sends twelve spies into the Promised Land, after the Jews have emerged from the slavery of Egypt, to see how it can best be conquered. The spies returned forty days later with bad news. The land was very bountiful, but there was no way it could be taken. There were giants there who would stop any effort the Jews made at conquest. Then the spies summed up their encounter with the giants who inhabited the Holy Land: "We

were in our own sight as grasshoppers, and so we must have looked to them."
Even in *their own* estimation they were cockroaches—and so others perceived
them in that way too. That lowly self-appraisal made it impossible for that
generation, who had still not outgrown the slave mentality they had absorbed
in Egypt, to conquer the land.

After this the people of Israel wandered forty more years in the Sinai
desert. The Sinai desert isn't that big. In forty years you could walk from one
end to the other tens of times. The Jews were kept there in exile to have one
generation pass and another raised in freedom, purged of insecurities and a
slave mentality, so that an independence-minded nation could go forth and
claim what G-d had promised their forebears.

Be Careful Not to Put Your Fears First

We also have to claim what is rightfully ours. A woman asked me to speak to
one of her friends who has been having a hard time finding someone to
marry. I'm not going to tell you that this woman would be judged by shallow
men as the most beautiful woman in the world, but she is extremely intelligent and well read, with a wide circle of friends who depend on her because
she's fiercely loyal and generous.

After a long conversation I asked her why she thought she was having such
a hard time dating. "Because I'm plain," she said matter-of-factly. To hear her
say this broke my heart. New York can be a superficial place, and many of the
men she'd met probably were looking for arm candy, but there are plenty of
less-than-beautiful women in relationships—and beauty is subjective anyway.
I was willing to bet that a lot of her difficulty had to do with the way she was
presenting herself on dates: fears first. I was sure that she was sitting down as
if she were second-best, the ugly stepsister with nothing to offer. The men
she was meeting were reacting to that. If she was plain in her own eyes, how
was anyone ever going to see her as beautiful? If she didn't want to be married
to herself, who was ever going to want to be married to her?

By giving weight to her fears that she wasn't good enough, she was allowing those fears to materialize in all their darkness. The solution was for her to
feel, as she did in her career, that she had something to offer. Self-confidence
is always sexier than a perfect figure. Marilyn Monroe was a size 14. But she
carried herself like a sex goddess and that is what made her into one. You
can't love a pretty face alone—or not for very long. You can love someone's
generosity, her sense of humor, her passion for social justice, and her devotion to you forever.

"Easier said than done," you may be thinking. Don't forget that we're in the business of creating our own reality. I suggested that this woman withdraw from dating temporarily and use the time to ask herself, "What do I have to contribute that will immeasurably enrich the life of another person?"

Once you know what contribution you have to make to the world at large, it shines through; because you know you have something to offer, you feel you have a place at the table.

You're confident because you know your contribution is essential. People want to feel at home with someone, and you can't make someone else feel comfortable unless you're comfortable in your own skin.

I suggested to her that she read a biography of Eleanor Roosevelt, whose story has always been an inspiration to me. This first lady was a homely, awkward child, crippled by shyness. Her mother, who was always described as beautiful, referred to Eleanor as "Granny"—reinforcing Eleanor's belief that she was unattractive and lacking in the necessary social graces. After her mother died while she was just a girl, Eleanor was raised by her father, Elliot, a rake and an alcoholic, who tragically died two years later. Eleanor overcame terrific confidence issues to become a great warrior on behalf of the less fortunate. She persevered, even when her political opinions were unpopular, even when her own philandering husband did not support her, and she was often pilloried in the press. She could have retreated into the role of a typical matron, but she refused to retire into conformity. She had to weather the cruelest of jokes and cartoons and indignities. She acted positively and with righteousness despite her considerable fears and ultimately conquered them by embodying divine principles on earth. She was named the most admired woman in America for thirteen years.

The heart of self-confidence is self-knowledge.

Each of us is special. Every single one of us is worthy of love. You are worthy of love because you carry a spark of the Divine, and no one can take that away from you except yourself by acting cruelly toward others. If you believe in destiny, which is to say that you know you were put on earth to do something to make this world a better place, then you have to be self-confident. If you're sure that you're always going to have to jockey for position, then you can never find a place of peace.

A woman got in touch with me, sure that she had married the wrong man. A federal prosecutor who had made a name for herself putting serious criminals behind bars, she told me that at thirty-five she found the pressure from her parents to marry so great that she chose someone she had been seeing casually and allowed herself to be bullied into marriage. "Even as I put on my wedding dress," she told me, "I had tears streaming down my cheeks. I knew it was a mistake." Since I believe in G-d's providence and matchmaking skills, I am not inclined to listen to those who would say that marriage is a merely capricious act and that we choose our spouses based on accidents.

When I met her husband with her a few days later, it was clear that he was a man besieged with insecurities. Every time he expressed an opinion, he turned to his wife to ask her if she agreed. He told me, "Look, Shmuley, you know a lot better than me what my wife is looking for. Will you tell me if I'm the one to provide it?" I was in shock. "I know a lot better than you? Are you mad? I've known your wife for all of four hours; you've known her for four years. How little do you think of yourself that you can even say such a ridiculous thing?" I told him, in his wife's presence, "The only way I can help you is if you can identify some essential quality, uniquely yours, that defines you, that makes you special. Once you find it, you'll give it to your wife freely and confidently. And she'll begin to appreciate you."

He came back with surprising assurance. "I'm not as exciting as my wife," he confessed, "and I may not be as bright, but I have a gentleness to me. My strength is that I genuinely care about people, and that's why I am liked in my veterinary practice. My wife needs that. She's tough and never unwinds. I could take care of her if only she would let me." His wife and I were both surprised by his confidence. Their marriage continues to be an uphill struggle, but it was in that moment that I began to see that their marriage could be saved, and it seems to be getting better every day.

It's Not About You

There's an even more compelling reason for confidence in your own abilities. Let's assume that your self-denigration is not about you. Rather it is about He who created you.

**Bowing your head in fear and allowing your insecurities
to dominate you is an act of disrespect.**

It disrespects the G-d who created you, the parents who raised you, the teachers who worked for lowly salaries to educate you, the woman or man who thought enough of you to marry you, the children who look up to you—and in the case of that lecturer, the people who came to hear you speak. Fear is fundamentally selfish, and caving to our insecurities is no exception.

Fearlessness or confidence is a gift you can give away. When you tell your assistant that she's done a terrific job, if she respects your opinion at all, she'll walk away from the interaction with her head a little higher. She's not just someone, she's someone who does a good job. In a sense, you've created her. G-d created the world with speech, utterances like "Let there be light." You create people with compliments like "My, you look radiant today." You make them feel alive and noticed. This is why it is so important to live a decent life, conferring dignity on each and every one of the lives with which you come into contact.

Confidence gives us the strength to have contempt for our detractors, to fight back when our allegiance to righteousness is challenged. I think we see this contempt often in those who have prevailed against evil. While I was at Oxford, I was honored to know Michael Aris, a distinguished professor of Buddhism and Tibetan culture. His wife is the Nobel Peace Laureate and nonviolent human rights activist Daw Aung San Suu Kyi. She had been under house arrest in Myanmar, and he had not seen her for six years by the time I came to know him. Their entire relationship took place over the phone. I asked him, "How can your wife be so fearless? Where does she find the strength to carry on?" "She thinks her tormentors are pygmies, unworthy of anything but her contempt," he answered.

I think this is one of the significant factors in the television host Bill O'Reilly's success. Whatever you might think of his politics or debating techniques, what impresses his viewers is that he holds no sacred cows sacred. There was a negative piece about the Fox News Network in the *New Yorker* magazine, one of the most hallowed icons of American journalism. When I saw O'Reilly a few days later, the *New Yorker* article came up in conversation. He said to me, "I don't care about them, don't care what their reputation is. I'm not impressed with any of that." That's what makes him O'Reilly, and that's why millions of people watch him. They like the fact that he challenges everyone, is intimidated by no one, and continues unafraid.

We are impressed by the fearless. O'Reilly makes it clear that he isn't moved by the big names and their traditions, and his message has resonated very strongly with many Americans as a result.

In order for you to build the foundations for fearlessness, you must recognize your insecurities for the fears they are.

When you're confident about your ability to contribute, there's no room for self-hatred and recrimination.

You must gain ground on these fears by looking at yourself and the things in your life as holy, deserving of reverence and respect.

26

Principle #16:
Connect Your Life with Others

As an adamant harder than flint have I made thy forehead: fear them not, neither be dismayed at their looks, though they be a rebellious house.
—EZEKIEL 3:9

Only connect! . . . Live in fragments no longer.
—E. M. FORSTER

You are your own first line of defense against fear. When I say that, I do not at all mean to suggest that you must undertake this struggle alone. In fact, strengthening your connections with other people and the outside world and feeling that you're important in relation to others is directly linked to overcoming a feeling of powerlessness. Whenever you feel that others care about you, you are granted a sense of destiny. Your life is intertwined with the fate of others, and you are no longer at the mercy of the elements.

The fear crusade in our culture is happening at a time when disconnectedness has become the norm. Stockbrokers get their bonuses at the end of the year these days; without that carrot, employers know they're likely to lose them to poachers from competitive firms earlier in the year. Athletes used to be closely associated with a team; can you imagine Joe DiMaggio playing for anyone but the Yankees? Now they bounce back and forth among the highest bidders and have no compunctions about disparaging their own teammates in the press.

My father used to tell me and my siblings a story because he wanted us to be close. A king asked each of his nine sons to bring a stick to his deathbed. He then asked them to break their sticks, which they did easily. He sent them out again for nine more sticks, and this time he put the sticks together into a bundle and asked his sons to break it. Of course, they couldn't. "Separate," he told them, "you are easily defeated. Together, you are invincible."

Certain external attachments are worthy of our cultivation and strengthen us against fear. I know a woman who is a physician with Doctors Without Borders. She's routinely in situations that would make ordinary people quail—situations where she's at risk from both serious illness and life-threatening violence. When asked what fortifies her when from her tent she can hear gunshots at night, she says she's fearless because she knows her husband, although far away, loves her. Now how can the love of a man four thousand miles away possibly protect her from the bullets of a rebel army? It can't, but it can make her feel fearless. She knows that she is the center of another human being's universe, a man who would move heaven and earth to support and protect her. She has internalized his love and loyalty, and it bolsters her. Even when she is alone, she is never alone.

Her situation is utterly different from that of the stockbroker I counseled, who needed to sleep with a different woman every night to feel good about himself. The doctor has internalized the strength and vindication that come from being loved and supported by a man who has made sacrifices on her behalf, who has chosen her to the exclusion of all others, and she has achieved a sense of strength born of interdependence as a result. My stockbroker friend has done no such thing. The well from which he's drinking doesn't give him any long-lasting satisfaction, so he must revisit it over and over again. He's dependent on it. He has no real relationships, just cynical acquaintances who use each other. He's a wanderer with no home, a nomad with no rest. How could he ever be at peace? The doctor, like a camel storing water, keeps the sustenance of her husband's love with her always, so she can draw upon her reserves when she encounters a challenge. The stockbroker, like a thirsty horse, most go searching from oasis to oasis.

**No one can fully immunize himself against fear
without help.**

We're not built that way. Solitude and loneliness build fear, they don't destroy it. Whatever advances I have made in my own personal campaign against fearfulness are largely the result of the help I have gotten from other quarters.

For example, I need my wife. I need her good opinion of me, her advice, her comfort, her counsel. I am not afraid to let her know that I need her. Many times I have told her how strongly it goes against the grain of men to become totally naked—stripped of every emotional defense—with a woman. But I have no compunction in doing so. I am nothing without her. I need her respect. If she gave her heart to another man, it would be hard for me to recover. I derive confidence from the fact that someone so special would choose me as her husband. She is a major armament in my own personal arsenal against fear. I don't feel alone, because she is devoted to me. I have noticed that when crises affect me in my life, I need her to be at my side, even physically in the room, so that I can meet the challenges ahead. In order to make her contribution to my life effective against fear, I can't be afraid of sharing anything with her. I have to overcome inhibition and tell her everything.

When you hold nothing back and can share the darkest corners of your soul, you learn not to be afraid, because the light has now gotten in. That's the importance of a truly intimate relationship.

Even my wife cannot immunize me fully. I need a hug from each one of my kids. I work hard to remain permanently attached to my parents and brothers and sisters. My siblings and I witnessed our parents' bad marriage, and it drew us closer. Today we are inseparable, and they are my best friends. Indeed, there are many things that my siblings can understand that my wife cannot fully. Real friendships that aren't about using each other are another must.

But more than anything, I need G-d. A secure attachment to G-d is the irreplaceable step in combating fear. This is your link to the eternal, to the source of blessing and life. As long as that attachment is secure, we can never be afraid, because we know that there will always be life.

G-d's love requires a leap of faith; it's celestial rather than tangible. This means that He can't physically hold on to us in times of trouble. G-d's love is experiential rather than sensual. Since we cannot apprehend G-d's love with any of our senses, it is therefore made manifest to us through the earthly love of spouse, family, and children. This is what is meant by "holy" matrimony. Our spouse, children, parents, and siblings give us unconditional love, and through them we experience G-d's love. It's not love we earn, or necessarily deserve, but love given freely as a gift.

As essential as unconditional love may be, it is also a dismissal of our uniqueness. It's not specific to us; we get it whether we're nice or not. So we need yet another kind of love to bolster us, our attachment to community. Our friends, our religious communities, our neighbors appreciate us even though we're strangers to one another, with only accidental ties like geography, or because of what we do. A community doesn't love us unthinkingly but appreciates us because of our contributions to it. Our neighbors love our kindness and hospitality, our willingness to carpool or to make cupcakes on short notice for the bake sale. When you participate in a community in a meaningful way, you feel valued and esteemed. That kind of conditional love, tenuous as it may seem, allows us to feel possessed of virtue.

We must seek out ways to increase our connectedness to others. In the Jewish religion, there is the concept of the mitzvah. Mitzvahs are rituals you do, good and holy deeds, that connect you to G-d and to other people. They aren't all extraordinary acts. Marrying, having children, and entertaining in your home are mitzvahs, as are charity, prayer, faith, good works, conducting oneself with humility, and stopping one day a week on the Sabbath to rejuvenate yourself physically and spiritually. Giving coins to a poor person who asks you on the street is a mitzvah. These are all strands in the rope that connect us to other people and, through them, to G-d—a spiritual umbilical cord.

This is how our crusade against fear becomes something more. I encourage you to increase your connectedness to the people in your life and to your spiritual source because it is wholesome and holy. As we shall see, these efforts at connectedness are also a very powerful immunization against fear.

**When we strengthen that rope to the divine,
we strengthen ourselves. We feel safe
because we're anchored and secure.**

The more candles you light, the more darkness is dispelled, and every candle we light allows us to see a little bit more bringing us further out of the darkness into the glorious, golden light of a future without fear.

27

Principle #17:
Do Good

Ye have feared the sword; and I will bring a sword upon you, saith the LORD G-d.

—EZEKIEL 11:8

It is every man's obligation to put back into the world at least the equivalent of what he takes out of it.

—ALBERT EINSTEIN

One of the easiest ways to connect your life with others in a way guaranteed to dispel fear is to do good works. Jews are commanded to give charity every day. Sometimes it's a substantial contribution to an organization we may believe in, while other times it means giving something smaller, like a dollar put into a charity box or half an hour spent on the phone with a friend who's having a hard time with her relationship.

These aren't such big things, but they enable us to form connections and illuminate the lives of others. The more we feel we're connecting, the closer we are to fulfilling our own sense of destiny, the plan that says that we were put on this earth to do good and make it more Edenlike.

It doesn't take a lot. I spend a good deal of time in Manhattan, and it's always astonishing to see how easily people walk by those in need. Midtown is filled with people—homeless, hungry, and desperate—asking for help, and yet the well-heeled walk right by, on their way to buy an expensive gourmet sandwich and bottled water. Does giving to the homeless "encourage" them, as some have argued? Perhaps, but that's hardly the point. If somebody asks, you give. Period. The obligation to be charitable has little to do with the recipient and everything to do with the benefactor. We are obligated to be good people and to give charity. And if you're worried that the recipient might use it for something like alcohol, then go in with him to a shop and buy him food. If a woman tells you she needs the money to buy diapers for her baby, go into a shop with her and buy the diapers. How can good people think nothing of sailing by someone clearly in bad shape? Why wouldn't you stop, to give something you can clearly spare, whether it's a dollar or the banana in your briefcase?

One of my friends has a theory that it's easy to ignore those people because we feel threatened by them. "There, but for the grace of G-d, go I." Are any but a very select few of us completely protected from that kind of ignominy? Is there really no combination of events that could end up with our losing everything, begging strangers for help? I think that we can turn that equation around. Instead of feeling fear when we recognize ourselves in someone desperate, we can use that recognition as a form of empowerment. When we ignore someone in need, we miss a tremendous opportunity—not only to do good, but to immunize ourselves against fear.

When we raise someone up, we benefit as well. Giving charity is more than simply throwing a lifetime out to other people. It helps the giver even more than the recipient. As the Talmud says, "A cow wishes far more to give its milk than the calf desires to suck." When the milk builds up and there is no outlet, the cow is in terrible pain. We too are ready to burst when we have much to contribute and nobody wants our gifts.

Giving charity, giving love, gives our lives purpose and helps us to participate in creating the kind of world we want to live in.

This is a crucial point, one that comes back to the idea of creating our own reality. If we give regularly to a charity, it contributes to our understanding of the world as a compassionate place, and that in turn allays many of our own anxieties. We begin seeing the world not through the lens of the paranoid, as a place out to get us, but through a human lens, as a place out to help us. Giving to charity is a way of confirming to yourself that people take care of each other. If I'm struck down by a terrible disease, G-d forbid, perhaps someone else will fund research to find a cure, the way I helped even when I had no need. If I go bankrupt, others, rather than showing me contempt for my failure, will help to raise me up, like a beloved brother. There's no need to be afraid. If I'm persecuted in my homeland, someone else will surely help me to relocate somewhere safe, the way I helped Russian Jews get to Israel.

This has been one of the secrets of how the Jews have learned to live without fear amidst being persecuted in virtually every land in which they have settled. They always looked out for each other. They always knew that they were not alone in their oppression. To this day a plethora of social service organizations, designed to help the neediest, is common in every Jewish community in every part of the world. And it was always thus.

If you meanly hold on to every dollar you earn, no wonder you're frightened. You're living in a selfish world of haves and have-nots, and you live in mortal dread that the wheel of fortune will turn and you'll be on the underside. Of course you're threatened by that homeless guy: he's you, minus a couple of paychecks, and no one is coming to his aid. He is despised and mocked for his poverty, treated not as a child of G-d caught in hard times but as a lazy parasite afraid to work.

When you give to charity, you participate in the creation of a world that is fundamentally benevolent.

Help becomes a possibility, so you're not so terrified about your own future.

In Judaism, of course, we are asked to tithe—to give at least 10 percent of our income to those in need. One of my friends insists that his children tithe as well. Even when they were very young, getting minimal allowances for candy and stickers, he asked them to put aside 10 percent of that money for a charity of their own choosing. He wanted to make giving to charity a habit in their lives, like studying or making the bed. By asking them to choose the charity, he made them feel a sense of ownership in the project. Participating in the decision-making process helped them to isolate the ills they felt passionately about healing and increased their connection to the good deed they were doing.

I ran into one of his sons at an event recently. He had just graduated from college and is living on his own. After we'd caught up, I asked him if he'd mind answering a personal question. "You're probably not making a whole lot of money right now. Are you still tithing every year?" He answered that he worked at an entry-level media position, but he still made a careful calculation of 10 percent of his income and supported his charities of choice. "I thought about stopping until I'm a little more financially comfortable, but I discovered that giving makes me less freaked out about money, not more."

I asked him if he was planning to continue the tradition with his own children, and he assured me that he was. "I sometimes resented doing it as a kid, but of course, I'm grateful for it now. It gives me a good feeling about who I am. It's also made me less materialistic, and I'll want my kids to have that good feeling too." That good feeling he describes is a fear-buster. As it contributes to his understanding of his place in the universe, it minimizes his frustrations and fears. By passing along this strategy, he inoculates his children as well.

Do Good

Sometimes just giving money is not enough to make us feel connected. A wealthy man I know told me that giving charity didn't move him the way it used to. He didn't get that fear-busting "good feeling" from it any longer. I politely refrained from reminding him that the point of giving to charity wasn't to make him *feel* good but to *do* good. Instead I invited him to roll up his sleeves and join the board of the organization to which he had contributed. They could benefit from his business acumen just as much as from his money, and he could benefit from a more hands-on relationship with doing good.

It may sound trite, but keeping yourself busy by doing lots of good things with your time literally leaves you with no time to worry or be afraid. We Americans have not mastered the art of leisure. We have far too much time on our hands, time that can leave our imaginations running wild into the irrational hands of fear.

The simplest thing we can say about fear is that it is an unaffordable luxury. If your life is consumed with good projects, fear becomes a luxury you cannot afford. If your environment is filled with good people, fear becomes a nuisance that is not worthy of your attention. Does a Special Ops soldier storming a cave in Afghanistan to hunt down Al Qaeda have time for fear? Can the boxer who is training day and night to defeat his opponent waste time or energy on the luxury of fear? Did Mother Teresa have the time to sit around and worry about contracting illnesses from those she comforted?

If we spend our time wisely, our busyness is more than just busy work. We counteract the feeling of nothingness by having a positive impact on other people's lives. If the greatest human fear is the fear that you don't matter, then by all means, start to matter. How? In the eloquent words of Ralph Waldo Emerson, one must make every attempt "to give of one's self, to leave the world a bit better, whether by a healthy child, a garden patch, or a redeemed social condition." By affecting the lives of others, we begin to be, and our fears recede accordingly.

One way that terrorism is fought, whether the terrorism is literal or figurative, is by increasing good deeds and making a positive impact on other people's lives, so that we feel that our lives really do matter and are not subject to the arbitrary whim of someone who might wish to snuff us out. A gust of wind can blow out a small candle, but it is powerless against a blazing flame. The more significant we feel on the inside, the more our insecurities subside on the outside.

We know that doing good will make us less afraid, because it's our first impulse. On the afternoon of September 11, people in New York City weren't huddled in their homes in terror and self-protection. They were on the street with jugs of water to refresh the dust-covered survivors streaming over the bridges into the outer boroughs. They were waiting in line to give blood in such numbers that the Red Cross had to turn them away. Instead of fleeing somewhere "safer," trained personnel came to New York from all over the world to help in the recovery efforts.

That was bravery in its truest form and the purest way to combat the fear that struck every New Yorker's heart on that beautiful September morning. Our first impulse, to do whatever we could to help, was the correct one, and it was instrumental in helping to banish our fear.

28

Principle #18:
Connect with Family

Then said he unto me, Fear not, Daniel: for from the first day that thou didst
set thine heart to understand, and to chasten thyself before thy G-d, thy
words were heard, and I am come for thy words.

—DANIEL 10:12

A mother is not a person to lean on but a person to make leaning
unnecessary.

—DOROTHY CANFIELD FISHER

If we're looking to anchor and secure ourselves by building connections,
then surely there's no better place to start than in our own homes.

Our relationship with our families secures us to the earth and affords us
the security of knowing that we have a permanent place in the universe.
Surely it's no accident that at this most fearful time in the West, the nuclear
family is a shambles. Although America is the richest country in history, it
also has the highest per capita rate of depression and anxiety. We are growing
more and more fragmented. Families live scattered all over the globe; grandparents are consigned to retirement homes or move away to the warmer cli-
mates of the South. Families are isolated even within themselves, as TV has
replaced family dinners and video games have supplanted conversation. The
more children feel isolated from their parents and unable to talk to them
about their anxieties and worries, the more they will turn to drugs, alcohol,
and early sexual relationships for the consolation they can't get at home.

It is any surprise that we frighten so fast?

This is not true in other, much poorer parts of the world. Even in places plagued by terrible political instability and poverty, normal people are going about their daily lives. It's not because they have less to lose—less money, perhaps, but their lives are worth the same to them as ours are to us. They just don't have all the fear-feeding accessories we do. They aren't as materialistic. They don't have alarmist media telling them their brains are going to turn to mush if they eat that mad-cow-diseased steak. Instead they are far more connected to tradition, tribe, and family than we are. Lacking technological innovations like telephones—unnecessary when everyone lives so close to each other—and televisions, they actually interact far more with each other, and by so doing counteract their own fears.

Reinstating the centrality of the family in America is crucial if we are going to free ourselves from the perpetual orange alert under which we currently exist.

The Power of Unconditional Love

Reconnecting with our families is especially important because familial love is unconditional. I had a conversation with an adoption activist a couple of years ago who told me that one of the biggest fears of an adopted child is that he'll be "sent back," returned to the agency like a defective electronic appliance. It's not a completely groundless fear; some adoptive parents, especially if the child has behavioral problems, do give up and ask for the adoption to be revoked. The very best adoptive parents, this activist told me, manage to convey to their children that their love for them is unconditional, that, as with a birth child, there's nothing they can do to get "sent back." Children raised with parents who communicate this effectively have much less need to test the waters, and they grow up with a much more secure sense of themselves.

The feeling that we can't get sent back is the real joy of the parent-child relationship. We love our children no matter what; we love them because they're our children. And we're loved that way too (at least until they hit adolescence). When a daughter looks at her father, she may see a flawed man, but as her father, he's perfect. The only person who's likely to share this opinion equally is that man's mother. When she looks at him, he sees his own reflection in her face, and it is a much kinder rendition of himself than the one he confronts daily in the mirror. At one level there is a temptation to dismiss a mother's soft-focus view of her son as blindness. But isn't it also possible that a mother sees a higher truth? That her son is a man who would like to do the right thing, even if he doesn't succeed every time?

It's hugely important for us to feel that we're loved and appreciated, no matter what we do or how much we make or who we know. It is important for us to bask in the rose-colored reflection of people who think we're terrific, even when evidence would seem to dictate otherwise. Surrounding yourself with loving relatives who care for you unconditionally pulls you away from the irrational fears for the future and into the promising warmth of the present.

Find Forgiveness

In order to fully participate in the richness of family life, we must first forgive our families. Even better, we should cease judging them.

We live in a constant state of blame and offense, and our families are the first line of fire. "My parents were cold and unloving, and that's why I have such difficulties sustaining a relationship." "My sister got all of my parents' attention and took advantage of their financial goodwill. There was never enough for me." The litany goes on and on.

I was speaking to a man who works with his father. His widowed dad had recently remarried, and the son hates the new wife. He considers her profligate in spending his father's money and is jealous of the primary place she has in his father's life. I said to him, "Look, we all need our parents' love. But if your dad wants to spend every last penny on his wife, that's his prerogative. Get over your jealousy. It's not your money, it's your dad's. And it's not your life, it's your dad's. You have to try to be happy for him, even if that now means that you occupy a secondary place in his life." This man would be far better served creating a life of his own by getting married and having children than begrudging his father for having found a new love after his wife's passing.

Today we look for almost anything to justify our alienation from key members of our family. We have to learn not to be so easily offended, and we have to learn to forgive. In fact, it is far better to apologize for something you haven't done than to compromise a relationship with a family member. I am astonished by the number of people I counsel who have severed ties with their parents, their siblings, their children over the most minor slights. I interceded between two women who were fighting about a piece of their grandmother's jewelry. This woman had come to America and built a life out of nothing—and two generations later, her memory was reduced to two whiners fighting over a shiny rock.

These relationships must be mended, and once you've done that, you can start to rely on those familial systems. You can turn to your parents in times of crisis for advice and a kind word. You can ask your siblings for their opinions on everything from finances to parking. Who better to talk to than someone who knows you as well, and loves you as much, as a close family member does?

We also have to stop fixating on the idea of our parents dying. I know that I've alluded to this before, but when I began writing this book, I was genuinely surprised to discover how dominant a fear this was in the people I talked to. I know many people whose relationships with their parents are all about death—even while the parents are alive. It's as if their parents are interred in their final resting places even while the family is sitting down to dinner. This attitude seriously interferes with the baby boomers' ability to have a natural relationship with their parents while the elders are still here.

I interviewed a woman who had written a book on surviving your husband's midlife crisis, and she said the single most pervasive trigger for one of these crises was the death of a parent. It's a reminder of our own mortality. The loss of someone to whom we may not have said everything we wanted to say sparks tremendous feelings of regret. It's perfectly natural that the death of a parent should lead to a reevaluation of your own life. When that evaluation leads you to the conclusion that your life is empty—and that a young mistress and a Porsche will address the deficit—it's tragic. You need to live life fully in the moment so that you don't have to be filled with toxic regret and resentment later. Rebuild broken relationships now so that you never have to fear not having done so while there was still time.

Much of what these men experience is the regret that they were not able to have a meaningful relationship with their parents while they were alive. Many people don't push their relationships with their parents, because it seems futile. "They'll never change," the thinking goes. And this may be true. But why should you be haunted by the ghosts of all the things you didn't say? The fear of the death of a parent is greatly heightened by the fear that it will occur before we have had our chance to speak our piece.

In the Jewish religion, a seven-day period of mourning follows the passing of a parent, during which the community comes by every night for prayer and comfort. A man who lives in our neighborhood lost his father.

Although I didn't know him well, I visited, and he asked me to sit with him. He looked like the saddest man in the world. "My G-d, my G-d," he said. "All I can think about are the things I never said to him that had to be said." I got a lump in my throat, and it made me think about my own relationships.

It's clear that we have to rescue our relationships with our families from the dutiful phone call. You must find the courage to address issues with your parents and to deepen those relationships. You have to put some energy, some life, some dynamism back into those relationships so that you can experience the benefits of loving and being loved in this way.

Pull Up a Chair

I believe that one way to pull family life back from the outskirts and into the center of our lives is to reinstate the family dinner. We have to get together, prepare a meal, sit down, and eat it together—if not once a day, then at least once a week. The African-American writer and activist Marion Wright Edelman talks about growing up in a religious household, where the entire family would gather for Sunday dinner after church. It was a time of food and laughter, sociability and responsibility, and she believes that it was an important fortification for a young black woman in a bigoted world. Everyone else may have been telling her that she wasn't valuable, but that wasn't what she was hearing from the people gathered around that table. She is now trying to reinstate the ritual with her own children and grandchildren. Weekly family lunches or dinners, where grandparents, cousins, and extended family get together, are an absolute must.

In the Jewish religion, Friday night Sabbath meals are the focal point of the family. In most Jewish families, even those that aren't particularly observant, Friday night meals are so sacrosanct that even grown kids know they dare never be absent.

Parents who allow their kids to drift away from them are just plain stupid. Is that why you raised your kid? To lose him to his friends? In general, I believe the whole emphasis on friends for teenagers is way overrated. Sure, you need the corroboration of your peers, but not at the expense of family. Yet I know families in which the parents would be lucky to see their teenage kids twice a week. And forget about ever having a meaningful conversation. The sense of disconnect is such that the only noise you hear in the house is the constant blare of the TV.

I think about all the new parents who are far away from their own parents. Hillary Clinton wasn't kidding when she said it took a village to raise a child; new parenthood can certainly be overwhelming, and devoted grandparents can be a terrific help. In fact, the period in the late afternoon when most very young babies get cranky is called "the grandmother's hour." Wouldn't we have fewer instances of postpartum depression if our mothers— and their mothers, if possible—were around us to walk the baby and tell funny stories of their own memories of new parenthood? Wouldn't that support allay some of the fears and isolation that commonly accompany this miraculous time?

Sometimes we can't battle fear alone and have to turn to other people to give us hope. This is why it is so important to surround ourselves with people who love us unconditionally, people whom we trust. Asking for help and support at a difficult time is a way of fighting back against fear. It's not weakness but the very opposite. Only the strong are robust enough to reach out to others in crisis, without the fear of becoming dependent or compromised.

29

Principle #19:
Develop a Primary Relationship

In that day it shall be said to Jerusalem, Fear thou not: and to Zion, Let not
thine hands be slack.

—ZEPHANIAH 3:16

Love is, above all, the gift of oneself.

—JEAN ANOUILH

Tolstoy famously began Anna Karenina with the line, "Happy families are all alike; every unhappy family is unhappy in its own way." I would argue that we are all afraid in the same way, but that we all love, and are loved, differently.

Love is inherently original, and it is the act of giving and receiving love that makes us unique. But fear is a copy-cat emotion that is always experienced in the same way.

Loving someone, and being loved by that person, brings out and celebrates our individuality. Why else would we marry? Why would we circumscribe our freedom, the way we must in a committed relationship? Why would we cut ourselves off from the possibility of romance with the four billion other people on the planet—some of whom might be better-looking or funnier or sexier than the person we've chosen? Why would we voluntarily open our lives to the scrutiny of someone else, the way we must in a marriage? It's not for the children: 40 percent of children in the United States are born out of wedlock, and many more of them have parents who are divorced. It's not for the sex: everybody knows that in this society married people are the only ones who aren't getting any. So why else would we do it?

Marriage, the decision to take that plunge into total intimacy with another person, is an act of superrational courage—with a big potential payoff. Since our core fear is that we don't matter, that we are somehow replaceable and ordinary, the true and committed love of one person can immediately alleviate those fears. When someone introduces you to a stranger as "my wife" or "my husband," the act confers on you an indelible sense of worth. Someone loves you enough to own you, to lay claim to you! Someone is willing to say, to the world at large, that you are so beloved that you are possessed utterly by him or her. You are your spouse's chosen one. Your spouse has said no to those six billion other people, for you. And if, G-d forbid, something happens to you, you have a guarantee that at least one person on this earth won't go about the daily slog as if nothing has transpired.

Someone's wanting to marry you is the ultimate proof that you're special. Those who live in a fulfilling relationship are significantly less afraid.

Marriage is more than being loved, it's being fully known. A loving husband blindfolded can find his wife in a room through her scent alone. He could identify her by the freckle on her left knee. He knows all her opinions and passions and prejudices, the trivial and silly along with those things so grave and private that she never imagined sharing them with another living soul. In knowing her this way, he reinforces all the things about her that make her unique.

Choosing Not to Choose

We love our parents and children, no matter what, and we can get to that place with our spouses as well. Marital love isn't—and shouldn't be— automatically unconditional. No woman wants to hear her husband say, "You're not beautiful, or special, or particularly smart, but I love you with all my heart anyway." What we want to hear is that our particular (and sometimes

peculiar) combination of qualities has won us that special place in the heart
of our beloved. Equally, no woman wants to hear her husband say, "I love
you because you're beautiful and special, but as soon as your hips widen and
your hair begins to gray, I'm afraid that'll be it for us."

**Marital love, then, is about exercising the choice
to love unconditionally. In other words, marriage
is the choice to give up choice.**

Love is transformative; we create our beloveds. I knew a student at Oxford
who met her soul mate. The relationship had taken off like a rocket ship, and
she radiated deep contentment. One day one of the other students, teasing
her, asked if her boyfriend was good-looking. I will always remember the look
of bewilderment on her face. "I don't know," she said. And I loved that. She
couldn't tell! What she meant was "I don't know if he's good-looking the way
that actor or this musician is good-looking. I just know that I'm attracted to
him." Her love for this man transcended our silly definitions of attractive and
unattractive and transformed him into someone she found beautiful. She created that reality with her love: he was beautiful because she loved him.

This is why being in a relationship that is intimate, honest, and open, with
a person around whom you can be totally natural, is one of the most comforting responses we can have to fear. It transforms reality into something
higher and transcendent. Love and fear are antithetical: the more of the former, the less room for the latter. Divorce rates are higher than ever before,
and a shocking 50 percent of professional American women aged thirty-five
and over are single. My single friends say that I don't know how hard it is to
find someone, especially in a meat-market environment like New York. This
is also one of the reasons it is so important to believe in destiny.

With the understanding that you have a place in the universe comes the
understanding that you don't have to be alone in it. When I counsel single
people, I hear the hopelessness in their voices. They don't believe that they're
going to meet someone. I tell them about the Jewish concept of the soul
mate, which is not only that there is a predestined partner out there, or-
dained since the beginning of time, but that you and that person, even while
separated, actually share one, indivisible soul.

If you haven't yet found that someone who places you at the center of his
or her universe, your fears are likely to be more pronounced. Your fears may
also be the reason you haven't found your soul mate. You're afraid of commitment, afraid that someone better might come along, afraid of intimacy,

afraid of being hurt, and afraid of having to compromise. So you continue your endless search, not realizing that you are the pawn of your apprehensions—and that these are, in fact, standing in the way of your being able to satisfy one of your deepest needs, to be loved and needed. Uncertainty is an immobilizer.

A relationship is dynamic, always changing, always interactive. Solitude is stationary.

It is possible to marry without making any impact on your fears and insecurities. Often the person you choose to marry is the living personification of the values you hold most dear. If you love money more than anything in the world, then you'll go for an heir or for someone who has a high-paying job. If you love the body more than anything else, then you'll choose the best-looking butt at the gym. If you love goodness and virtue, then you'll choose the kindest person you meet. I did not choose my wife based on luck but on principle. I knew the sort of woman I wanted to marry, someone who was kind, gentle, humble, and magnanimous. (In other words, the exact opposite of me.) I was looking not for a clone but for a complement.

Since so many people today are plagued by low self-esteem and riddled by insecurity, one person will often find another who is equally plagued by doubt. Soon the two of them are running to every cocktail party in Manhattan because they both so deeply crave acceptance, rather than comforting each other and creating a deep and emotional relationship.

When you are a damaged person and you marry someone equally damaged, your marriage will exacerbate rather than minimize your fears. That's why you must search for a complement rather than a double.

I knew a rich man who divorced his wife of twenty-two years and took up with a girlfriend thirty years his junior. It was the perfect relationship—not of convenience but of fear. He was afraid of getting old and, like many rich businessmen, had colossal insecurities that he was still worthless. Every morning he'd look at his wife, and instead of seeing life and love, he, like the Jack Nicholson character in *About Schmidt*, saw deterioration and death. Her wrinkles reminded him constantly that he was a few steps away from the grave himself. Rather than learning to overcome his obsession with death, he got rid of his wife, replacing her with a young body who made him feel young as well. The girlfriend, for her part, was not a stupid or shallow woman. Nor was she after this guy's money, although she certainly enjoyed the lifestyle he provided. She was just as afraid as he was. There's an abundance of single women in New York, and dating such a well-known businessman gave her a name. How sad that two people who were so desperately in need of love found nothing but fear in one another instead.

Modern Marriage Does Not Seem to Allay People's Fears

Marriage is a primary arena for self-validation. If a woman is prepared to take your last name and have your kids, then you must be one special guy. Lately, however, marriage seems impotent in providing a corroboration of our uniqueness. Men and women get married, but they remain workaholics, trying to impress the world before each other. They have affairs, because they don't feel they get enough love and excitement from their unions. This is another way our fears sneak up and ruin our lives.

**If you have a poor opinion of yourself,
then the person dumb enough to marry you
must be worthless as well.**

And how can someone who is inherently a loser ever make you feel good about yourself? Such a person can make you feel loved, but not special.

I counseled a woman who told me that nothing about her husband attracted her. "His shoulders are hunched instead of square. He's too effeminate. He's socially awkward. I'm not even interested in having sex with him. A man should be more than his wife, but my husband is less than me." I knew that these silly arguments stemmed from something deeper. She came from a prominent family of politicians, and her uncle was a senator. She was raised to prove herself worthy of the family name, and part of that meant marrying someone who could lift her up rather than pull her down. Amazingly, when she did marry, she chose what she really needed rather than what the family needed: a nice, sweet guy who had no problem being in her shadow and loved her more than any other man could. Since she lived in the constant fear that she would not add luster to the family name, she projected her fears onto her husband. Since she saw herself as a failure, she saw him as one too.

When you choose the right person, and really open yourself up to a relationship, the results are miraculous. When you have a significant other, a primary relationship, a person who has given up all others on your behalf, then your unique gifts are corroborated. You feel cherished and special. You are now strong and invincible. And you know no real fear, because you don't have to contend with loneliness.

Come Clean

Building a strong, real relationship with your spouse is an essential step in developing fearlessness, and it's much harder than it sounds. As someone who spends a great deal of time counseling married couples, I can tell you that there is a tremendous amount of fear standing in the way of most marriages. I would guess that the average husband knows less than 40 percent about his wife's total being. He would, for example, refrain from asking her if she found their sex life adequate for fear of hearing she doesn't. He would never ask her if she fantasizes about other men, because he couldn't handle it if she said she did. Rather than taking it as an erotic sign of his wife's womanhood, and as a romantic invitation to him to win her over again just as he did when they were single, he would take it to mean that some other guy is more of a man than he. Conversely, a lot of wives take the approach that ignorance is bliss. Although they see that their husbands close their eyes and tune out mentally while having sex, they never ask them if they're thinking about other women, because the answer would be too painful.

In my book *Why Can't I Fall in Love?* I argued that most of us never make it past the first stage in marriage. We end up like two cities connected by a river, two autonomous people united, for the purposes of commerce and kids, by this institution called marriage.

What we should aim for in our marriages is deep integration and inextricable attachment.

As long as our marriages are governed by fear, they will continue to be lonely.

When fear guides your relationship, instead of being a blessed respite from the outside world, your marriage becomes just another trap, another arena for exhibiting a surface personality. Such a relationship isn't regenerative, it's simply another drain on your emotional resources.

For instance, many of the men I counsel are terrified that they are going to lose their jobs and the ability to provide for their families. This is a terrible fear for a man. These men tell me because they feel that telling their spouses would diminish them in their wives' eyes. All this secrecy does is compound their fears. There was even a French movie recently about a man who got up and pretended to go to work every day so he wouldn't have to tell his family he'd been laid off. This is a perfect example of the way our fears misdirect us. This man's self-worth could have come from the knowledge that he had a devoted wife who stuck with him through every vicissitude, even in his darkest hour. Instead of confiding in her, he chose external props of self-esteem, his wingtips and briefcase and commuter train, and in so doing, he multiplied his own feelings of isolation and worthlessness.

> **There is no point in having a big house if it
> is simply haunted by fears.**

I spoke last year to a woman who had been avoiding an unpleasant money conversation with her husband of fifteen years. "I don't want to know that he's frightened about the state of our finances, frankly. I'd just rather not know how bad it is. Ignorance really is bliss." Here we have a perfect example of the horrendous effects of refusing to confront your fears. Not only is this woman choosing to live in ignorance about something that directly affects her—and something that's within her control—but she's allowing it to destroy her marriage as well. Imagine how her husband feels, shouldering the burden of their insecure financial state himself. Imagine how he dreads the day when some external event—a shop's refusal of her credit card, a creditor's call during dinner, the threat of losing their house—drags her out of her denial into the cold, harsh light of reality. Imagine how much strain this situation—not just their financial woes, but the distance between the two of them about the situation—is putting on their marriage.

Imagine that this woman were to approach her husband and say, "Honey, I know we've got money trouble, and I know you're keeping it from me, but I'm in this marriage for the good and the bad. I don't want you to worry about this alone. Why don't we sit down tonight and go through the bills together? We'll figure out exactly what we owe, and then, together, we can start to figure out how to get ourselves out of this mess. But don't worry, because it's going to be okay.

Of course, this is difficult. She would first have to confront and conquer her own fears. In the process of going through the bills, she might hear things she'd rather not. She might end up canceling their much-anticipated vacation or starting the search for a smaller, more affordable house. But look at the rewards she would reap. Her own fears would be diminished as soon as she looked at them critically: a smaller house wouldn't be the end of the world. On the contrary, their big house is simply an arena to be haunted by the ghosts and goblins of her fears. By joining her husband in coping with the scary situation, she'd come out of her own isolation, providing him with comfort as well. They don't have to be solitary and afraid. If she can join him in the trenches, they will both be strengthened, and their relationship will be reinforced as well.

I believe in full disclosure in a marriage. This is always true. I told a husband who was drawing too close to his receptionist to choose the right time to share with his wife that he feared the consequences of the growing attachment. After his wife's initial shock and upset, they devised a way to make the situation better, and the trust that he engendered by being so forthright with his wife deepened the bond between them. These are the hardest conversations that couples can have. They take a tremendous amount of courage. Only when you are completely truthful and naked with one another can you achieve a sublime state of companionship.

Fear drives us to secrecy, and secrecy will drive us apart.

I spoke with a man and a wife who were going through a very rough period in their marriage. He had had an affair about five years before, and the secret festered in him. He had to create a room in his heart for this secret and to keep it under lock and key. He could no longer be completely natural around his wife, and she began to notice the distance. She tried to get his attention in a negative way, by being mean to him. When that didn't work, she struck up a friendship with a man she met at Starbucks. She hadn't actually been unfaithful, but she was spending hours having coffee with this man, pouring out her heart and soul to him. Here, at last, was a man she could talk to. And then she would go into a closet with her cell phone to confide in me. Imagine this—a woman who goes into a closet to talk to a marriage counselor.

Seeing them in the same room together, I knew that they loved each other, but their secrets were coming between them. I told the husband that he was going to have to come clean with his wife about the affair. He was going to have to open that secret room in his heart for his wife's inspection. "No way," he said. "She has zero tolerance for that kind of thing. She'll kill me. She'll leave me, take the kids, and move into her mother's house." I spoke to the wife separately about disclosing her relationship with the man from the coffee shop. "You're only talking to this guy because you feel you can be open with him. Be open with your husband, and you won't need this guy anymore," I said. She answered, "Are you kidding? My husband would kill him—and me—if he knew."

Here were two people who thought that they were married to ax-murderers. Although consecrated in marriage as one flesh, they were more afraid of one another than they were in love with one another. It's not hard to see why they were afraid. Both of these people were stuck putting the "I" in front of the "we." I was asking them to dedicate themselves to something bigger than themselves—in this case, their marriage.

When you come clean, you and your spouse can then attack the issue together; instead of being adversaries, you're motivated by a common goal. Here's a situation that I've encountered often in my counseling sessions. A wife turns to her husband and says, "You feel distant when we're in bed together. You're not looking at me; you don't say my name. Are you even thinking about me? If not, what are you thinking about?" Invariably the man rushes to reassure her that of course he's thinking of her all the time. All three of us know that he's lying.

He'd say that he's protecting his wife from the very painful knowledge that his attraction to her is waning and that he cannot perform sexually unless he is thinking about other women. He's also protecting himself. He thinks that if he's honest with her, she'll leave him or stop sleeping with him altogether. He should give his wife more credit. She's an adult, and she's motivated to fix the relationship. If the two of them could talk about their sexual issues, they could renew their eroticism and their attraction.

In fact, telling her is the beginning of a solution. Let's say he's been fantasizing about a nurse at his hospital. This gives us something to work with. What is it about the nurse that he finds attractive? Is it the flirtation he has with her? Flirting is sexy and fun, because it connotes unavailability and youthful playfulness. Married people often stop flirting with one another, and it's deadly for the relationship. So his wife can learn to flirt with him and add a little unavailability to her repertoire, and we're on the way to a solution. Or maybe his receptionist makes him feel powerful and worldly because he's in a position of authority over her. Maybe he's turned on to her because she's compliant. Maybe it's just the simple attraction of new flesh. Or maybe in his mind he associates his wife with kids, with responsibility, while associating the nurse with sexy stockings and an erotic uniform. All these things are fixable.

> **Sexuality is entirely in the mind, and the mind can
> be manipulated to transfer erotic attraction
> onto nearly any reasonable target.**

In my book *Kosher Adultery* I devised plenty of ways for a husband to perceive his wife erotically as a new woman by bringing sinfulness into an all-too-legal marriage. As long as his desires are out in the open, we can work toward satisfying them in the context of his marriage. But if they're never articulated, how can they possibly be fixed?

It takes a tremendous amount of courage to say, "I think about someone else when we're making love." It takes a tremendous amount of courage to hear it. Frankly, it takes a lot of courage to be in the same room with people who are having this kind of conversation. If you realize that it's a step toward improving your sex life, and maybe saving your marriage, you'll find the courage to do it. Your marriage is a third party, a separate entity, one that's poisoned by your secrecy. You must dedicate your actions, however painful, to your marriage. "I know this may hurt, but our marriage cannot continue if we keep sweeping this under the carpet. When you think about it that way, you're motivated by the knowledge that there's something bigger at stake than your embarrassment or your hurt feelings. You're moving away from the "I" to the "we."

> **Successful marriages involve moving away
> from the "I" and toward the "we."**

We can do better. In fact, we must. I would like to promote openness in relationships. By opening our lives to include someone else, by sharing our fears, and by confronting them together, we launch a counterattack against trepidation.

Are You Trustworthy?

If you're fortunate enough to be in a relationship, it is your duty to help your significant other drag his or her own fears out into the daylight. If one very important reason to pursue and sustain a marriage is to have someone who understands and reinforces everything that is unique about you, then it stands to reason that an enormous part of being in that relationship is returning the favor. This brings to mind another virtue that has been lost in this culture: trustworthiness.

If you want complete openness in a relationship, you have to be worthy of the trust your partner puts in you.

The first issue, of course, is fidelity. Though the statistics are strongly contested, the consensus among researchers in the United States is that about 50 percent of all husbands are unfaithful, and wives aren't that far behind at about 40 percent. Some statistics even have the wives, over the past ten years, overtaking their husbands in the number of affairs. When you open your life completely to someone and believe him when he tells you you're special, then it is utterly ruinous for him to find a replacement and to lie to you about it. When you cheat on your spouse, you're saying, "I found someone better: someone sexier, someone cuter, someone richer, someone who does what you do for me—only better." There is nothing more erotic in life than to be found desirable. Conversely, there is nothing more soul-destroying than to be rejected, particularly by someone who once wanted you. Especially when it's the person whose name—and whose children—you've borne!

Trustworthiness must extend past simply keeping your pants on. When someone takes the courageous step of showing themselves completely to you, you have to make a promise, to yourself and to that person, that you will not use what he has shown you against him. It's well known among attorneys that the most vicious breakups take place not between business partners but between lovers. Lovers killing each other account for one of every three murders in the United States. One of the reasons that so many divorces are so vicious is that the parties know exactly which buttons to push to make their soon-to-be ex-spouses crazy. Those buttons, of course, correspond to their fears. Can you honestly say that you don't throw the most vicious thing you think of at your spouse during a fight?

I counseled a couple who fought all the time. It was excruciating to be in the same room with them, and I would often have to intervene just to keep the conversation civil. Their speciality was throwing their fears in one another's faces. The husband had grown up very poor, a farmer's son in Nebraska. Though he had made a lot of money through years of work as an attorney, he was still deeply insecure about failing. He had grown up with nothing, and he feared he'd go back to nothing. He had become a miser who complained about every penny his wife spent. His wife, on the other hand, had grown up in a wealthy family that owned a video chain store and had spent most of her life secretly worrying that her friends were only her friends because of her deep pockets and the prestige of her last name.

The husband's insecurities also caused him to be controlling in other ways. He insisted that she quit her job as a buyer at Bloomingdale's and stay home with the children. The wife, five years older than her husband, accused him of immaturity and petty jealousy. "He wants to know where I am every second of the day. He wants to veto every decision I make about the house and the kids. He becomes insane if I so much as talk to another man." Whenever she felt controlled by him, she would find a way to cut him down. She would exacerbate his jealousy by telling him that he was the worst lover she had ever had and was under-endowed, to boot. He in return would call her a spoiled bitch—and the fighting continued.

Once when the husband was honored by a school for agreeing to endow a classroom, his wife told him that she would not be attending the award dinner. "You only gave that money because your biggest client is the president of the school. It was a business decision. You couldn't care less about those kids, only about yourself." In return, he was more than happy to remind her that her friends, who listened for hours to the long list of his shortcomings, were parasites and that she didn't have a single real friend in the world. These two went straight for the jugular with each other. Instead of acting as an antidote to fear, this marriage was a catalyst to it. Rather than smoothing the rough edges of life and making both feel unique, this marriage was doing the exact opposite. The message each spouse sent to the other wasn't "You matter" but "I feel I don't matter, and I want you to feel that way too."

Each felt disempowered and was unfortunately sure that the way to feel in control was to maximize the other's fears. I had to make them see that their premise was impossible. You don't gain control over people by magnifying their fears, because that is a betrayal of your own insecurities. By manipulating your spouse's fears, you're ultimately exacerbating your own. This is always true.

In history it has always been the most frightened people who insist on using fear to control others.

Stalin killed his entire officer corps out of fear of a coup; Hitler had Ernst Roehm and other Nazi leaders killed, lest they diminish his power; Saddam

Hussein never slept in the same bed two nights in a row for fear of assass-ination.

The real tragedy of this besieged marriage is that it would have been very easy for this husband and wife to improve the situation. All she had to say to begin the healing process was "I don't care if you win an award from a school or not. I don't love you because of the medal you come with. You're impor-tant to me, not your achievements." And he could say to her, "I never married you for your money. I married you because I wanted you to love me and I wanted to take care of you." But neither of them could manage to say some-thing kind, because both were afraid they'd be capitulating and compromis-ing the righteousness of their own positions.

A crisis like this calls for a redefinition of roles. If you are in such a predicament, you must decide that your primary role in your marriage, from here on in, is not to be the breadwinner or the person who remembers to buy the toilet paper or the one who gets up for the baby in the middle of the night.

Your primary role in your marriage is to tell your spouse— in word and in deed—that he or she matters. Your principal purpose in your marriage is to allay your spouse's fear of unworthiness and to confirm through the constancy of your love that he or she is profoundly significant.

Men and women do each other a disservice by discounting the fears specific to our sexes. I was talking to a woman expecting her first child about her hus-band's reaction to the pregnancy. She wanted him to participate more fully in the nursery preparation and to read the books she was reading about preg-nancy and parenting, but all he seemed to want to do was work. I asked her if she'd considered that perhaps he was concerned about providing for her and the baby. She laughed at me. "Don't be ridiculous! It's the twenty-first cen-tury. I don't have some cavewoman fantasy about being taken care of. I'll be going back to work in a couple of months." A week later I received a call from her. "I talked to him about what you said, and you were right! The baby's expenses are freaking him out, and he was really worried about being able to live up to his responsibilities." No matter how many women flourish in successful careers, I think it is still true that men bear the brunt of the fear about supporting the family.

Women have their own specific concerns. For instance, I think women are very afraid of not being as attractive as other women and of losing their

looks. Unfortunately this fear isn't completely unfounded. It is hard to maintain self-respect and confidence in a culture that scores women almost exclusively on the way they look and the lengths to which they will go to exploit
themselves sexually. A number of magazines have recently focused on the
prevalence of pornography on the Internet. Men are just a few clicks away
from a silicone Barbie doll performing the most explicit acts, and I was
chilled to read interviews with a number of guys in *New York* magazine (October 20, 2003) saying that they'd rather go home and masturbate to pictures
on the Internet than have sex with their girlfriends. Pixels never say no, and
they never have a bad hair day. This is tremendously degrading to women,
not to mention to the men themselves.

> **A husband who uses pornography or any of the socially
> acceptable soft-core alternatives is fueling his wife's
> fear that she is not enough to excite him.**

An emotionally intimate marriage, one based on trust, full disclosure, and
mutual compassion, is one of our most powerful defenses against terror, and
one of the very great pleasures afforded to us in this life. I can only recom-
mend that you not squander this wonderful gift but use it to immunize yourself and your spouse against fear.

30

Principle #20:
Raise Fearless Children

O man greatly beloved, fear not: peace be unto thee, be strong, yea, be strong. And when he had spoken unto me, I was strengthened, and said, Let my lord speak; for thou has strengthened me.

—DANIEL 10:19

The happiest moments of my life have been the few which I have passed at home in the bosom of my family.

—THOMAS JEFFERSON

I'd like to share with you one of my own best defenses against fear. It's not an SUV with the global positioning system and the sophisticated airbag technology. It's not a state-of-the-art alarm system for the home. It's not a diversified blue-chip mutual fund portfolio. It's my six-year-old daughter.

I remember watching the news one night when it seemed that every story was uglier and more disgusting than the one that had preceded it. After half an hour I was awash in corruption and scandal and mean-mindedness and gossip and disaster. Rochel Leah came over to me. She wanted to show me the picture she'd drawn of a "woof." She'd made it blue because she knows blue is my favorite color. And that's what made me feel better: a blue woof. The feeling of the sewer, though not totally gone, was lifted. I looked at my daughter's innocence, and I transcended all the celebrity scandals and corrupt corporate shenanigans and stories of people killing each other over five-dollar vials of crack.

Having children if you don't have them yet, or spending time with the ones you do have, will embolden you immeasurably.

**It may be true that your life on earth is limited
and ephemeral and will inevitably pass.**

If you use that time to create something that lasts, your life is more than a life sentence. If it is important to be loved unconditionally, it is also important to love that way as well.

Children remind you that your life is more than the simple span of time you spend here on earth, eating hamburgers and mowing your lawn. Having children gives you the luxury of making your life into a collection of principles, a series of convictions. In the same way that an understanding and knowledge of your history anchor and support you, having children enables you to send an arrow into the future. The patriarch Jacob never died, the Talmud declares: his children's children's children are still populating the earth and continuing his belief system. Though I'm certainly not comparing myself with one of the great patriarchs, it does give me some comfort to imagine one of my daughter's children telling her own child a story about her grandfather Shmuley, crazy nut that he may have been, to illustrate a point about decency.

In our roles as parents we are offered the greatest chance we have to act as a bridge between the celestial and the terrestrial. As parents we are more than simple caretakers, ensuring that our helpless offspring make it to eighteen intact. We parents all have the dream that we will be able to communicate some truth about life to our children. And there is no better teacher than our own good example.

**By having children and communicating to them
your beliefs and principles, you are transformed
from a mortal human into an eternal idea, an idea
that your children can pick up and be inspired
by for the length of their days.**

When my children see me stop to give a homeless person money, they learn about giving. When they see me fast on a religious day, even if they're too young to join me, they learn to connect with the sufferings of the Jewish people as well as their own glorious heritage. And I am that link. In me the tenets of my faith come alive for my children to adopt. When they see me make time for a couple whose marriage is in trouble, they learn about caring. These are things that will enrich their lives, as they have enriched mine.

"So what," you may be thinking, "does this have to do with fear?" It's simple: influencing who my children are and the way they behave in the world gives me the chance to make a lasting impression on the world, one that extends beyond my years on the planet and whatever other contributions I make while I am here. And the more I connect with eternity, the less I fear my own transience.

Parent Fearlessly

It is not enough simply to have children. We have to rededicate ourselves to active, compassionate parenting—for our children's sake, and for our own. We must parent fearlessly, immunizing our children against the constant and corrosive influence of fear that affects our own generation.

> **Parents who love their children will educate them
> to fear none but G-d alone.**

If we can't give our children a completely safe world, let's at least give them a completely secure inner world. It is in our power: we can teach them to fortify their internal defenses instead of relying on externals and cheap possessions.

When we think about our responsibilities as parents, we think of raising our children to be good people. We teach them to be responsible, civic-minded citizens. We teach them to be financially responsible. We teach them to have respect for their elders. We think about teaching our sons to honor women and treat them with dignity; we think about teaching our daughters to value themselves. We should add another quality to the values that we attempt to impart to our children: never to be afraid.

How can we raise children who are immune to fear? Our children, supposedly the great lights of our lives, are all too often the locus of our fears. When we feel fear on their behalf and convey that fear, we are passing on a terrible legacy. We are condemning them to unhappy lives.

**Don't parent defensively. Teach your children
what they should be. Never speak of your fear
of what they might become.**

When we allow our fears to dictate what our children do, we cheat them out of important experiences and full, rich development. On a hot day last summer, my children asked me if they could stand on the street outside our home with two of their friends and sell homemade lemonade. The group pledged half of all their proceeds to charity and decided to divide the other half among themselves. I was only too happy to reward their wish to be enterprising and philanthropic, especially since it got them outside on a beautiful day. They stood on the corner outside our home for four hours and made fourteen dollars. I don't know what precipitated their change of heart, but when they came back in, my daughter said, "Tatty, we've decided that we want to give all the money to charity, not just half."

Later that afternoon I received a call from their friends' father. "Shmuley, we're friends, so I feel I can speak bluntly. It was the height of irresponsibility for you to allow my kids to stand out on the street like that. The news is filled with the stories of all these crazy kidnappings. I wanted to believe that I could trust you with the safety of my kids. You had no right doing that without calling and asking our permission."

I thought to myself, "What a shame." Our children had worked hard, and they had worked together. They had come to the conclusion, of their own accord, that they wanted to donate all of the proceeds of their efforts to a worthy cause. In other words, I felt that they had demonstrated a grasp of some of the most important lessons in life, without any adult prompting at all. I was proud of them.

And yet this man was allowing the bogeyman to rob them of a legitimate sense of pride. They were being told that, rather than having done something good, they had done something bad. What his children would remember from that day was not the satisfaction of hard work or the gift of being able to work well with others or the joy of giving the fruits of their labor to people who need it more than they did, but instead a narrow escape from things too terrible to contemplate. With the best of intentions, this father had allowed his fears to rob his own kids of a feeling of competence and worth.

A recent statistic suggested that 86 percent of girls have had sex by the time they graduate from high school. If you talk to them, as I have, you find they regret it. Why did they do it? They did it out of fear. Some boy said to them, "If you don't do this, it means that you don't love me." "If you're a prude, then I'm not going to hang around." "Do this or I'll date Allison." These girls give in because they have no little voice inside them that talks back. There's no inner voice that says, "Drop dead, creep. I don't need a boyfriend to know that I matter, and neither, frankly, does Allison." Without the benefit of any kind of internal immunity that would reassure them that they have intrinsic value, they have already begun to rely on those unreliable externals: their bodies and the good opinion of somebody who just wants something from them.

From experience I know that I'm going to be counseling these girls ten years down the road, listening to the terrible stories of their poisonous relationships, hearing how they never know whether the man they're with really loves them or not. They will not have been to the library since high school, but they will have been to the gym every night. They will have dug themselves deeper and deeper into their fear bunker, and it will be too late for them to get out. We can imbue our children with an inner immunity to fear, and we have every responsibility to do so.

**The first step in protecting our children from
our own fearfulness is by refusing to show fear
in their presence.**

Children are great imitators. When our kids see us gnawing our fingernails in front of CNN, they'll take that as a cue for their own lives and behavior. When they see us fretting about going to the doctor, they think there is something seriously wrong. I'm not suggesting that we hide our fears from our children. I'm suggesting something much more radical: we must refrain from being afraid, so we have nothing to hide from them at all.

Isn't one of the very real pleasures of parenting the feeling of confidence, competence, and control you derive from the knowledge that someone trusts and depends on you completely? When your child wakes you up to tell you that she's heard a noise downstairs, you put on your slippers and go to see what the disturbance is—and you become a hero in her eyes.

**It's important that your children see you as fearless
and try to emulate that fearlessness. You can only
really accomplish this if you *are* fearless.**

Otherwise, your kids will someday be faking it in front of their children in turn.

Fearlessness must be taught. Kids are afraid of everything. They're afraid of taking a shower (if they're boys, that fear lasts into their adult years) and of the clothing rack that looks like a monster when the lights are off. One of the very real duties of parenting is to take the time to understand and then defuse these fears. They may be tiny to us, but children's fears are life-size to them. Children have to be shown, carefully and patiently, that washing their faces won't drown them and that the clothing rack is just a place to hang their skirts and jeans.

Stop Worrying

We worry, chronically and endlessly, on our children's behalf. At some point we Americans started to see our parental role as that of caretakers, over and above any other responsibility to our children.

Protecting our kids has become more important than inspiring them.

Most of the parents I know spend a considerable amount of time worrying about their children's safety. They worry about household accidents, guns in the schools, molesters in the playgrounds, and kidnappers in vans. I realize that this statement is controversial, but I do think we have to stop worrying so much about our children's safety—*for our children's sake.*

A man came out with a video showing children how to elude kidnappers and sexual predators, including various techniques for squirming out of their grip. I had him on my radio show. After much thought, I ultimately decided not to show the video to my kids. It's not that the information wasn't valuable. But I felt that in teaching them to avoid predators, I would also be teaching them to be afraid. Introducing the idea would carry its own danger. Instead of offsetting fear, learning these techniques would create an "I'm next" feeling. I refuse to inculcate a victim mentality into my children. However, I might have shown them the video if I thought my kids were in a higher-risk bracket (if, let's say, I was a high-profile politician or involved, G-d forbid, in an unpleasant divorce with someone I thought might try to kidnap them).

The threat of violence against Jewish targets since 9/11 has led to increased security at synagogues. Most Jewish schools now have permanent security at their doors. What message does that send to children? It tells them, every time they walk into their place of learning past an armed guard, they are targets. That guard reinforces the fear that they are likely to be picked out and picked on because of their religious and ethnic identities. This isn't the message we should be sending to children. If security is necessary, then let it be less obvious. Even the president's security detail consists of men in regular business suits rather than army Special Ops with giant machine guns.

When I was doing my radio show with Peter Noel, I would often chasten members of the black community who are in the habit of crying racism at the slightest provocation. It sent the wrong message to their children, who are always watching their parents for clues. Why would you want your kids to grow up believing that they are hated and reviled because of the color of their skin?

I give the same advice to my Jewish brethren. In the Jewish community you will often hear, "Scratch a non-Jew, find an anti-Semite." After two thousand years of slaughter, many in the Jewish community are permanently suspicious. I am opposed to this victim mentality. I don't want my own children to grow up with a chip on their shoulder, because that chip does nothing but handicap them. I know that anti-Semitism and racism, both covert and overt, is alive and well, especially in Europe, and I will not be able to permanently protect my children from it. Though anti-Semitism may sometimes find me, I won't go looking for it. To be sure, I am fully behind organizations, like the ADL and the Simon Wiesenthal Center, that serve as watchdogs against the rise of anti-Semitism. But I know that the most important organizations in the Jewish community are those that promote Jewish education and identity.

It does not benefit the Jewish community to see anti-Semitism everywhere. If you see anti-Semitism in every remark, don't you send the message to your children that their religious heritage is a potential liability? Why would you want your kids to identify as victims instead of feeling empowered by their heritage?

We must avoid preventing our children from fully experiencing life by being constantly afraid on their behalf.

Fear's paralysis is a terrible and unfair punishment for our children. Since we're still making choices on behalf of our kids, it's our responsibility to be fearless for them. If your children don't do anything, you don't have to worry about them. In this instance, fear lets us win the battle, but we lose the war.

A friend told me about a conversation she'd had with another mother while pushing her infant daughter on the swings. When she mentioned that she was starting baby swimming lessons, the other mother recoiled in horror. "That's a terrible idea," she said gravely. "Children who have had swimming lessons often feel overconfident about their abilities in the water, and they can get into very serious trouble."

This woman was saying that my friend shouldn't teach her child to swim, because the little girl would acquire an inflated sense of her own prowess. She was saying that the child should sacrifice all the benefits of learning to swim—the acquisition of a new skill, physical fitness, the self-esteem that comes from active participation in sports, even the frivolous fun of pool parties in her future—simply to appease her parent's own fears. Of course, children should not be allowed to play unsupervised around a body of water before they have sufficient skills; that would be insanity. But we must make the distinction between vigilance and paranoia.

> **We cannot restrict our children to reduce our own fears. We're missing the point if we keep our kids inside, playing violent, misogynist video games and watching mind-numbing TV shows instead of getting out and throwing a ball or playing games that require actual creativity and imagination.**

In the same way that your fears impede you in love and your professional life, fear gets in the way of effective parenting. Your constant concerns for your children do you—and your kids—no good. Instead of embracing your role as parent, you hamstring yourself, and your children are less happy and less well behaved as a result.

Just Say No

One of the major problems I see in this culture is that our children are growing up too fast. I know that every generation complains about this, but it has never been so true—or such a problem. A mail-order catalog for a retailer that caters exclusively to girls in their early adolescence arrived in our mail the other day, addressed to my thirteen-year-old daughter. The underwear section is filled with photographs of thirteen- and fourteen-year-old girls modeling lingerie. Not underwear, but lingerie—frilly, lacy lingerie. Why do these children need sexy underwear? Whose pleasure, I would like to know, is this lingerie for? And yet there's a market for it. There are children buying sexy underwear, and parents permitting them to wear it. According to a *Time* magazine statistic, 40 percent of high school girls wear thongs, with many wearing the elastic band over their jeans so that it's distinctly visible. Nobody at home is saying to these girls, "Absolutely not. Not under my roof. You'll dress like a lady, young lady." These girls are embracing exploitation for fear that they would be otherwise ignored. Fear, rather than confidence, is dictating their actions.

The clarion call of childhood right now is "treat me like an adult." A sturdy, happy, healthy childhood is one of the major underpinnings in a solid foundation, the kind of foundation we need to create if we have any hope at all of resisting fear. When we allow our children to bypass childhood, we're allowing one of the most essential underpinnings to be stolen from them.

If they don't have the strength of a sturdy childhood behind them, children will grow into unsteady and frightened adults.

It is your job as a parent to stop your children from growing up too fast. You must do it for their own good, in the same way that you stop them from eating an entire box of sugared cereal or staying up all night watching TV. They are too young to know that they will regret bypassing this crucial stage; it is your job as a parent to put the brakes on, to know better than they do about what's right for them.

In order to do this, you have to trust your instincts and assume a leadership role.

Parenting fearlessly also means that you can't be afraid of your kids.

I watched one of my daughters' friends and her parents negotiate a bedtime, and it was like watching them hash out the treaty at Yalta. I couldn't believe it took this much give-and-take for a parent to get a kid to go to bed. "I want her to feel like she's participating in the decision," the mother said to me. My own house is much less of a democracy. My children go to bed when they're told to go to bed, because I'm the father and they're the children. Sometimes they rebel (I can hear their feet pattering). But the principle is established, even if its implementation is sometimes ineffective. And my daughters will never wear thongs. They are ladies, not entertainment for pimply pubescent youth. I am not their friend, I am their father. In life, I hope that they will have many friends, but they will only ever have one father.

It is a parent's job to give children as strong a foundation as possible. You educate them. You travel with them. You throw a ball around with them and teach them to drive. You try to instill your values in them. And yet, in this incredibly important arena, we are falling short. We are raising children who lack bold, courageous initiative. American kids are increasingly lazy; they plunk themselves down in front of a TV for hours on end, even if there is snow outside to play in, if there are bikes to ride and friends to visit. When we raise children without initiative, the only thing left to them is to be adventurous in unhealthy ways. Instead of escaping into nature or athleticism—because we're afraid they'll be eaten by a bear or hit their heads—they escape into video games and flirting on the Internet. I want instead for my children to be formidable, independent, and courageous. Don't you?

How will we create these independent warriors? I'm not the first to observe that children don't come with an instructions manual. Some things, though, are just common sense. There's no substitute for talking to your children about their fears—and that may mean that you have to push through a few of your own in order to hear them. One of the major roadblocks preventing you as a parent from having honest, open communication with your children is not sullen teenage angst or lack of time but your own fear of how that conversation is going to go. You're afraid that your children are going to ask you questions you don't know how to answer. You're afraid that your kids might point out your inconsistencies and hypocrisy, the fact that you tell them to do one thing while you do another. You're also afraid of the subject matter. It's damned uncomfortable talking to your kids about sex. You're afraid of what you might find out: what parent really wants to know that his kid has experimented with drugs? Yet even if we don't have the answers, it's our job as parents to wrestle with the questions.

No Matter What

Probably the most important thing you can do to immunize your children against fear is to make sure they know that you love them unconditionally. You're thinking, "Of course I love my kids unconditionally." But is that actually the message you're sending to your children?

I don't think we realize how much kids need to be told and shown that they're loved—no matter what. We don't realize how many conditions we put on our love. Our kids need to hear that we won't love them any less if they score poorly on their spelling test or if they test their new crayons on the hallway wall. I'm an advocate of discipline, maybe more than most parents these days, but my kids never wonder if I love them.

I had a child-rearing expert on my radio show, and I asked her, "How do I make sure that my five daughters are Daddy's girls?" She said to me, "Be affectionate and demonstrative with them always: hug them and kiss them whenever you see them." What great advice! I have implemented it, even with my teenage daughters, who give me grief about how uncool it is to hug their dad in front of their friends. "Tough," I tell them. "You're my Daddy's girl. You'll be married fifty years, and you'll still be my Daddy's girl. There is no escape." And there isn't a night when they come home from school when I don't ask them, before anything else, to give their short, hairy father a kiss, no matter who is around. They know that they deserve my love just because they exist, not because of their accomplishments and their scores.

**Every time you tell your kids that you love them,
you're giving them a little more ammunition
in the war against fear.**

I have a theory about why adolescents rebel against their parents: it's a way of dealing with the anger that accompanies the realization that our happy childhoods were a lie. Let me explain. We're all born communists. Bill Gates's kids play in the sandbox next to other kids; they don't know that their house is bigger or that their father is richer. If you've spent any time with young children, you know how justice-driven they are; they're meticulous about fairness and equality. In their eyes, everyone's important and can be expected to be shared with.

As we get older, we start realizing that everything is not as equal as our parents told us. Susie is smarter; Jennifer is prettier; John comes from a wealthier family; Herman is stronger. And these adjectives have measurable effects. Since she's smarter, Susie gets called on more often. The teachers like her better and put her in charge of the class when they're called out. Since Jennifer is prettier, she gets more attention from boys. John's parents buy him anything he points to, so he always has the newest toys and the coolest clothes. Herman's heft makes him the hero of the football team. It gradually becomes clear that to the world we're not all equal and worthy of love just because we exist. Some people do better, some people look better. The stories told to us in the sandbox were a lie.

Isn't that why teenagers rebel? They're reacting to the dawning realization that they've been fed misinformation. That's why they're in such a hurry to grow up, so that they can repudiate all of the falsehoods told to them in childhood and prove that they're not naïve after all. As adults, we're used to inequality; we're hardened to the realities of life. There's nothing revelatory about it: some people have summer houses, some people don't. The news that we're not all equal hits teenagers like a ton of bricks, and everyone reacts differently. Some kids become positive-feedback junkies: they dedicate their entire lives to getting good grades or being popular with the other students or achieving athletically. Others look for the nearest escape: tons of television, cheap sex, video games, drugs.

> **Your job as a parent is to ease that transition
> between the idyllic world of the sandbox and the
> cold world of adulthood as much as humanly possible.**

You have to offset the heavy dose of insecurity and fear that comes with the realization that the world is not as perfect as it once seemed. What's the big deal that Susie won the merit award and John's parents bought him a new car for his sixteenth birthday? We love you and will love you no matter what. We want you to try to do well at school to make the most of your potential, not to get into a good college. You don't have to dress like a prostitute to get the attention of the boys in your class; your value isn't determined by whether or not someone asks you out for Saturday night. You matter. You matter intrinsically and infinitely—no matter what.

One More Inoculation

You have to show your children, even as you are learning yourself, how to immunize themselves internally against fear. Religious education has provided my children with a sense of destiny. They know that G-d is watching over them and loves them, just because they're his children. You can't actually protect your children from things that may frighten them, but you can give them the sense that their existence is part of a bigger plan, that there's order in the universe.

Religion certainly makes it easier, but even the nonreligious can learn lessons from it. For instance, Jews celebrate a festival called Purim. It commemorates the victory of the Jews against the genocidal plans of the wicked Persian prime minister Haman. To celebrate it, children dress up in costumes and spin noisemakers whenever the prime minister's name is mentioned in the scroll's text. While it's a fun holiday, it is laden with important themes: the courage of Queen Esther, who risked her position at court in order to protect her people; the heroism of Mordecai, who stands up for what's right and refuses to bow before Haman; and the ultimate triumph of good over evil. Children prepare baskets of food and drink to send out to friends and neighbors, and everyone is obligated to give two presents to the poor. The focus is on giving, as opposed to getting and consuming. Purim is also a feast day, when families and friends and neighbors gather to break bread together, with all the attendant teasing and conversation and communion that such an event inspires.

Is there any reason we can't imbue some of the American "Hallmark holidays" with equivalent meaning, replacing the empty sentiment and empty calories with something purposeful and holy? Why not turn next Halloween into an excuse for a feast? Instead of just ghosts and goblins and running around to neighbors for candy, make it something family-oriented. Use the holiday as an opportunity to gather. It can also be a good time to teach your children the meaning of charity. Perhaps they could use part of their allowance to buy candy—or food cans—for poor families and find a way to distribute these without causing indignity to the families. Or they could visit a home for the elderly in their festive costumes. Or, at the very least, parents can have their children focus on an important moral lesson that can be derived from the holiday. The singer Michael Jackson once told me that the reason he takes his children trick-or-treating is so that they witness the kindness of strangers.

The more your child feels connected to a solid family with solid values, the less adrift she will feel in the world. The more connection she has to a community grateful for her charitable contribution, the easier it will be for her to subdue the insecurities that grip her in the lunchroom. When she understands that she is loved unconditionally, by her parents and her G-d, she won't have to seek unwholesome and unhealthy facsimiles of that love elsewhere.

Imparting an immunity against fear to our children is especially important in this culture. It is the job of the parent to provide a healthy, wholesome countermeasure to the dose of fear doled out every time your child watches television or checks out a Web site. And this is why it's so sad to see our culture littered with broken families, children growing up without a strong, mature, dual parental influence. You have to maintain enough influence to make a difference in your child's life. The family structure is there to reinforce against fear. If there's no structure, how will children ever learn?

This, of course, is a challenge well known to religious parents hoping to raise their children in a wholesome environment. Being religious means that my kids will, G-d willing, marry early and be spared all the heartache that accrues in today's crazy love-'em-and-leave-'em dating scene. My daughters won't dress in ways that dishonor them, and they won't hang out at parties with boys. They will be encouraged to reject that which is shallow and frivolous and choose instead those things that are eternal and deep. My sons will be raised to honor women and honor commitments. It's my job to make it clear to them that the trade-off is worth it, that the benefits they'll reap from a religious life far outweigh the temporal pleasure of lip gloss, boyfriends, and girlfriends. I do not think that this responsibility should be restricted to religious parents. It belongs to all parents everywhere.

Our home lives must provide a wholesome counterweight to the corruption of the culture.

It is in the first order of our responsibilities that we represent the other, more wholesome side of the coin.

31

Principle #21:
Build Your Community

And it shall come to pass, that as ye were a curse among the heathen, O
house of Judah, and house of Israel; so will I save you, and ye shall be a
blessing: fear not, but let your hands be strong.

—ZECHARIAH 8:13

The bird a nest, the spider a web, man friendship.

—WILLIAM BLAKE

My young cousin is a soldier in an elite Israeli combat unit. He has spent much time in Judea and Samaria fighting terrorists. He has had bullets whiz by his head, and he has witnessed two members of his unit—both in their early twenties—killed before his eyes. He is a brave man, so I asked him his secret for staying strong, even when he knew terrorist snipers were right across from him. He told me, "You don't understand. You're with all your friends, and they're there to protect you. You sleep with these guys, you eat with them, you train with them. They're like your brothers. As long as they are with you, you're never afraid."

The only people who talk about this kind of community in America seem to be the gallant people in the military, probably because these people are often finding themselves facing possible death. Many veterans of World War II have likewise told me that they miss the sense of camaraderie that existed in the military and that they have never fully duplicated in this civilian life.

Indeed, how many of us have anything like that sense of camaraderie today? How many of us really prioritize our friendships? Although we need these community connections more than ever, we're unwittingly moving away from them. We're too busy to return calls; we hate hanging out with that couple since they had the baby; that single woman's dating trials and tribulations bum us out. Communities are increasingly fragmented as everyone retreats behind walled suburban homes. We don't go to church anymore. Even friendships have become more functional than heartfelt. We're more likely to make time for a drink with a business acquaintance than we are for an old college friend.

Look at the way we spend our leisure time. How close are we to other human beings when one of the principal forms of getting together with friends is going out to a movie together rather than catching up, sharing information about our families, our work, our dreams? TV especially has killed off a sense of community, since it provides an artificial feeling of communal connectedness that simply isn't real.

**You may think that since you and seventy million
other Americans are watching the Super Bowl,
you're enjoying great communal cohesion,
but in truth you're just one more couch potato
sitting alone in his living room.**

This is one of the things I miss about England. In Britain friends and family go to the local pub together after work. It's not unusual to see children playing with each other there while their parents talk with each other and with friends. There's music, but it's music to sing along to, not to drown out all possibility of conversation. In America we go to a bar to pick up and get picked up. We go to see and be seen. It's certainly not a place to bring your children. The idea of a bar's being family friendly is inconceivable.

More Money, More Problems

The West is wealthy, but wealth, for all its blessings, is by its very nature isolating. In fact, isolation is the very thing that many seek to purchase with their wealth. You begin in a tenement, where you know everyone in your building, and you think nothing of asking your neighbor to watch your child play while you run to the corner store. You graduate to the suburbs, where you know two of your neighbors. Your car gets bigger and more impenetrable.

Instead of sending your child to day care, where she can interact with other people's children and build a community of her own, you hire a babysitter, who watches your child alone. And then you hit the jackpot and buy a private estate that's totally cut off from the outside world. Wealth buys you your own plane, so you don't have to sit next to the chatty traveling salesman. It takes you to the front of the line at an amusement park, so you don't have to wait in line next to someone else's sticky babies.

All this money is buying us fear rather than relieving us of it. Our expensive security systems and the guard in front of our gated community don't make us less afraid, but a community that cares about us will. If your home is used to shut people out rather than to bring them in, it becomes a prison. If you won't lend your brother your snazzy new car because you can't take the risk that something will happen to it, your car becomes something that destroys connections instead of enhancing them. And your fears for your car will just increase. Besides, how dumb are you that your stupid car is more valuable to you than your brother, anyway? What kind of pathetic life are you leading when you're afraid that something will happen to your car? Eventually your beautiful possessions cease to enrich your life; they become a source of worry rather than evidence of blessing. As the ancient rabbis said, "The more possessions, the more worries."

When you open your home with hospitality, it becomes a bulwark against fear. With a large family, my wife and I often face real financial pressures. Whenever that happens, we try to make a point of inviting ever more guests to our home. We have even started a regular communal prayer service that meets in our home on the Sabbath. I figure if G-d was kind enough to give us a nice home, then I'm going to use it for something communal and it's going to be everyone's house. Rather than worry about it, I'm going to use it. To be sure, this leads to a lot of wear and tear on the house. My kids are always pointing out things that are breaking and warning me to duck when the rafters of the ceilings come loose. But those problems are nothing compared to the feeling that the house is blessed: with friends, with children who see that material objects must be consecrated to a higher cause, and with a sense of a community where I feel we belong.

Contrary to what the television executives would have you believe, real community, rather than the virtual variety, is important. You need to feel that there is a wider context to your life. You need to feel that you make an impact on your environment, that you change and enhance it. You need to feel that you are a vital part of a greater whole. You need to feel that you make a contribution, a contribution beyond the personal, one that is valued even by strangers.

The Importance of Conditional Love

We've spoken about the importance of unconditional love, the kind of love that exists between a parent and a child, as we grapple against fear. We've spoken about the importance of unconditional love conditionally given, the kind of love that first brings together a husband and wife. And we will talk about the importance of a strong spiritual love, a tie that binds us to the infinite. The love we receive from the community is another kind of love, a conditional love, and this is precisely what is valuable about it.

Your community requires a contribution. You can't greet your friends in your bathrobe, the way you do your family. Your mother will call repeatedly until you return her calls, but your friends will eventually stop calling. In order to keep your position on the board, you have to spend the month between meetings sending the e-mails you promised to write. When a couple invites you for dinner, you reciprocate. There is a social contract.

**The community requires something of you,
but it keeps its end of the bargain by appreciating
your efforts on its behalf and including you
in its framework.**

Americans must return to communal life. Finding a community is straightforward if you're religious. When you're not, you have to take responsibility for building and maintaining your own. That can be difficult, given our busy lives. In an age of petty affronts, it's easier to be insulted than to join up. But it's not as hard as you might think, simply because so many others out there are starved for a sense of community as well.

**You must undertake one action a week
that fosters community in your life.**

Some suggestions that I would offer include first and foremost attending church or synagogue. Volunteer at your local library for readings and recitals. Offer to coach Little League, and make sure to bring along your own kids, of course. Many communities have a volunteer fire department and neighborhood watch. One of the most important steps you can take is to join groups that visit the elderly and people in the hospital, a mitzvah which in the Jewish religion is one of the most important commandments. Invite people to your home for dinner—which Jews usually do every Sabbath night, and in considerable number—as well as hosting a play group. Participate in food drives, and anonymously leave satchels of food on the doorsteps of needy families. Arrange classes and speakers at your home, and invite your friends to hear them, an activity which is again fairly common in the Jewish community. We call them study groups. Start a salon in your home, where you aim to bring together people with similar interests and those who might even benefit from professional contacts. And, of course, you can join your local school's PTA and help run boys' and girls' clubs.

After a month, I think you'll be impressed by the effect on your anxiety level.

A Secular Sabbath

I've spoken before about the importance of gathering family for meals, and I think this is a good way to foster community as well. Jews are encouraged to invite many guests to join them on Friday night for the Sabbath meal. When we marry, we do so not at an altar but under a wedding canopy, emblematic of the tent of Abraham: a roof with no walls and no locks. There is nothing to keep people from entering. Hospitality is a central part of our tradition. The Sabbath is a time to relax and review the events of the week, to laugh with friends and talk to other people's children, and to eat well and drink wine and have a glorious time. Sabbath dinner in our house is an absolutely sacred time.

Sabbath makes for an essential break. Americans are on call 24/7. We're connected to our work all the time. The noise never seems to stop. Eventually it seeps into the soul, and we become permanently restless. We take a conference call on our way to work, check our e-mail as soon as we get home, leave our kids to throw the ball among themselves when our BlackBerry vibrates. All this frenetic activity is dedicated to upward career mobility. To what end? So our clients can come visit us on our deathbeds? So our children can tell their children how low we bought Nextel?

Americans have already experienced the wonder of the Sabbath, whether we knew it or not. In August 2003 there was a massive blackout that took out most of the power grid supplying the northeastern United States and Canada. New York, Toronto, Detroit, and most points in between went black. As the afternoon wore into evening, a silence descended. Cell phone batteries gradually began to die, and laptops powered down. Movie theaters were shut, and every shop was closed. There was finally peace, a respite from all the things in our lives that beep and jingle and vibrate. And suddenly, all we could hear was ourselves.

Something mysterious happened. In New York, a city known for world-class whiners, almost no one complained. Tens of thousands of people climbed out of the stopped subways and walked home. If they couldn't get home, they found food and shelter and community where they were.

Our air conditioners didn't work, so we fled to our stoops, talking to strangers—our neighbors—often for the first time. We couldn't tune into our favorite sitcoms or check the status of our eBay bids, so we talked to our families instead. CD players didn't work, so people sat out on their steps with guitars and sang. We borrowed candles from storekeepers and the better-prepared. We didn't check our messages once. The noise pollution that usually makes us so jittery and easily shaken was silenced. And it was terrific. It was unifying. It was fun.

Where had the fear gone? It had been absorbed into the ambience of community and had been neutralized by the feeling of brotherliness. It was one great, memorable evening. For religious Jews it was less of a revelation; rather it seemed that the Sabbath had come a day early. For us every Friday night is a time of peace and quiet. All creative work, including the operation of electrical appliances and the combustion engine of a car, is off limits. Moses told Pharaoh to "let my people go." African-Americans had Martin Luther King Jr. to shout, "Free at last." The clueless inhabitants of the world's richest city had to settle for a short circuit as a liberator, a coerced Sabbath that arrived as an uninvited, yet not completely unwelcome, guest.

We all know what's important in life, but it seems that the important is usually superseded by the urgent. The gift of the blackout was that all those things we thought were so urgent had to wait until the next morning. Abraham Joshua Heschel said that the sin of modern man, with his orbiting rockets and huge real estate developments, is to value space over time, possessions over special moments.

> **Time has been devalued as mere currency**
> **by which we acquire property.**

Our labor-saving devices aren't relieving us of work—just of our silence. They're marketed as liberating ("You can check in with the office from a red rock peak in Colorado!"), but they're actually incarcerating ("You should check in with the office, even if you're on a red rock peak in Colorado!").

What price do we pay in fear when there is never any respite from the external pressures of our lives? How can we help being frightened when the whole world tells us that the things that make us strong and fearless—our families, our communities, our spiritual life—aren't as important as the things that keep us on perpetual edge, like reality TV and the fluctuations in the stock market?

Judaism conceives of life differently. "Remember the days of old, consider the years long past" (Deuteronomy 32:7). Time is life's most precious gift. Life is measured by the years we live and the connections we make during that time, not by the things we own.

> **Your most valuable possession is the time you
> spend with loved ones and the lasting memories these
> moments create. Wealth should be used to acquire time,
> rather than time being used to acquire wealth.**

The Sabbath is designed so that we can spend six days working and worrying, getting our troubles out of the way, so that on the seventh we can enjoy a totally tranquil and uninterrupted interval dedicated exclusively to human connection and divine closeness.

> **The Sabbath is a day when we put relationships
> over riches, introspection over exertion, people over profits,
> and raising a glass in friendship over
> raising one's social status.**

Perhaps this is why the Jews have been so successful at overcoming fear. On the Sabbath we become one large family, meeting in the synagogue and inviting other families into our homes so we can connect with one another while our children play. If you walk around my neighborhood, which has a large number of Orthodox families, on any Saturday you'll see much more foot traffic than you normally see in a suburb. Orthodox Jews don't drive on Saturday, so the streets themselves become a community, filled with pedestrians going back and forth to synagogue and to one another's houses for lunch. There's a feeling of real strength, of restfulness and benevolent interdependence. It's a beautiful thing, a small-town feeling just outside the busiest city in the world.

I read that in order to prevent another electrical meltdown, New York State might initiate rolling blackouts of the type seen in California. I'd like to propose a better idea: Persuade America to rediscover its lost Sabbath. One day a week, turn away from the tyranny of the TV, shut down the shops, and go home. Have candlelit dinners, and ask people from your community—people you don't know—to join you. The energy conserved will be enough to replenish not just our national reserves but our personal ones as well.

32

Principle #22:
Knot Your Spiritual
Umbilical Cord

So again have I thought in these days to do well unto Jerusalem and to the
house of Judah: fear ye not.

—ZECHARIAH 8:15

The wise man in the storm prays to G-d, not for safety from danger, but for
deliverance from fear.

—RALPH WALDO EMERSON

Insecurity is our first emotion, for we are born completely helpless and dependent. We deal with that insecurity by latching on to things—our parents, our teddy bears, and later in life, our figurative security blankets.
Eventually we become more independent, in one of two ways. We let go of
our parents and either transfer our dependence onto some other set of externals or begin to find our own footing. We either grab on to the life preservers
that life throws us—our jobs, our homes, our cars—and commit to a life of
dependence, or we find internal security, an inner sense of purpose and
meaning. When we choose that second option, we bypass the lie that we are
transient beings with ninety years on this earth if we're lucky. Instead we become part of an eternal story, part of a chain in a higher continuum of existence.

**The ultimate way for us to reaffirm our
connection to the things that tether us to
the world is to reconnect with the divine.**

I would like to return to the example of Martin Luther King Jr. saying that he was not afraid to die the night before he was assassinated. His understanding of his place in the universe helped to contribute to that lack of fear. He knew that his work had helped millions and would help millions more. King was also a deeply religious man, and a religious leader; he never went by any title other than Reverend. He felt he had been called upon by G-d Almighty to end the immorality of segregation. I believe that he was immunized from fear by that deep connection to a higher source—and that it was a connection that even an assassin's bullet could not sever.

**When we are content within our relationship with G-d,
we know that we're never alone. G-d accompanies us
always. His providence surrounds us like a warm
blanket, his grace warms us like a hot bath.**

When we have a spiritual center, we understand that life isn't transient. Look at all the saints who went to their deaths without fear. They weren't afraid, because they knew nothing could kill them. They would simply transmute their existence from one mode to another. The Talmud says that "the righteous, even in death, are alive, while the wicked, even while alive, are dead." The righteous are connected with the source of all life even after they have left the earth, while the wicked, who destroy this earth and are connected with only the flimsiest physicality, are dead even while they walk and breathe.

The more spirituality people have, the more their lives are illuminated and the less they are afraid. Indeed, of all the qualities most associated with saints, serenity and inner peace are at the top of the list. The converse is also true. Of all the qualities most associated with psychopaths and evildoers, outer turbulence and inner turmoil top the list. Just look at the speeches of Adolf Hitler or Benito Mussolini. Do the speakers strike you as secure souls? People like the Lubavitcher Rebbe, the Dalai Lama, and Pope John Paul II always speak in calm and tranquil voices that reflect the peace at their centers.

Rabbi Akiva, one of the Talmud's leading figures, had the skin combed off his body with red-hot metal as a punishment by the Romans for his participation in the Bar Kochva revolt of 133 CE. His students couldn't believe that he showed no pain or fear. They asked him if he was a ghost. He answered, "I have waited my entire life to give my life to G-d. I am now at peace."

Rabbi Elchonon Wasserman, one of the great Jewish sages in the period of the Holocaust, was marched out by the Nazis in Lithuania to face a firing squad for no other reason than having been born a Jew. He put on his finest Sabbath clothing so that he could meet martyrdom with dignity. He delivered a speech to his fellow Jews who were about to die alongside him. He told them that they should hand no victory to the Nazis by displaying any kind of fear. "We will all soon be with G-d, and He will avenge our deaths. Now, let us do our duty and die as proud believers."

Countless Christian saints went to their deaths in the Roman Colosseum with utter serenity on their faces. Even the Roman lions and bloodthirsty gladiators could not frighten them. Their strength was an inner strength, impervious to Roman cruelty. Later it was the Christian faith that survived and the Romans who went down into the dust of history.

In the same way that we must reconnect with ourselves, our families, our friends, and our communities, we must reconnect to G-d. Doing so is essential to allaying our fears. You then understand that you are a child of G-d and that you contain within you a fragment of the divine that lends you infinite significance—even if you don't marry someone with an impeccable pedigree, work for a blue-chip company, or live in an enormous house.

**If you feel connected to G-d, you understand
that you are here on earth to serve a purpose, to
fulfill a destiny set out for you as part of a larger plan,
and you can never feel unmoored and alone.**

Religion as Superstition

This isn't a universally shared opinion, of course. Bertrand Russell acknowledged the connection between religion and fear, by proclaiming, "I regard [religion] as a disease born of fear, and as a source of untold misery to the human race." Of the many remedies, or opiates, man has invented to dull the pain of existence, Karl Marx argued, religion was the greatest drug of all.

Friedrich Nietzsche took this idea further, arguing that the Jews—a weak and vulnerable people—invented morality as a ruse to enfeeble the strong Teutonic knights, the *Übermenschen*, encouraging them to renounce violence and substitute for it moral strength. These individuals maintained that ancient man, alone in a vast and impersonal universe, and conscious that death could strike at any moment, conjured up G-d to comfort and empower him against the capricious forces of nature. But they got it all wrong. It wasn't religion they were talking about, but superstition. True belief undermines your fears; superstition reinforces them. Belief in G-d makes you strong and independent. Superstition makes you dependent on a furry rabbit's foot.

**G-d is not the godfather, and religion is not a lucky
rabbit's foot protecting you against bad luck.**

People who confuse religion with superstition approach G-d not as the Father but as the godfather, a being who protects them from danger. They don't love G-d so much as fear death; they don't observe tradition so much as ward off evil. Throughout history religion has sadly and often been used to augment rather than combat people's fears.

The more fearful we are, the more easily we are manipulated. For many today, religion has become synonymous with superstition. But whereas religion makes us strong and independent, superstition merely makes us weak and dependent. True religion immunizes us against fear. The more connected we are with G-d, the more we can walk against the current of popular opinion, secure in our ability to *do* the right because it *is* right. Whereas religion inspires, superstition alarms.

**While religion connects us to the heavens, superstition
focuses us on the grave. While religion helps us transcend
human limitations, superstition traps us
in a prison of our own anxieties.**

A Jewish superstition that has caught on in the popular culture big-time is the piece of red string that celebrities are wearing, encouraged by their teachers at the Kabbalah Centre, in an effort to ward off the evil eye. The belief in an evil eye in Judaism is a device that is meant to help you to be humble so that no one will be jealous of your blessings. Societies are undermined through boastfulness, which sows enmity and slowly erodes human cohesiveness. Humility is the only way to ward off the evil eye. If the frightened and desperate stars of the world really took that message to heart, they'd take the stupid red strings off and exhibit some genuine humility instead. By promoting a red string in place of ethical meekness, the Kabbalah Centre is preying on people's panic.

But listen to the kabbalist on the Kabbalah Centre's Web site: "The Red String protects us from the influences of the Evil Eye. Evil Eye is a very powerful negative force. It refers to the unfriendly stare and unkind glances we sometimes get from people around us—Kabbalah teaches us that we can remove intrusive negative influences by using tools such as the Red String!"

This, of course, is pure drivel, and the writer is guilty of robbing Kabbalah of a moral or ethical dimension. Are we really to believe that we ward off people's envy not by living modestly but by driving our overly expensive cars while wearing a red string?

Be careful, when you turn to belief to help combat fear, that you don't end up with superstition instead. I go out of my way to break my silly and shallow superstitious beliefs, and so should you. Show that you're not a prisoner to irrational fears and shallow superstitions.

> **Open an umbrella in your home. Walk under a (safe) ladder. Break a mirror if you have to. And show that your belief in G-d is wholly unrelated to the fearfulness of superstition.**

Religion Teaches Contempt for Evil

It was no accident that the iron will of Abraham Lincoln was sustained, as he said, in the darkest years of the Civil War by his reading the Bible almost daily, while the utterly fearless General George Patton read the Bible every night before he retired. I do believe that Mother Teresa's strong faith in a merciful G-d allowed her to embrace lepers and to clean their weeping sores with her bare hands.

> **The more attached you are to G-d, the more you become contemptuous of evil.**

Surely Avraham Netzach, who was imprisoned by the Russians for setting up a network of Jewish schools and brutally punished for his refusal to work on the Sabbath, was bolstered by his religious faith. He carried himself with such an air of G-d-given confidence that his enemies feared him. The belief that he was the human channel for a concept—Judaism and, more specifically, the idea that the Sabbath should be kept holy—empowered him to act without fear.

Once when Martin Luther King Jr. was giving a lecture, a white racist ran up to him at the podium and punched him so hard in the chin that the hundreds of people present heard the horrible thud. King was knocked to the floor, but he quickly regained his feet and yelled out, "No one harm him. Let him be." King then spoke to the man, asking him the reasons for the violence. The man stopped yelling "nigger" and started telling King about how he had suffered awful events in his life and how no one had ever cared for him. It was on that day that King's followers witnessed King's true personal commitment to nonviolence and the utter fearlessness of their incomparable leader. It is no coincidence that King derived his inspiration and fearlessness from the Hebrew prophets, whom he quoted incessantly. "Let justice flow like a river, and righteousness like a mighty spring" (Amos 5:24).

Life Is to Be Lived

If fear is the only thing that motivates our religious feeling, it can turn that religious feeling into something very dangerous. Take religious people who focus on the idea of an afterlife, a world much sweeter and more rewarding than the one we live in here on earth. These people are fully focused on that other, better world—to such an extreme that their real lives in the here and now might as well be meaningless. They take risks, knowing that something might happen to them, but they are fearless because they believe that the world that follows this one is superior in every way to the one we live in. Their fearlessness is not based on having tapped into something higher but is rather motivated by a denigration of all things physical.

You can see how a single-minded focus on spirit might lead to a denigration of the physical world—not a desirable goal.

When you start thinking that the next world is better than this one, you forfeit your commitment to making the earth a more G-dly place.

In fact, this is the thinking that motivates many of the acts of terrorism around the world. You'll die now, but if you die with Allah's name on your lips, you'll be rewarded with virgins and sex orgies in the afterlife. Beyond being an abomination—how else can we describe sex for murder?—this type of thinking is entirely self-serving and has nothing to do with G-d.

Connect Through Prayer

There is another way for you to connect with the divine, in a way that is genuine rather than superficial. You can open up a line of communication with G-d through prayer.

> **Prayer is the articulation of all that we should aspire to in life.**

Prayer is a way to align yourself with righteousness. It's an act of dismissing the petty concerns that suck out the marrow of life as you reach for something higher. The more connected you feel above, the less you can be defeated below. The more your life is suffused with meaning, the less susceptible you are to capricious forces. The more secure you feel in your own direction, the better you feel about your standing in G-d's eyes. It naturally follows that the better you feel, the more morally centered, the more principled you feel, the more fearless you become. When you pray, you feel that you are in touch with a higher power; you are not cosmic dust, blown hither and thither at the mercy of the elements. Prayer says that you believe in a higher plan and understand that you play a part in the cosmic drama.

It is also an opportunity to reconnect with your deepest values. When we pray for the health of our children and the success of our marriage, we remind ourselves that those are the things we value most in life, and we are inspired to come home early from the office and nurture them rather than pursue a life of empty materialism.

> **Prayer is a way of reaching both outside and inside yourself, to touch the heavens and to connect with your own spirit.**

It is another way that we can connect the earthbound with the divine. As Dorothy Bernard said, "Courage is fear that has said its prayers."

Prayer is also an act of defiance. We have talked about fighting the darkness, refusing to accept an unfavorable prognosis, and the importance of standing up for yourself in the battle against fear. Isn't this what prayer is? Rather than accept a cruel decree, we dare to try to change it. To say a prayer in the face of hopelessness is to light a candle in the enveloping darkness.

Prayer is, in itself, an act of hope.

You cannot be completely hopeless and pray. A belief in the human ability to shape and mold events is the foundation of the very act. Prayer is an act of supplication that cannot be offered unless it is assumed that it can be heard.

**Rather than being merely a religious ritual,
prayer is a psychological need. When you pray,
you empower yourself with the belief that
you can overcome fate and create destiny.**

**Resignation in life comes about as a reaction
to things in the past, but prayer is the
human capacity to will our own future.**

I am concerned when I hear how much emphasis many religions place on fearing G-d's wrath and punishment. This is an outcropping of the same superstitious foolishness that has Madonna and Britney Spears wearing a red string. It's a belief that cheats good people of the relationship with G-d to which they are entitled.

I asked my friend Phoebe, not a religious person, if she believed in G-d the way she believed in the existence of a country called Liechtenstein. She said she did. And then I asked her if she thought He would protect her and her family. She said she didn't feel confident about it, because she wasn't righteous enough. I thought this showed an astonishingly low sense of self-esteem. She believes that she won't get the miracle she deserves because she doesn't deserve one. She really believes that G-d will only look out for her if she goes to church every Sunday.

This is a rejection of the entire notion of G-d's unconditional love, one of our most powerful armaments in the war against fear. It says that G-d only protects the righteous. I hope to have made it clear throughout this book that our righteousness is not only for G-d's sake but also for our own. We practice righteousness so that we can find purpose and attachment in our own lives, even as G-d unconditionally showers his bounty upon us as His children. So long as we never cross into the world of the truly cruel and wicked—in which case we are severed from G-d—He will love and bless us. People like Phoebe see their relationship with G-d as a quid pro quo: you burn the incense, I'll save your kid's life. Again, that's not religion, it's superstition.

G-d isn't a deal maker. He shows love to His creations and rains abundance on His children, no matter what—and that's why believing in Him and doing things to strengthen that relationship is a tremendous antidote to terror. I asked Phoebe to whom she was comparing herself when she found herself coming up so short. This is a woman who does her best to be a good wife and mother, someone who takes pride in doing good and important work, someone who gives to charity and is kind to small children and animals. What phenomenal lack of self-esteem had led this person to believe that she was undeserving of G-d's love? What religious tradition led her to believe that G-d is more fickle and easily offended than a human parent? And what religion gave her such a low opinion of herself that although she was not wicked or evil, she still felt cut off from her Creator?

I know that many religious people have a relationship with G-d that is dominated by fear. Is this really any relationship at all? Imagine a relationship between a man and a woman in which fear is what she feels, first and foremost? Can there actually be any love at all in such a relationship? Can there really ever be any trust? Of course not; it's fundamentally corrupt.

Fear of G-d, many will argue, is one of the cornerstones of every religious faith, and that is true. Hundreds of Biblical verses attest to this fact, some of the most prominent being "My covenant was with him of life and peace; and I gave them to him for the fear wherewith he feared me, and was afraid before my name" (Malachi 2:5) and "Then they that feared the LORD spake often one to another: and the LORD hearkened, and heard it, and a book of remembrance was written before him for them that feared the LORD, and that thought upon his name" (Malachi 3:16).

But here is a crucial caveat:

**Judaism has always understood fear of G-d
to mean not fear of punishment but fear
of being distanced from G-d through sin.**

A husband may refrain from cheating on his wife because he is afraid she will chop him up with a machete, or he may refrain from cheating because he doesn't want to alienate a woman he loves too much to live without. It is in the spirit of this latter motivation that we are meant to fear G-d.

**We do not refrain from sin for fear that G-d will
strike us down with hail and brimstone, and we do not
refrain from idol worship for fear that He will turn us
into a pillar of salt. Rather, we do so because
the proximity we enjoy with G-d would turn
to distance once we broke His covenant.**

Those who wield the sword of the fear of punishment, and who portray G-d as a vengeful Being with a spear ready to strike at the first perpetrator of iniquity, undermine the love inherent in religion and make it instead into an instrument of fear.

**People who relate to G-d as if he is violent and
angry embody those cruel attributes and
make life hell on earth for others.**

It's yet another scare tactic, designed to keep people coming back for redemption, the way an abusive husband controls his wife's money and self-esteem.

> **Any religion that must invoke fear in order to safeguard the adherence of its flock is betraying its lack of confidence in its own message, just as a husband who threatens to beat up his wife if she cheats has clearly given up the idea that her actions might be motivated by love.**

Instead of empowering people with a sense of destiny, this type of religion hamstrings people. It forces them to be much more conscious of what they *don't* do than of what they *do*. It's a contingent rather than an essential way of looking at your existence, and it makes people feel very, very bad about themselves.

I believe in a G-d who's genuinely forgiving and loving and long-suffering. I do believe that G-d will catch up with wicked evildoers, like Hitler, Yasser Arafat, and the Washington snipers. I believe that we must serve as the instrument of his justice and safeguard the lives of innocents.

I also believe that the vast majority of us are not wicked or evil, even if we are not completely righteous. I believe that G-d patiently waits for us to do the right thing rather than striking us down for doing the wrong thing.

> **The G-d to whom I pray is a loving G-d, or He would not be worthy of my prayer.**

He is G-d who has granted me a mission on this earth and will be patient with me as I mature into that role, becoming less selfish, materialistic, and self-absorbed as I progress. If you believe that G-d is the punisher, then every time you make a mistake, you wait to be fried by a bolt of lightning.

Just as a victim of domestic violence must leave a relationship to survive, we have to free ourselves from the misconception that G-d requires us to be afraid of Him. Then, and only then, will we be free to revel in the strength we can derive from a connection to G-d that is life-affirming, death-denying, and liberates us from fear.

CONCLUSION

Living Life in the High Places

And I will come near to you to judgment; and I will be a swift witness against the sorcerers, and against the adulterers, and against false swearers, and against those that oppress the hireling in his wages, the widow, and the fatherless, and that turn aside the stranger from his right, and fear not me, saith the LORD of hosts.

—MALACHI 3:5

None but a coward dares to boast that he has never known fear.

—FERDINAND FOCH

Fear is a question: what are you afraid of, and why? Just as the seed of health is in illness, because illness contains information, your fears are a treasure-house of self-knowledge if you explore them.

—MARILYN FERGUSON

We are right now living in a desert of fear. We spend our lives picking our way across the dunes of money troubles and hair loss and professional envy to get to the occasional oases that life provides us: our marriages, our children, our G-d. Occasionally we spot something that looks like an oasis, but when we reach the palm trees, there's nothing but sand in our hands. These are the false antidotes we apply to our fears: the trophy wife, the Botoxed brow, the platinum card. Instead of alleviating the thirst of our fear, the disappointment of these mirages makes our journeys much more heartbreaking. Only by reconnecting to a sense of our own destiny and dedicating our lives to causes greater than ourselves can we bring water to the desert that is our anxious existence.

When you live in fear, you have already lost the battle, but when you recognize fear for the immobilizing trap it is, you are finally engaging the real enemy. When you begin to confront your fears, you gain a foothold against an insidious emotion. You can isolate the rational from the irrational, take precautions to protect yourself and your loved ones, and gain the courage to move on.

When you change your orientation from the inward
to the outward, when you find reasons to matter that
are valuable in a selfless and an eternal sense,
you shake off fear's cold hand.

When you begin to do something worthwhile and positively affect the lives of others, instead of allowing fear to paralyze you, you become a moving target, hard to hit, difficult to incapacitate. And when you fortify the relationships that give you a sense of your own inner value—with yourself, your family, your community, the world at large, and with G-d—you become invincible.

When you eliminate the graying dullness of fear,
the world emerges in splendid color.

You can fall in love without fear of hurt; you can enjoy the sound of your children playing without concern for their deaths; you can enjoy your work without fearing exploitation; you can be intimate without the trepidation that your vulnerability invites pain. Finally, you can move on in your life with boldness and promise.

And when you shed the burden of a life lived in fear, everything changes for the better. Your professional life improves as you begin to carry yourself with confidence, unrestricted now by insecurities. Your personal life blossoms as you joyously seek connections with new people, not out of loneliness but out of the positive sense that you have something to contribute to their lives. And your spiritual life is strengthened immeasurably as you connect with G-d, not out of fear of his wrath but in gratitude and love for his grace.

**No one who has truly lived is ever afraid of death,
and no one who has really loved
has ever been frozen in fear.**

It is only those who have squandered their opportunities on earth who fear death, the ultimate confirmation of their suspicion that they are of little value or significance. If you have learned to love, laugh, and hope through all the trials of life, you have discovered that the secret to immortality lies not in overcoming death but in overcoming fear.

ACKNOWLEDGMENTS

M y battle with fear being ongoing, I wish to thank, first and foremost,
the man who made me better confront my fears by giving me the idea
for this book. Robert Gottlieb, my literary agent and friend, is a fountain of
wisdom and experience. Even when I was not sure that fear should be the
subject of my next book (I was afraid that it would not sell as much as my last
book), he was adamant. Many believe he is the best in the business. Once I
got into writing the book and discovered an indescribable passion for the
subject, I understood why.

Diane Reverand, my editor at St. Martin's Press, is a woman of refine-
ment and grace, high intelligence, wide erudition, experience, humanity, and
humility. She has made me feel valued at every interaction in our relationship, and I am grateful to G-d for having found an editor who is on the same
page as I (forgive the pun).

Laura Tucker, who edited, refined, and helped to shape this entire manu-
script, also gave me penetrating ideas about how to combat and overcome
fear. Laura is one of the finest young women I know. A brilliant editor, her
literary talent is eclipsed only by her goodness. What a pleasure it is to work
with someone I so deeply respect and admire.

Ron Feiner is my counselor, friend, crutch, and a supreme repository of
life's wisdom.

My wife, Debbie, is the inspiration behind everything I do. It is no exag-
geration to say that more and more I find myself living simply to be worthy
of her. A woman whose fearlessness is inspired by an unassuming righteousness, she is my lioness of courage.

My children are my light and, after my wife, my greatest pleasure. Their
having come into this world has given me purpose. When they walk in after
school each day, I feel less afraid. As a father it is my job to love them. But

equally it is my job to be a model of fearlessness and to inspire them to outdo their father in living courageously.

My late spiritual master, the Lubavitcher Rebbe, sent me to Oxford as a rabbi when I had just turned twenty-two. I was frightened of being inadequate, but having the confidence of a great and saintly man is a magical elixir in combatting fear. It is now ten years since his passing, but his glorious spiritual legacy, as well as the countless religious institutions he left behind, continues to illuminate the globe.

G-d Almighty is He to Whom I aspire to draw ever closer. May my life prove worthy of His blessings, and may fear be banished from this earth.

—Shmuley Boteach
April 2004